Things Past

Things Past

MALCOLM MUGGERIDGE

Edited by
IAN HUNTER

WILLIAM MORROW AND COMPANY, INC.
NEW YORK   1979

Library of Congress Catalog Card Number 78-71376

ISBN 0-688-03445-4

Printed in the United States of America.

First U.S. Edition

1   2   3   4   5   6   7   8   9   10

To J. H. H.
Qui viam illuminavit

Contents

Introduction

Between the first and last entry, this anthology spans half a century. To have perturbed, entertained, scandalized and illumined one's fellow mortals over such a period is a journalistic achievement unrivalled in our day. As one turns the pages and the years are there any unifying characteristics in this prodigious output?

Foremost is the compelling readability of Malcolm Muggeridge's prose. It is tart and pointed - whether discussing people or events, Muggeridge has always preferred to risk malice to mincing - never dull, never pedantic. How unfortunate that so much of it, particularly from the early years, should have been so long buried away in nearly inaccessible sources. True, there have been two previous anthologies: *Tread Softly For You Tread On My Jokes*, published in 1966 (known in the USA as *The Most of Malcolm Muggeridge*); and *Jesus Rediscovered*, his best-selling collection of religious essays, published in 1969. But both drew primarily upon writings from the sixties, and the early Muggeridge remained almost unknown. The chronological arrangement of articles in this anthology, which begins with his very first publication, allows the reader to explore the genesis and development of his views.

Malcolm Muggeridge was born 24 March 1903 in Croydon, near London, the third of five sons of Henry Thomas and Annie Muggeridge. His father was secretary of a London firm of shirt manufacturers, and an early Fabian who, in 1931, was elected as Labour MP for Romford.

After local grammar and secondary schools, Muggeridge entered Selwyn College, Cambridge in 1920. His previous training obliged him to read Natural Science, a subject in which he professed no interest then or since. After four desultory years 'the most fultile and dismal of my whole life', he emerged with a degree, and set out for India to teach at Union Christian College in Alwaye. Here his writing career began, auspiciously enough with an exchange of correspondence with Mahatma Ghandi published in *Young India*, and then with his short story, 'An Elderly Teacher', published in the *New Statesman*.

After three years in India, he returned to England and, in 1927, married Kitty Dobbs, a niece of Beatrice Webb. Together they set off for Cairo, this time to a teaching post at the Egyptian University where Muggeridge held forth on English literature before classes 'of stupefied faces and inert minds' in a commodious classroom which had formerly housed a harem. Muggeridge's first son, Leonard, was born in Egypt. He also wrote a play, *Three Flats*, later to be performed in London. After sending some articles, mostly of political commentary, back to the *Manchester Guardian*, they responded by offering him an editorial position which he immediately accepted.

From 1930 to 1932 Muggeridge righted the world's wrongs from the *Guardian*'s editorial corridor, preaching the vain hopes and pretensions of its editor, C. P. Scott, to an unheeding world. His first novel, *Autumnal Face*, was published to favourable reviews.

On the first day of 1932, C. P. Scott died and his son, Ted, a close friend of Muggeridge's, took over the editor's chair. Tragically, Ted Scott drowned only four months later, victim of a freak boating accident. Muggeridge was grief-stricken and at loose ends; when the *Guardian*'s Moscow position came open, he leapt at it. In Moscow those socialist principles, imbibed since childhood from his father and his Fabian circle, were at last to be put into practice. There was to be a classless Utopia, there a future that would work, a kingdom of heaven on earth where exploitation would end and the weary be at rest. There he and Kitty went, burning en route their degrees, marriage papers, passports and other intimations of the dying bourgeoise society on which their backs were turned.

The intensity of Muggeridge's disillusionment in Moscow is evidenced by the selection of articles here included from this period, and it is vital to understanding the later evolution of his views. By the time he left Russia in 1932, he was appalled by Stalinist repression and contemptuous of the *Guardian*'s doctoring of the truth, which concealed it from their readers. *Winter in Moscow* (the conclusion of which starts on page 38) expressed the former view. *Picture Palace*, a novel satirizing the *Manchester Guardian*, the latter; however at the review stage, the *Guardian*, staunch defender of free expression of opinion, managed to obtain an injunction to prevent publication on the ground of apprehended libel.

In 1934 Muggeridge returned to India as assistant editor of the *Calcutta Statesman*, leaving his family (now three children) in London. Finding neither the editor nor the paper to his taste, he spent most of his time writing a biography of Samuel Butler, subsequently published as *The Earnest Atheist*. After eighteen aimless months, he rejoined his family and secured employment on the *Evening Standard*.

Until the outbreak of war, Muggeridge contributed to the

Londoner's Diary in the *Standard*, wrote essays and book reviews, another novel (*In a Valley of this Restless Mind*, reissued by Collins in 1978) and a social history of the decade, *The Thirties*.

His wartime exploits as a spy in MI6, are recounted with zest and self-deprecating wit in the second volume of his autobiography, *The Infernal Grove*. He portrays himself as a fumbling innocent, an Inspector Clouseau in a world of espionage, ruse and double-cross. In fact he regarded his life as so degraded and absurd that he attempted suicide by drowning. He was ultimately saved by a mystical realization that man is but a sojourner in time whose destination and habitat is eternity, and by an awareness of the unity and benevolence of all creation, not excluding even a dispirited man seeking death. He finished the war in Paris responsible for assisting French citizens falsely accused of collaborating with the Germans, 'the only worthwhile thing I did in the whole war'. He was decorated with the Legion of Honour, the Croix de Guerre with Palm and the Médaille de la Reconnaissance Française.

War's end found Muggeridge back on Fleet Street, this time on the *Daily Telegraph*, where he wrote editorials, served a stint as Washington correspondent and, in 1950, became Deputy Editor. In January, 1953 he was invited to become editor of that hardy English perennial, *Punch*, the first outsider to occupy the chair in the paper's history. The next four years were spent in the sombre pursuit of 'trying to discover what, if anything, was funny enough to make the English laugh'.

The advent of television in the fifties – a medium Muggeridge has lost no opportunity to flay but on which he has regularly appeared - made his face and inimitable voice known even more widely than his pen. As probing interviewer or acerbic panelist, he acquired a reputation as an unrepentant skeptic and agnostic, an impression only partly offset by his more recent television biographies - for example about Mother Teresa of Calcutta (*Something Beautiful for God*) and his study of the seminal Christian thinkers, *A Third Testament*.

Readers acquainted only with Muggeridge's later writings frequently inquire when he became a Christian, a question based on the premise that one becomes a Christian with the same calamitous finality as one learns of a terminal illness. The most casual perusal of any of the extracts here included from the 1930s will demonstrate that this question cannot be answered in such terms. Similarly, many reviewers of *Jesus Rediscovered* played variations on the theme of a sudden, Damascus Road conversion.

The truth is that his early writings disclose the same themes, the same doubts and preoccupations, the same parched thirst for living water. Even so, it is doubtful that this collection will do much to weaken the prevalent misconception about a sudden, dramatic conversion. Fantasy is clean cut and symmetrical; reality tends to be angular and complicated. And myth evinces greater staying power than reality.

Too many of Malcolm Muggeridge's readers have sought answers when they should more profitably have noted his questions. 'He who searches for God, finds Him' wrote Pascal. So, for Muggeridge, the search is its own sanctuary, the question its own answer, the journey its own destination. Oddly enough, it is precisely because there was no Damascus Road conversion that many of his readers have felt compelled to invent one.

As this collection demonstrates, Muggeridge's life has been a restless quest for faith which has even yet attained few certainties. Whether early or late, his probing, skeptical intellect spurns the easy answers to which the comfortable cling. His disillusionment with power, and its factota of all ideological persuasions, came early. Nor has he been much attracted by any of the Kingdoms of the Earth which the Devil, noting that they were in his gift, offered to Christ, an offer which Christ spurned. Throughout his life Muggeridge has sought, with maturing conviction and orthodoxy, that kingdom which is not of this world.

This anthology then has a two-fold purpose. First to make available a selection of the best of Malcolm Muggeridge's writings spanning half a century. Secondly, to demonstrate that his preoccupation with what might broadly be called 'religious' questions is no recent quirk of advancing years. Fortunately these aims proved compatible. When I first began to search his early writings, I came upon a lode so rich and untapped that some criteria for exclusion other than lucidity (the man is apparently incapable of dull writing) became essential to determine what must be omitted. The more I read, the more it seemed that there was a theme running through all his writings – a pilgrimage in quest of faith. Like Bunyan's pilgrim, Muggeridge's path through the twentieth century has traversed diverse earthly Kingdoms, Vanity Fairs, and Sloughs of Despond. Not a few Giants Despair have sought to imprison him in castles of social, ideological or religious conformity. But whatever the climate, however fascinating or menacing the surroundings, he has invariably folded his tent and made off '. . . with some notion, however indistinct, that at last one will see the Holy City set upon a hill'. Reflecting on this theme, it seemed appropriate to select a title for this collection derived from Bunyan's beloved classic.

It will no doubt be contended that some of the pieces here included (particularly those snippets of satire and invective which I find irresistible) indicate less a pilgrimage than a vendetta. But even Bunyan's pilgrim, Christian, skirmished occasionally. We read that he battled Appollyon's darts with a sharp two-edged sword, although it may be doubted whether his adversaries emerged from a fray any less lacerated than those on the receiving end of Mr Muggeridge's stinging jibes.

For those who find Muggeridge's prose irresistible (and that includes many who do not share his views) here is a prose banquet. For those who strive to understand our strange time, here is a chronology written athwart those memorable and bizarre events which shaped it. For those embarked on a pilgrimage in the same direction, here is companionship, perhaps even illumination, along the way.

In acknowledging the contribution of others, it is obvious that my obligation to Malcom Muggeridge is unique. I owe him too many debts to itemize here, and in any case such debts are un-repayable.

I would be remiss not to acknowledge, with gratitude, the assistance of Bruce and Jacqueline who arranged, Joyce who typed, and Elizabeth who has borne all things past with gracious equanimity.

Ian A. Hunter
March 1978

I will talk of things heavenly or things earthly, things moral or things evangelical, things sacred or things profane, things past or things to come, things foreign or things at home, things more essential or things circumstantial, provided that all be done to our profit.

John Bunyan, *Pilgrim's Progress*

An Elderly Teacher

Mr Alfred Twistead was a teacher in an elementary school; and every day he played the hymn for the morning assembly. He had been doing this for nearly forty years, so that he knew all the hymns in the book without looking at the music. Besides being a teacher, on five evenings each week he was the pianist in a jazz band that played in a tin-roofed building adjoining a chapel. On these occasions he wore a faded dress suit, which would long ago have fallen to pieces had it not been for the careful attention of Mrs Twistead, who kept it in a press, and who fixed a second seat to the trousers to make them stronger. Mr Twistead had taken up this extra work in the first place to get money for the education of his two sons. He had wanted them to have polish; to be gentlemen. But they did badly at the select private school to which he sent them, and had to go away to Australia. Even then, when the money was no longer necessary, he went on with the band largely through habit.

As the time for his retirement drew near Mr Twistead became very excited. He was tired of playing the hymn at the morning assembly; and a new headmaster had come to the school whose ideas about education were incomprehensible to him. None of his colleagues knew of the warm delight that was growing up in his soul at the thought of his coming freedom. They saw him only as he had always been: shabby and tired and dull; painstakingly respectable; peering inanely at them over the top of his spectacles; and, even in the driest weather, carrying an umbrella. 'Poor old Twistead,' they would say. 'He belongs to the old school; but he's nearly finished his time now.'

He had planned what he was going to do with his leisure when it came to him. There was a lot that needed doing in the garden; he wanted, for instance, to build a little shed for his tools and the lawn mower, if he could pick up some timber cheaply; and then there would be evening strolls with his wife, and an occasional game of bowls in the park – altogether plenty of ways of filling up his time.

When the last Friday at school came, however, he felt rather sad. He knew the place so well that somehow or other he had become a part of it. His life had been lived in that dull red building, standing grimly and coldly in its piece of asphalt playground, and the break at leaving it for ever was painful. It seemed almost incredible that he really was standing for the last time in the shabby school-hall, with its stale smell, with 'Play the Game' framed over the headmaster's platform, and with insipid pictures of country scenes and battles hung round its walls; and that such inevitable parts of his life as playing the hymn and teaching standard three were finished with. He thought of his first lesson as a pupil teacher to a class of eighty boys. Now he had reached the last. All the intervening ones seemed just a grey waste in which nothing stood out as being different from anything else.

After the hymn the headmaster took prayers. He made a drill of it, saying: 'Hands together,' and 'Eyes closed!' like a sergeant-major. Then, as was his custom, he made a little speech. 'Boys,' he said, 'two airmen started this morning on their tenth attempt to fly over the Atlantic. This is the Columbus spirit again.'

Mr Twistead played a march to which the boys went to their classes. His first lesson was scripture, but instead of this he generally took mental arithmetic. Then came writing. Writing had been the single passion in Mr Twistead's life. He loved beautifully-shaped letters that were round and ample, and he always tried to make his pupils keep their exercise books spotlessly clean, teaching them never to cross out a mistake but always to enclose it in brackets. When they were working at an exercise he would walk round amongst them, pausing here to praise, there to condemn; and sometimes he would sit by a boy to give him special help, pushing his tongue forward between his teeth as he moved the pen.

At four o'clock he took from his desk the little stick he used for conducting in singing lessons, and his Bible, and his book of tables, and a few specimens of good writing, discoloured through having been hung on the walls, that he wished to keep to remind him of his best pupils. He made these things into a small bundle, and then went to say goodbye to his colleagues.

'Goodbye, Twistead, old man,' they all said. 'The place won't be the same without you.'

The more elderly amongst them were already looking forward to their own retirement, and half envied him; while the younger and more enthusiastic ones, who were new to the work, had a moment of cold fear as they wondered if they would be like that when they retired.

He shook hands with all of them, smiling in his wistful and rather colourless way. Miss Smalden, who bounced as she walked, and who had original ideas on the teaching of geography, and who believed in free discipline, said: 'What are you going to do with yourself, Mr Twistead?'

'Oh, I've got the garden to look after, you know,' he answered. 'And really I feel rather like a little rest.'

Miss Leather, who specialized in basket work and expressionist dancing, pressed her thin lips together and said that she hoped he would be happy.

'Oh, yes,' answered Mr Twistead.

The young headmaster shook hands with him heartily. He had closely-cropped, spiky hair, and a large chest, and an authoritative voice. 'I hope you'll look in and see us sometimes,' he said. 'We'll all miss you.'

But really Mr Twistead knew that he was glad to see the last of him, since he wanted a younger and more vigorous man in his place, who would help to get the school on; and he laughed inwardly thinking, 'One day, despite your energy and your self-confidence, you'll be old and tired like me; then they'll throw you out, too.' But all he said was: 'Oh, yes, thank you.'

The boys were playing in the street outside. He had seen many of them playing there in his time, and had loved them in a way. It had hurt him personally when they would not learn to write properly. But, like the headmaster, they saw him walk away without any feeling of regret.

In the evening he sat in his garden. It was spring, and the buds on the trees were just beginning to come out into leaf. Birds were singing, and in the recreation ground nearby he could hear the municipal band playing. The grass of his little lawn was soft and green, and the creeper over the back fence was taking on a new life, while against the sky was a line of runner beans. As the golden light of the setting sun poured on to his withered dry skin, Mr Twistead felt vaguely sad to think that with him life was over; that there was no spring to follow.

Mrs Twistead shouted out to him once or twice in her shrill voice, telling him to be careful not to take cold; but he sat on, smoking his pipe and watching the stars come out one by one. It struck him then that until that time he had never in all his life had leisure to watch them carelessly, with his mind untrammelled and at ease; and it seemed a pity, for as he watched them now he found in them something he had never known before; something which made the school, and the band, and his dark, shabby clothes seem mean and stuffy. And tears came into his eyes as he thought of the weary struggle it had all been – the getting up early; the going to bed late; the stinting and the saving; the patching and the hiding – shouting at little boys; playing noisy tunes in a hot room with the silly couples dancing, dancing, dancing; going home at midnight and heating up a cup of cocoa; hearing his wife breathe heavily while he was undressing – all for nothing, the stars seemed to say; for nothing.

He almost made up his mind that even then there was time to begin again, just for his last few years of freedom; but as he sat at supper with his wife watching her mouth working precisely as she ate he realized that for them it was all over.

She put away the crockery carefully in the sideboard – hours of my life in the sideboard, he thought – and brushed the crumbs off the table, carefully throwing them out of the window for the birds; and then, soon after, they went to bed.

Mr Twistead was in the habit of getting up in the mornings to make an early cup of tea. His wife smiled when she noticed that the next morning he did not stir, remembering how unnecessary it was now for him to be up in good time. Then she saw something peculiar in the way he was lying, and touched him and found him cold and began to cry quietly; for he was dead.

[1928]

Europe, 1934

It would be safe to say that, unless something very unexpected happens, if no vent is found for the pressure accumulating in Germany, another large-scale European war must break out within the next few years whose consequences will be even more ruinous than the last. The structure of post-war Europe is crazy, but not elastic. It will not bend into a more reasonable shape and attempts to make it secure – notably the League of Nations – have only served to increase its dangerous rigidity. So rigid a structure cracks explosively. Who would dare to prophesy the possibility of its continuing to withstand the strain of an arming and soon armed Germany? It must crack sometime. The question is, where? If in the West then we shall all have to fight again, and, in fighting, destroy what remains of European civilization, leaving its debris, as they have always calculated, to the Bolsheviks.

Roots

People need a certain basic security if their lives are to have any dignity or substance. They need at least to imagine that tomorrow and the day after will have a certain continuity with today and yesterday. When everything is shifting they look back and see chaos and look forward and see chaos, they become chaotic themselves. Everything has to be worked out from first principles, even from no principles. Nothing can be taken for granted. Their personal lives and their lives as members of a society are incoherent and so aimless.

The Sear, The Yellow Leaf

Mr Bates arrived at the public library at exactly ten o'clock. Being punctual made going to the library to see the newspapers, seem like a real occupation. When he was a clerk in a shipping office, and before the office went bankrupt and had to discharge all its staff, he had been noted for punctuality. It figured in his thumbed testimonial: 'Mr Wilfred Bates is reliable, industrious and punctual.' The newspapers took him about an hour. He went conscientiously through their advertisements, having lost interest for some reason in their news and their leading articles and their special features. Even the most startling events left him indifferent. He turned over amazing disclosures – murder and adultery and sudden death – without even a glance, and hurried on to columns of close print which announced vacancies for smart salesmen and for intelligent ladies skilled in professional corsetry, and openings of all sorts for go-ahead young men. Any of these which might, by any stretch of the imagination, apply to him, he noted down. This, too, was a fiction, since he had long ago given up wasting postage on answering advertisements, and time on copying out in his laboured, precise handwriting the brief tale of his achievement. His qualities as enumerated in his testimonial, though excellent, were too common to have a market value; and his age was against him.

From the library he went to the park, nodding a good morning to the gardeners and attendants. He saw the same faces day after day in both the library and the park, and came to feel a sense of fellowship with them. They lived the same kind of life as he did, and frequented the same places. Whereas busy people in the streets seemed hostile (perhaps only because he envied them), they were friendly and sympathetic – a curious company in different stages of decay; mostly aged; all without hopes or duties or responsibilities; all, Mr Bates thought, waiting to die, and meanwhile turning over the back pages of newspapers and airing themselves in the park. He sat on a bench, the collar of his overcoat turned up to protect him from the chill of autumn, and listened to the quarter hours striking until it was time to fetch his grandson from school.

Sitting there and watching with careful attention a man paint a lamp standard green; vaguely noticing passers-by, classifying them, he felt that in a way he was privileged to be so removed from the world's business. It set him apart, and gave him a chance of looking objectively at his own life, and at the mass life to which he had belonged, but felt himself as belonging no longer. Going to and from a shipping office right to the end, he thought, I might never have seen it as I see it now – trams gliding by like dreams, and faces bobbing along streets like sticks and old tins on the surface of a stream, and the noise of traffic like the monotonous wash of the sea on a shore. His face was as grey as the thin irregular moustache which straggled over his upper-lip; his eyes as faded and shabby as his clothes, and his hands, folded in his lap, worn and uneven like a much-scrubbed kitchen table.

An old man with an infirmity; a curious lurch in his walk; stopping every now and again to throw out his arms and jerk upwards his chin, pointed angrily at a tramp asleep on a bench with a sack over his head. 'It's a scandal,' he muttered. 'You don't tell me that nowadays he couldn't get a clean-up. I've heard on the wireless . . .' His voice trailed off into incoherence. The tramp was always there asleep. Stockinged feet protruded from the sack, occasionally twitching. Otherwise he gave no sign of life until noon, when he awoke, yawned and stretched himself, and then went round the rubbish baskets, making his lunch on what he found in them that was edible. His beard and hair were overgrown, fantastic; his clothes miscellaneous; his whole appearance ribald and defiant. Mr Bates had a kind of respect for him. The tramp's withdrawal from the world was so much more complete, he thought, than his own. He had the courage to forgo every standard; even cleanliness; even decency. Beside him, Mr Bates and the others were pitiable figures; timid old men crouching fearfully inside their shabby overcoats and bowlers. They continued to shave. They brushed their boots and their clothes, and hid their decay under a show of respectability. Even though they had been outcast from society, they continued to observe its rules and proprieties. He spat in its face. Asleep under his sack or limping round from rubbish basket to rubbish basket, the tramp, it seemed to Mr Bates, put the rest of them to shame.

As he waited with a little group of women, the only man amongst them, outside the infants' department of an elementary school, Mr Bates was shy and uneasy. He imagined that the women looked curiously at him, wondering how he came to have the leisure to fetch his grandson each day. They were hard-faced, bitter women, conscious of dinners cooking in their ovens and anxious to get back to them. Their attitude towards one another, Mr Bates fancied, was hard and suspicious, and towards him contemptuous. In their world there was no place for a man – even an elderly man, with nothing to do. They pounced on their children with ferocious tenderness when they came out of school, and went off with them. The scene there – the grey asphalt playground with the red school building rising out of it, and these women waiting impatiently for their children – gusts of warm, musty air coming through the open door from the corridor within, had become a part of Mr Bates's life. He saw it again and again – sleeping and waking – its colour and smell and sensation – until it was swollen and exaggerated – an obsession.

Fetching his grandson from school was a duty that he undertook in return for board and lodging, and the five shillings a week pocket money that his three children contributed between them; not as their equivalent, but as a trifling service which, as his daughter-in-law put it, was the least he could do. The child dawdled on the way home, and Mr Bates did his best to coax him along. He had no affection for the child, nor the child for him. It was curious, but he felt more kindly disposed towards any urchin playing in the park than towards his grandchild. There was no blood feeling even. He took no pleasure in the thought of his seed being continued. His own children were strangers to him, and had always been strangers. He had forgotten his wife, her very appearance, all the years he had spent with her, almost as soon as she was dead. It was as though his life and hers had never really touched, so that when she no longer existed, when he no longer saw her, nothing remained to remind him that she had once been his wife. Though he went on living amongst the same furniture and sleeping on the same bed and seeing around him faces that were partly her and partly himself, her presence never re-created itself. Death obliterated her as far as he was concerned.

Dinner was noisy. His daughter-in-law – an untidy woman with protruding teeth; pretty in a feeble, disorderly way – carried in steaming dishes and served them. The meal was somehow strained and disorderly, like an appointment just kept, a train just caught. Mr Bates's three sons were there; one of them slightly deformed; his back unduly broad and his arms unduly long. They lived all together because it was cheaper. Mr Bates ate greedily, his morning in the park having whetted his appetite, and idleness giving to food an extra importance, as though, lacking other occupation, his body took a special delight in being nourished. His body took a special delight in being nourished, but his soul denied the need for food at all. Thus his greed was reluctant and unhappy. He wanted each mouthful, and, when it was finished, regretted it. As he ate he was aware that his daughter-in-law noticed the helpings he took, and stored them up in her mind as one more grievance against him.

In the afternoon, when his three sons had gone back to their work and his grandson been taken back to school, he drowsed over the fire. It was the emptiest part of the day, interminable and aimless, when he could put no barrier between himself and the fact that he had nothing to do; no reason for being alive; no part in anything that was going on in the world. Drowsing over the fire, replete, sometimes dreaming confusedly and sometimes staring round at the little room with its shabby furniture and half-drawn curtains, still faintly flavoured with the meal that had just been eaten, he longed for darkness to come. As it came gradually, dissolving so much that he hated to see; bringing people back from work to laze like himself over fires; transforming the room from being bare and exposed to being snug and secluded, he shook off his melancholy. If only it would always be dark! he thought, and admired the tramp's sagacity which led him to sleep during the day with a sack over his head, and to prowl the streets at night.

Mist made the darkness more enchanting because more adequate. It rolled over everything, turning people and buildings into vague shadows; their noise into a remote echo; their light into a dull glow. Mr Bates could live amongst shadows and echoes without suffering. The streets tempted him when they were misty and dark; and he was glad when his daughter-in-law asked him to go to the shops and fetch her four lamb cutlets for supper.

The stream of people was against him. He was setting forth, and they were returning; a day's work behind them; the cosy evening they had earned in front of them. Some were as old as he was. Some even older. Not age has outcast me, he thought; a disease within myself; a lack of vitality; sterile aspiration that became paralysis. He remembered how always, from the very beginning; at school; as an office boy; as a lover, a husband, a father, he had felt himself to be a stranger amongst strangers. It was the same now. Though he knew the street perfectly; each turn and curve; each shop and pillar box and hoarding, he picked his way along it cautiously like a blind man in an unfamiliar place.

The shop where he was to buy his lamb cutlets blazed with light, and resounded with shouts, and was thronged with people. scarlet meat displayed on white tiles, raw and brazen, glared shamelessly like rouged lips under arc lamps; and women swarmed round it (the same women who waited each day with him outside his grandson's school), prodding and touching, their eyes intent. Mr Bates got his cutlets and, as he left the shop, noticed a placard – 'Another Tube Suicide'. After that he saw the placard everywhere. The street was festooned with it – 'Another Tube Suicide'. Newsboys were shouting it – 'Another Tube Suicide'. Moving electric letters on the top of a building wrote it – 'Another Tube Suicide'. People, it seemed to him, whispered it in one another's ears – 'Another Tube Suicide'. He whispered it to himself – 'Another and Another and Another Tube Suicide'.

He saw the train whizzing out of its tunnel like a snake out of its hole; two lights approaching; a man detaching himself from the regiment of waiting men and women and, as the two lights got nearer and nearer, hurling himself at them. After that, darkness. He heard no shout of horror or sound of jamming brakes; saw no mutilated body; no blood spattered over steel lines. Darkness engulfed the scene after the suicide. It was an end. There were no consequences. Mr Bates's imagination stopped short at the act of destruction.

The blue lights of an underground station twinkled invitingly through the darkness and fog; and the entrance hall was thronged with people like the vestibule of a theatre or cinema. Amongst these people Mr Bates thought he saw the tramp; beard and hair curling; eyes sparkling. 'We'll go for a ride on the inner circle', he would say to him, taking his arm. Then, 'Have a lamb cutlet', thrusting all four into his pocket. He would find out how the tramp spent his nights, rambling with him through deserted streets, dancing with him along the Embankment, cooking the cutlets over a night-watchman's fire in a spacious, empty Trafalgar Square; find out who were his companions and where were his haunts; learn the secret of his courage and happiness, and be able hereafter to sleep through the day with his head in a sack instead of fetching his grandson from school, and drowsing over a fire through interminable afternoons, and living amongst the debris of a past that had no substance.

When he came actually to take the tramp's arm and propose this excursion, he could not find him, and so took a penny ticket for himself. Still he was travelling against the stream. His moving stairway was empty; the one coming up, crowded. He strolled up and down the platform waiting for his train; impatient for it to come like a man with an urgent appointment to keep. It was curious how the few things he had to do, like eating meals, became more and more feverish as the spaces between them grew longer and emptier; like an actor with one line to say waiting in the wings through scene after scene; then, when his moment came, blurting out his line incoherently.

The world now was a tube with advertisements curving round its sides; lightlessly lighted; airlessly aired. Mr Bates walked up and down the platform, regretful that there was no regiment of waiting men and women from which to detach himself; wondering whether he ought not to have left a letter behind to be read out at the inquest, and afterwards published in the newspapers. It would have been an opportunity to try and explain himself. 'I take my life because I have lost it.' He was ready with a formula. Then, 'After thirty years of work with one firm, during which time I was never once admonished (this to stab the hearts of his late employers), I found myself, through no fault of my own, unemployed and a burden on my relatives (this to stab the hearts of his sons and his daughter-in-law), and existing loosely in a society which, having no place for me, no use for me, seemed hostile (this to stab the hearts of everyone). My days were aimless and tiresome, and I decided to bring them to an end, since thereby I inflicted no loss, pain or inconvenience on anyone (this to stab his own heart). Signed, reliable, industrious, punctual Bates.'

He wished he had written the letter; taking trouble over it; getting it just right. It would have fulfilled ambitions he once had when secretly he scribbled on pieces of paper; took a correspondence course at a school of journalism; posted bulky letters, and received them back addressed in his own handwriting. There was no time now for the letter. Like a snake from its hole; a distant rumble; two lights getting nearer and nearer – was it absolutely true, no loss, pain or inconvenience? His daughter-in-law would be glad; his sons indifferent; but what about the faces he saw each day in the library and the park? They might mind, he thought, knowing that he was lying to himself. Even if they knew, they would be indifferent. They had their interests; bought sweepstake tickets; followed football results; loved their children and grandchildren. He was as separate from them as from everyone else. The rumble was louder, the lights nearer. Without an audience, and without having left a letter behind, Mr Bates prepared himself to jump; then faltered. The train was in the station, and its doors opening. He got in and rode to the next station, and hurried home to receive his daughter-in-law's reproaches for being so long with her cutlets.

[1934]

To Friends Of The Soviet Union

Who are you, dear Friends of the Soviet Union? You are the righteous minority; upholders of the ideal; denouncers of tyranny and injustice; lovers of truth and liberty; pacifists and saints and free-lovers and philosophers and socialists – in short, the elite or vanguard of the nation. When Jews are oppressed in Germany you raise your voices in protest; Sacco and Vanzetti, the Meerut prisoners, the Scottsboro prisoners – these and a thousand other injustices you condemn with eloquence and conviction. The British Raj in India and the Japanese occupation of Manchuria seem to you to be intolerable, and you make the wrongs of all subject peoples your own. Yet – and here precisely lies my problem – you bow your heads in the dust before the dictatorship of the proletariat as established in Russia and as revealed unto men through the agency of Marx the Father, Lenin the Son, and Stalin the Holy Ghost; and this despite the fact that the dictatorship of the proletariat has every single characteristic that you so hotly condemn elsewhere, and regards you and all that you stand for with open and unrestrained contempt.

That is to say, the dictatorship of the proletariat is cruel and arrogant; scornful of truth and liberty; indifferent to the suffering of individuals and classes and communities; incompetent and megalomaniac; ruthlessly intolerant of personal and corporate loyalties; hypocritical and stupid and corrupt, and has reduced a large population to a condition of poverty and misery and hopelessness that has to be seen to be believed. Nonetheless, dear Friends of the Soviet Union, you sniff round the dictatorship of the proletariat with craven adulation like dogs round ordure.

It may seem a little impertinent on my part to speak so confidently of the nature of the dictatorship of the proletariat. You too have visited Russia, and what you saw there served in most cases only to confirm your opinions and enthusiasms. Nearness lent enchantment to your view, and you returned from your conducted excursions to write and lecture and orate with, if anything, increased fervour. Who am I, you may well ask, to back my judgement and observation against, for instance, experienced, though aged social investigators like the Webbs, or talented journalists like Maurice Hindus, or distinguished scientists like Julian Huxley, or famous men-of-letters, like Bernard Shaw? Here I have to be dogmatic. It is a question of my word against theirs; and naturally, unless I was absolutely convinced of the rightness of my opinion, and had been able to confirm it again and again in the light of actual facts and experiences, I should hesitate flatly to contradict such reputable testimony.

After, however, spending some eight months in Russia; after going about the country a good deal; after a large number of conversations with all sorts and conditions of people; after seeing a lot of plays and films; after reading a lot of newspapers and listening to a lot of speeches; after generally, as the Americans put it, 'making contact' with the dictatorship of the proletariat, its personnel and its victims, I came to the conclusion that if it existed anywhere else and in any other terms, you would find it even more intolerable than I do; condemn it more emphatically; hold meetings and write joint letters to the Press protesting against it at least as fervidly as you do against, say, slavery in Liberia or police excesses in India.

This curious contradictoriness in you is, to me at least, more interesting than the Soviet regime. Indeed, the Soviet regime as such is not particularly interesting. Its precise historical significance will only be calculable when it can be looked back on from a decent distance; and its present absurdities and tragedies strikingly resemble, and are only more exaggerated than, the absurdities and tragedies of the contemporary world in general. There is nothing new about its theory or its practice; and, for my own part, I agree with an American professor who said that he liked the earlier phases of the Soviet regime because then it was one big, jolly racket, but that now it had split up into a lot of little rackets he found it very much like any other regime, only more disorderly and inefficient. It is probable, I think, that future historians will find the dictatorship of the proletariat entirely in keeping with the unreality and extravagance of the times, and will see in the Five Year Plan a grotesque and characteristically Russian equivalent of American Big Business.

Be that as it may, your attitude towards the Soviet regime is, at any rate for the moment, more significant and illuminating than the regime itself. Why do you dote on it so, dear Friends of the Soviet Union? What are you after? What's your game? You like peace and the League of Nations, don't you? But, dear Friends of the Soviet Union, the bellicosity of von Papen is as a voice piping in the wilderness compared with the bellicosity of the dictatorship of the proletariat. You like people to have the vote and to be able to say what they think, don't you? But, dear Friends of the Soviet Union, in Russia no one can speak or write or even think anything at all distasteful to six or seven megalomaniac and not very intelligent bosses without risking his life. As for voting – it is a forgotten institution. The political and social and economic rights of a Soviet worker or peasant are less, infinitely less, than those of a Negro in the United States. In fact, he has no rights. In fact, even more than in Oriental countries, he exists to carry out the will of a handful of masters; in the last resort, of one master. You like people to have enough to eat and to wear, and somewhere tolerable to live, don't you? But, dear Friends of the Soviet Union, in Russia the vast majority of the population lacks an adequate supply of the bare necessaries of life, and a good proportion of the population is starving. You are people of taste who deplore vulgarity in art, and sensationalism, and sentimentality, aren't you? But, dear Friends of the Soviet Union, in Russia, practically speaking, no art that is not vulgar and sensational and sentimental is allowed.

What, then, is one to make of you? At home you despise the taste of the general; in Russia, where no other taste is permissible, you are in ecstasies. You turn up your noses when the popular press exploits, for circulation purposes, the obscene details of some murder or divorce case; in Russia, when, by means of a State trial, the dictatorship of the proletariat exploits the same emotions, only in a more savage and unrestrained form, you exult. Tom Mann gets six months for refusing to promise not to disturb the peace, and you pour out righteous indignation with a warmth and sincerity that does you credit; the dictatorship of the proletariat 'liquidates' millions of kulaks, hundreds of thousands of priests, everyone who has your social background and who shares your views and aspirations, and you glorify its name.

Again, putting aside opinions, take your reactions to actual facts. I am certain that if an elementary schoolboy of average intelligence got into a train at Moscow and travelled across the Ukraine, even though, like you, he was accompanied by obsequious Intourist guides, by the time he reached Odessa he would be aware that he had passed through a melancholy, famished country whose agriculture was derelict, whose fields were weed-ridden and unploughed, whose population was wretched and starving; yet you, the flower of our intelligentsia, writers of books, editors of newspapers, lecturers and givers of wireless talks, instructors of public opinion, professors and enlightened politicians – you travel across the Ukraine and return with golden tales of success-ful collective farms, of a happy, ardent, well-fed, class-conscious peasantry.

How, dear Friends of the Soviet Union, do you come to be so easily gulled? Given the fact that your predilections are all in favour of the dictatorship of the proletariat, and that Soviet salesmanship is adept, and that your stay in Russia is usually short, and that most of it is occupied with conducted excursions – even then, to hear scientists with international reputations naïvely repeating statistics so fantastic that they have become popular jokes amongst those whose prosperity they purport to express! To hear famous economists draw ponderous conclusions from the 'stability' of the rouble which has been so recklessly depreciated that, when I left Russia three months ago, its exchange value was two hundred to the pound, and falling rapidly! To hear earnest social workers describe in glowing terms the manner in which Soviet children are cared for when, so appalling is the under-nourishment in Russia, it will take, on a moderate estimate and assuming conditions improve in the immediate future, two generations for the population to recover from its effects!

I have collected a number of these absurdities, and will quote two from Professor Julian Huxley's book, *A Scientist Among the Soviets*.

'While we were in Russia,' the Professor writes, 'a German town-planning expert was travelling over the huge Siberian spaces in a special train with a staff of assistants. Where cities are to arise, he stops for a few days, picks out the best site, lays down the broad outlines of the future city, and passes on, leaving the details to be filled in by architects and engineers who remain.'

'Highly placed personages,' he writes further on in the book, 'now and again give a good example by taking part in a *subotnik* (that is, voluntary labour). Congestion of unloaded goods wagons in the cities has been a frequent source of food-shortage and economic trouble in Russia. Accordingly unloading food from trucks is a favourable object for these volunteer gangs; and one is told that Stalin himself sometimes comes down to the Moscow goods sidings to help.'

Presumably, if a fellow scientist told the Professor that he had devised an apparatus that demonstrated the practicability of perpetual motion, he would, before advertising the discovery, ask to see the apparatus, or at least make some rather searching inquiries about it; the above statements, palpably ridiculous, proved so conclusively by the most superficial investigation, he accepts at their face value and faithfully records.

No one supposes wilful deception. You do not know that you have been gulled, dear Friends of the Soviet Union. You believe what you say and write. Only how does it happen that you say and write such nonsense? How does it happen that your newspapers and periodicals such as the *Manchester Guardian* and the *New Statesman*, in other respects truthful and conscientious, publish news and views about the Soviet regime that are less related to the facts of the case than the wildest scare stories of the popular press?

The answer, I believe, is terribly simple. A ghastly, fearful answer. You are indulgent towards the dictatorship of the proletariat because, in a sort of way, you are, or would like to be, a dictatorship of the proletariat yourselves. You are frustrated revolutionaries, and the spectacle of a revolutionary government in actual existence so intoxicates you that you fall on your knees, senses swooning, in awed worship. Like plain and reluctantly virtuous women fawning on brazen promiscuity you fawn on the dictatorship of the proletariat. When you hear of comrade so and so being taken for a ride you unconsciously lick your lips over the prospect of taking councillor so and so, who opposes your scheme for giving free milk to elementary school children, for a ride. The dictatorship of the proletariat is all-powerful and mouths your aspirations; and you, who have for so long had to be content with spinning your ideas into words, see in it the possibility of translating them suddenly into deeds. Seeing this, you adore; and adoring, you easily become propaganda-fodder.

At home you are, after all, a little community existing on its own and apart from the great mass of your fellow-countrymen. However confident you may be of representing all that is most advanced and enlightened in the nation you are still a minority, and take little direct part in the business of government; are essentially lookers-on; talkers and thinkers and agitators. The 'broad' or 'toiling' masses are, on the whole, strangely indifferent to your concern for their welfare and advancement. It is with difficulty, and rarely, that you can get yourselves elected to Parliament, let alone entrusted with absolute authority. If, on the other hand, you became a dictatorship of the proletariat you could afford to be indifferent to the 'broad' or 'toiling' masses. They would not matter then.

Here, it seems to me, lies the real attraction of the Soviet regime in your eyes. It shows you an attainable bridge between the abstract and the concrete. It shows you a means of putting your ideas, not approximately, but exactly into practice; how you can become men of action without having to compromise or to lay yourselves open to the reproaches of your less successful, and therefore more consistent, comrades; a way of enjoying unrestricted power without sacrificing one iota of your faith.

How much more agreeable it is to write decrees than to write pamphlets! How much more agreeable to give orders than to canvass constituents! How delightful to fashion, instead of project, a world fit for an enlightened intelligentsia to live in, and to prove the excellence of ideas, not by argument, but by sitting in the Kremlin and commanding their adoption. You have fed for many years on the consciousness of your own superiority. It is not a wholly satisfying diet, and leaves a man in old age lean and bitter. Add to it power, a vitamin, and you become swollen and magnificent. You become a dictatorship of the proletariat.

The fact is, dear Friends of the Soviet Union, the Soviet regime is you; and when you visit Russia you are delighted not so much because of anything you see there as because it is, for you, a home from home. In so far as you have tried to put your ideas into practice the results have been mostly unsatisfying. Your tilts against marriage with promiscuous lechery have left you exhausted rather than triumphant; Russia is a land where divorce and abortions are free for all, and the Moscow trams still run. Your political careers have been short and unproductive; Russia is a land whose legislation embodies your ideas, and the streets of Moscow are still crowded with people coming and going. Your enemies, who got seconds where you got firsts and were reckoned dull dogs where you were reckoned brilliant, find their way to the House of Lords, and you live in obscure neglect; Russia is a land where the mighty have been put down from their seats and the humble and meek exalted, where you have been exalted. At least so it seems to you. Actually you have long ago been slaughtered. Since, however, the slaughter was carried out in your name, and in accordance with principles that you approve, you cannot be expected to relate it to yourselves.

'There is nothing more dangerous,' writes Taine, 'than a General Idea in narrow, empty minds. Being empty, they are incapable of questioning it; being narrow, before long it becomes an obsession. Thenceforth, it takes complete control of them. They are no longer their own master, but become in the most literal sense, possessed.' Karl Marx and you have provided the General Idea, and the dictatorship of the proletariat has provided the empty, narrow mind. The result is the Soviet regime before which you grovel as people once grovelled before a casket containing Marat's heart.

When I consider how your fatuous idiocies have mocked the unhappy Russian population, and aroused false hopes and expectations amongst victims of economic distress in other countries, and in some cases led them, to their subsequent bitter regret, to emigrate with their families to the proletarian paradise you have so fulsomely advertised, there to starve and suffer and curse your names; when I recollect that Bernard Shaw gaily assured a Moscow audience that neither they nor any other Russians were short of food, and that Sidney Webb 'hotly repudiated' the malicious slander that there was forced labour in Russia notwithstanding the fact that the Soviet Press boasts of what has been achieved by political prisoners working under the direction – that is, the guns – of the Ogpu; when I reckon up your private and published reactions to the Soviet regime, you, with your General Idea, seem to me more contemptible, if not more dangerous, than the dictatorship of the proletariat with its empty, narrow mind.

No worse fate can befall a society, dear Friends of the Soviet Union, than to fall into your hands. A General Idea is the most terrible of all tyrants. Individual tyrants have their moods, and must at last die; it is inflexible and immortal. Individual tyrants only require a sense of personal supremacy, only destroy whoever and whatever challenges their personal supremacy; it destroys everything and everyone, is the essence of destruction – in towns, a darkness, a paralysis; in the country, a blight, sterility. Shouting monotonously its empty formula – a classless, socialist society – it attacks with methodical barbarity, not only men and classes and institutions, but the soul of a society. It tears a society up by the roots and leaves it dead. 'If we go,' Lenin said, 'we shall slam the door on an empty house.' '*Nous ferons un cimetière de la France,*' Carrier said, '*plutôt que de ne la pas régénérer de notre manière.*'

. . . I cannot imagine any worse possibility even in this unhappy uncertain time than that you should be able to enthrone your General Idea elsewhere. The fact that its first meal would be you, though just, would be no compensation for its subsequent ravages. Your attitude towards the Soviet regime shows how little you realize the General Idea's potentialities. Even so, I notice that few, if any, of you venture to exchange the capitalist tyranny you denounce for the proletarian bliss whose praises you sing so lustily; and it is gratifying to find that working class organizations with which you are connected profoundly distrust your General Idea and the political programme you deduce from it.

You are unquestionably one of the marvels of the age; and I shall treasure as a blessed memory the spectacle of you travelling with radiant optimism through a famished countryside; wandering in happy bands about squalid, overcrowded towns; listening with unshakable faith to the fatuous outpourings of carefully trained Intourist guides; repeating, like school children a multiplication table, the bogus statistics and dreary slogans that roll continuously – a dry, melancholy wind – over the emptiness of Soviet Russia. There, I used to think, an office-holder in some local branch of the League of Nations Union; there a godly Quaker who once had tea with Gandhi; there an inveigher against the Means Test and the Blasphemy Laws; there a staunch upholder of free trade and speech; there a preventer of cruelty to animals; there scarred and worthy veterans of a hundred battles for truth and freedom – all, all chanting the praises of the dictatorship of the proletariat. It was as though the Salvation Army had turned out with bands and banners in honour of some ferocious tribal deity, or as though a highbrow critic had hailed *Cavalcade* as the greatest masterpiece since Shakespeare, or as though the organ of a vegetarian society had issued a passionate plea for cannibalism.

[1934]

Utopias

My time in Moscow made me realize the difference between Utopias and Heaven, and understand the greater appeal of the latter. A Utopia is simply a place where a different set of people are important, whereas in Heaven everyone is important. Thus mankind has, very creditably, for the most part plumped for Heaven. It has been rightly suspicious of Utopias, and only allowed Utopias to have their innings when things got very bad indeed.

Plus Ça Change

Insofar as the tendency among liberals to look sympathetically on the Soviet regime is based on the supposition that it is now as greedy, class-ridden, imperialistic and unequalitarian as any other, they are justified. To each according to his need has long ago been replaced by the more usual and respectable slogan – to each what he can grab.

London Bridge Is Falling Down

Ever since I can remember thinking at all about the circumstances in which I found myself, it seemed to me that I was in contact with something which was running down. Roots had no life in them, though the trunk was still seemingly massive enough. Institutions like Parliament and the Church had a twilight air; projects to mature hereafter were only fanciful. The future could not be mapped by projecting the present, but was mysterious, unknown; the road which lay ahead might lead anywhere, or nowhere. I was lost, and my fellows lost with me. We had lost our way together; and of the many voices raised, persuasively, angrily, confidently, timorously, none could guide us. London Bridge is falling down, falling down – this old refrain became newly poignant; poetry, much beloved, might be said over, but no more forthcoming.

Such an attitude of mind is often blamed as pessimistic. It is a natural tendency to bury despair under strident hopes and cancel bewilderment with aggressive confidence. Decay is the best soil for Utopias, which are usually planted in winter rather than spring, and flourish in darkness rather than sunlight. The Gadarene swine throwing themselves to destruction probably imagined they were making for an easeful plain by the shortest route; sunset can be taken for dawn, and the day expected when night is coming.

To materialists, Christianity, indeed any religion whatsoever, must seem pessimistic, because to be religious implies a recognition that to seek to satisfy desire is a vain pursuit; that the work of human hands must soon perish – work and hands alike; that there can be no finality here on earth for individuals or communities, no finality at all; that we only exist precariously – perfection imperfectly expressed, eternity contained in time, a measure which will not contain it.

Yet if religion seemed pessimistic to materialists it is also true that it alone has provided the possibility of lasting hope. The past is littered with dead hopes – hopes of what was to be achieved when that war was won, that revolution triumphantly realized, that Act of Parliament passed and enforced; but the hope of life everlasting so briefly, so simply, proclaimed, survived from generation to generation. Material hopes cannot survive because they are material – that is, subject to corruption; but out of a realization of this is born a hope which cannot perish.

Thus I only began to hope when I ceased to be a materialist, and understood that men were not made happy or unhappy, serene or unsettled, by their circumstances whether physical or social or economic, but according to their sense of sharing a destiny which transcends their earthly circumstances, and consequent brotherliness between one another. I only began to hope when I became truly hopeless as far as this world is concerned, and saw that the profoundest of all truths was expressed by the saying that except a man lose his life he cannot save it.

Now the world and what was happening in it took on a different complexion. These institutions, which were running down, this present which would not project into the future, this way of life so obviously disintegrating, this darkness and destruction which loomed ahead, all became comprehensible. Men had tried to live by bread alone, and could not, men had tried to live in order to die instead of dying in order to live, and could not. If it had been possible to live by bread alone, if faces could have been lifted into immortality and spirits psychoanalysed into serenity, then would have been an occasion for despair. The failure – chaos deepening as statistics multiplied, war approaching as everlasting peace was ever more stridently proclaimed, misery increasing with bank deposits and sterility with sexual indulgence and savagery with humanitarian sentiments – was most blessed.

Never before had so much knowledge been made available, never had ignorance been so abysmal; never before had thought been so scientific, never had superstition been so crude and easily believed; devotion to freedom, prosperity, progress, all good things, never had men been so enslaved and so deceived. There in Russia, enlightened persons eagerly insisted, was a new civilization visibly coming to pass; there in Berchtesgarten, not so enlightened persons insisted, was a great gentleman dreaming dreams; there in Italy, trains were running on time; there in Geneva, what wonders were being performed; there in Paris and in London the voice of the people was heard through their elected representatives, was heard and was supreme. Yet in spite of new civilizations, a great gentleman, punctual trains, wonders truly performed, people's voice duly heard, with relentless inevitability, like a sleep-walker approaching a chasm down which he must fall, we have moved nearer and nearer towards, now at last have almost reached, an unexpected goal – destruction, all energies spent on destroying, all purposes directed to that end.

It had to be. When the foundation is gone, the house must fall. Perhaps ingeniously prop it up for some months, some years even; perhaps walk airily under its doomed roof loudly insisting that it is as secure as ever it was. Sooner or later it must fall. The foundation of any human society which lasts, which provides the individuals who compose it with whatever security is attainable for them, must be reality. On falsity nothing can be built but pretence; in falsity there is no strength, whatever arms and wealth may be at its disposal.

To reality, men must sooner or later return; but they will only return to it through suffering, and with humble and contrite hearts. Blood must be shed and humiliation endured before they again understand that sacrifice, not satisfied desire, is the way to fulfilment; that work, not money, is the measure of achievement; that fruitfulness, not pleasure, is the end of passion; that strength, not stratagems, is the basis of authority; that faith, not knowledge, is the way to understanding; that duty, not indulgence, is the path they must tread, and their common humanity, not their unique ego, what will hearten them to tread it.

After suffering and humiliation, they will discover heaven, and find that thereby they have also discovered the earth; rediscover God, and find that thereby they have also rediscovered one another; looking back with wonder on us and our strange circumstances, picturing to themselves those little, frail houses and cinemas rising like cathedrals from among them, hearing the many voices which have spoken to us – aged, quavering one proclaiming peace in our time, lunatic, frenzied one proclaiming war in our time, many, many voices; turning over printed words – brave little Manchuria, brave little Abyssinia, brave little Austria, brave little Czechoslovakia, there will be no war, there will be no war, there **is war**, brave little Poland, brave little Finland, brave little Norway, brave little . . .

The suffering and humiliation cannot be avoided. Evil cannot be blockaded into surrendering; nor can battle be left to others to fight, or money be made to serve when blood is necessary. Men lose contact with reality, imagining that symbols are veritably what they symbolize. A tempest roars, and they reach for a cheque book; famine comes, and they meet it with invoices. Contact is lost with reality, but not for long. Cheque book provides no protection against tempest; invoices provide no nourishment. Back, back, men are forced into the reality of their existence – the earth they must turn over, the passion they must expend, the mystery they must ever try to formulate, at best seeing through a glass darkly. As it happened before, so it must happen again, though we, perhaps, shall not see it. For us, perhaps, the darkness, now tangible; the blackout.

[1935]

Winter In Moscow

(In the preface to Malcolm Muggeridge's polemical first novel, *Winter in Moscow*, published in 1934, he admits that, as a result of his tour as *Manchester Guardian* correspondent in Russia, he took 'a great dislike to the Dictatorship of the Proletariat and, even more, to its imbecilic foreign admirers'. While ostensibly fiction, the story is patently autobiographical (Muggeridge is Wraithby) and it traces his growing disenchantment not only with the State which somehow never withered away, but also with any grandiose scheme to fashion a kingdom of heaven on earth.

These extracts are from the concluding chapter entitled: 'Who Whom?' which begins with Lenin's inscription: 'At bottom, the question of control is really the question: Who is it that exercises control? That is to say, what class controls and what class is controlled?')

Wraithby sat over a meal looking at Claud Mosser. 'The newness of it! That's what I like,' Mosser said. A world fit for Mosser to live in. 'Look at their prison system. Look at their divorce laws. Look at their courts and their schools and their crèches. Back of it all, youth. The ardour and courage of youth. Outsiders may be shocked; even repelled. But they've got to respect the flaming courage of youth that's back of it all.'

'The only thing I like about Bolshevism,' Wraithby said, 'is its antiquity. There's nothing older than Bolshevism. It takes you back to the beginning of time. Before history. Before animal life. Before matter had any shape. It takes you back to when the universe was a chaos of energy.'

Mosser saw that there was sales resistance to be overcome. He eased his cuffs and smoothed down his waistcoat.

'Look at the way they've abolished prostitution,' he said. 'Why, I was reading the other day in a book by Maurice Hindus a description of a home for reformed prostitutes. Listen to this. Can you beat it?'

He took the book out of his pocket and began to read:

As you go into this house now you are greeted by a man who offers to check your coat and rubbers ... This gives you a feeling that the place has a dignity of its own, like a theatre or an opera house ... A place of no small consequence, then ... This feeling heightens as you mount the freshly painted stairway and enter the office ... A young man of about thirty is at the desk. ... He wears a modern suit of clothes, complete with collar and tie, and, what is more astonishing, spats ... Communist though he is, he deems it essential to keep up as presentable an appearance as the scanty supplies in the Moscow haberdashery shops permit.

'No, I can't beat it,' Wraithby said.

'Think of the way prostitutes are treated in other countries,' Mosser went on. 'Outcasts. The lowest of the low. And here – check your coat and rubbers; freshly painted stairway; young man with collar, tie and, what is more astonishing, spats.'

His face glowed with enthusiasm. 'Where else would you find such an institution?' The idea stirred him; a genuine romantic, like the idea of a king or a president or a prime minister taking tea in a humble cottage. 'Mrs Peabody bobbed a curtsey and without any embarrassment asked His Majesty whether he took one lump or two.' 'A building once perhaps the home of one of the Czar's mistresses; now houses prostitutes. Outcasts. The lowest of the low,' he went on.

They went together to the circus. The attendants were dressed in gold uniforms, now shabby. It was a ghost of a circus; the animals aged; the apparatus battered; the performers jaded. 'Back of it all, youth. The ardour and courage of youth,' Wraithby whispered to Mosser. Was this the real Russia? A circus whose splendour had faded. No change except that its energy was spent. Nothing new about the circus except its disorder and shabbiness. The horses did their tricks stiffly like old men kneeling down in church; and the trainer's whip cracked without conviction.

'This is the past,' Mosser whispered back. 'In process of being liquidated. Sad, perhaps; but necessary. The past being cleared away.'

'Where do I find the present?' Wraithby asked.

'Out in the factories; in the great collective farms; in the theatres with their living revolutionary art; in concerts where workers meet to listen to the best music, afterwards to discuss . . .'

His question set Mosser off on to a great tirade. He fled from Mosser. The enemy, he thought; the destroyer, more dangerous and terrible because he deems it essential to keep up as presentable an appearance as the scanty supplies in the Moscow haberdashery shops permit.

. . . He tramped about day after day looking for a room in the real Russia; passing through buildings alive with human beings as with vermin; human beings packed densely together and forming a paste. 'Are you ever alone?' he asked a woman. 'Sometimes,' she said, 'I long even to be sent to Siberia because there at least I'd be alone.' He had foreign money to pay for a room. It was tempting; and offers were made to push back a little further the flood of human beings; wall off a little space; build a dam behind which he could live. He refused these offers. Here and there he found whole flats occupied by Communist officials or by members of the Ogpu. Oases of luxury like his hotel.

A Bulgarian barber helped him in his search. He was a young

man who had lived for ten years in Chicago. A belted tweed overcoat, his initials on the buckle, and wide-bottomed trousers that
overhung his shoes, were a relic of this time. Also a photograph in
a leather case of himself on a spree with his girl in the country.
'She's swell,' he said when he showed the photograph to Wraithby.

'How do you like it here?' Wraithby asked. He looked up quickly
like an animal; eyes afraid and alert.

'I sleep with de boys. Ten in a room, and not much eats.'

As he waited for a meal to be served in the hotel restaurant his
saliva overflowed.

'I was in partnership with my uncle,' he went on between bites;
'but dey wouldn't give me American nationality. I'd come in over
de Canadian frontier for two hundred and fifty dollars. Chicago...'

His dark eyes melted at the thought of Chicago; and he pulled
out his photograph and looked at it.

Wandering about in this teeming misery; looking for a corner
of it to live in, Wraithby understood the difference between ideas
and reality. He understood that every sort of idea was an unreal
simplification. Reality flooded into his mind like light, revealing
there a litter of ideas. He swept away this litter; and his mind was
clean but empty. 'After all,' he heard himself saying; lounging on
coloured cushions; drinking hot tea and eating buttered toast,
'there are worse things in life than starving.' That was an idea. In
reality there was nothing worse than starving. It was an ultimate
misery. 'I went to see *Uncle Vanya* the other day,' a Russian said to
him; 'and I wondered what they were all bothering about since
they'd got plenty to eat.'

The litter of ideas in his own mind was the litter of ideas outside. Rootless, unreligious ideas. What a blight they had been!
Piling up into shadows whose darkness cloaked a reversion to
savagery. Piling up into a Dictatorship of the Proletariat. Howled
out of loud-speakers. American bathing girls with ideas tattooed
on their bottoms. Triple portrait by the Kremlin wall; Lenin on
the left; Marx in front; Stalin on the right. 'After all,' he heard
himself saying, lying in bed by Anne's side, 'the family has to be
abolished. Property has to be abolished. Otherwise...' In a warm
bed, in darkness, he had abolished the family and property. The
Dictatorship of the Proletariat had also abolished the family and
property. Now he wandered amongst the teeming misery that was
left looking for a corner of it to live in.

He searched painstakingly for the real Russia; up and down

boulevards where children skated and played, and where old decrepit men stood with their cameras offering to photograph passers-by against a sea front or in a cardboard motor car, or sitting on the painted steps of a marble palace; in cinemas and libraries and museums and shops and government offices and clubs and restaurants; by the frozen river and amongst the pages of newspapers. Perhaps, he thought, there is no real Russia. Only an organization and organized force existing like signposts and barbed-wire fences in a stretch of wild country; only statistics and slogans shouted from the Kremlin and then lost in space; only waves of showmanship that pile up to wash a Bernard Shaw or a Lord Edderton or a Mrs Trivet over Russia. Was Mosser real Russia? Was Ouspenski real Russia? They danced, bespatted; consequential, on the surface of reality for a little while like company promoters and intimate biographers and film stars. With Jefferson hanging on to their skirts they got away with this and that for a little while. Then reality engulfed them. He saw Mosser and Ouspenski and Nollet and Mrs Eardly-Wheatsheaf and Mrs Trivet and Lord Edderton dancing on Russia; leaving foot-prints – famine, terror, heavy industry – but not really touching Russia. It was beyond their reach.

When he went to see Bulgakov, a Ukrainian with a round, wist-ful face that still seemed full of sun, Wraithby generally took a bottle of wine in his pocket. He and Bulgakov and Bulgakov's wife would talk together in whispers, because three children were sleeping in a corner of the room. If he got a little tipsy Bulgakov talked about the Ukraine. 'You should go there,' he whispered. 'Even now, when there's no food. It's a lovely country. Even now. But before . . .' He cracked his finger-joints and described how happy life had been once in the Ukraine. 'Of course, we didn't think it was particularly happy then; but I can see now . . .' His wife, fearing an outburst that would wake the children and perhaps be overheard, changed the subject.

'Won't you have some Soviet cake?' she said, fetching out part of a loaf of black bread; the only food they had.

'Happy,' Bulgakov went on, 'because our lives were connected with something. The poorest. The wretchedest. There were occasions in the year; Christmas; Easter; marriages and funerals. Based on absurd superstitions, perhaps, and on absurd social customs. But gay.'

Now, Wraithby thought, a pendulum swinging ponderously backwards and forwards, and demonstrating the diurnal revolu-tion of the earth. A live superstition replaced by a dead one.

Bulgakov pointed at three pictures on his walls. They were by a peasant. One was of five solemn men with heavy black moustaches sitting at a table and drinking; one of a bearded priest on a donkey with an umbrella over his shoulder, and one of a squat child garlanded with flowers.

'You see what I mean,' Bulgakov said.

It was the first proletarian art Wraithby had seen in Russia. He remembered the picture galleries he'd been through with their fatuous notices:

These twelfth century ikons mark the early stages of the struggle between kulaks and big landowners.

In Rubens the development of capitalism reaches a decisive phase, and the toiling masses realize their decisive role;

and the heavy portraits of Soviet personalities; glaring and lifeless as portraits of Christ in newly-founded Asiatic churches; and the pretentious machine-cult posters that Mrs Trivet took home to hang in her drawing-room.

'Yes, I see what you mean,' he said to Bulgakov.

The only place he could find on the train going back was on the little iron platform between one carriage and another. Just before the train started a man carrying a box joined him there. He was short, with a peaked face and three or four days' growth of blond stubble on his chin. Also, he was drunk. They went rocking through the snow; icy cold; the distances between stations getting longer and longer, until there were stretches of whiteness and clusters of black trees. The man lolled on his box, and seemed unaware that his position was precarious. He even dropped off to sleep. Wraithby, anxious for his safety, nudged him and asked, 'How's life?'

The man looked up curiously like an elf; head on one side; eyebrows raised. 'When there's bread I eat it; and when there isn't, I starve.'

Another, Wraithby thought, who'll outlive the Dictatorship of the Proletariat. 'The Revolution . . .' he began. The man growled angrily and spat. Wraithby reached across the little iron platform and hugged him. Arms round one another and shouting, they went rocking through the snow from one station to another.

The road from Wraithby's station led up past a row of wooden houses; then by a little church coloured pale blue and gold; then through a copse of trees; smooth snow untouched and gleaming

in the moonlight. Passengers from the train distributed themselves in the wooden houses, not speaking; moving silently; black
figures on white snow. Real Russia? Wraithby wondered, and
began to run; his blood warm and his face glowing, and happiness like a fire inside him.

Wraithby fell asleep in an old-fashioned sleeping-car. He woke
up, and, peeping through the window, saw a wide sweep of
country. It gave him a great sense of relief; and he realized that
Moscow was sombre and shut in, and that the dreary propaganda
that unceasingly washed over it had been oppressing his spirits.
Now he saw a horizon again. Stalin on Leninism, he thought;
Lenin on Stalinism; Molotov on Molotovism. Pah!

He went from place to place and found an intenser and more
passionate and simpler misery than in Moscow. In a German
settlement, a little oasis of prosperity in a collectivized wilderness, he watched peasants asking for bread. They wanted to be
admitted to the settlement. They knelt down and wept and
pleaded. Whatever else I may do or think in the future, he thought,
I must never pretend that I haven't seen this. Ideas will come and
go; but this is more than an idea. It is peasants kneeling down in
the snow and asking for bread. Something I have seen and understood.

The Germans showed him their settlement. They walked with
him through pigsties; stirring up one fat pig after another. They
caught sheep between their legs and parted the wool to show him
its thickness. They spread grain over the palms of their hands,
and gingerly opened the stables of horses and bulls. Their scarred
faces, cruel and clumsy, were sensitive to the nature of fertility.
They brought the smell of fertility to his nostrils. Barbarians,
too, he thought; but belonging to the earth. The barbarity of
Mosser and of the Dictatorship of the Proletariat was abstract.

In the evening the Germans put a military march on their
gramophone. They all stood up; stiffly; absurdly, spurred heels
clicking together, faces obtusely solemn. A barbarism, Wraithby
thought, that may, and probably will, make war on civilization.
Not, like the Dictatorship of the Proletariat, on life.

He walked through the streets of Rostov with an elderly
Intourist guide. Her face was crumpled into a perpetual smile. A
bib with a collar attached covered her chest and neck. They had
been together to a tractor factory, and to various buildings; some
completed and some uncompleted. She had been showing him over

Ouspenski's promised land; demonstrating the general idea.

'How do you like our Union?' she asked; an elderly spinster who ought to have been serving tea; putting the cosy on the pot between one cup and another, instead of demonstrating the general idea. An elderly spinster whose store of bibs had lasted since the Revolution. For fifteen years.

'Not very much,' he answered gently.

'I get meat three times a week,' she went on.

'I'm glad,' he said.

'And then we women are free.'

She said it very quietly. 'We women are free.' Her triumph was unassertive. She used, Wraithby thought, to attend meetings in connection with the emancipation of women. She used to demand the vote. Sowing the wind. Such a little piping wind! And now the whirlwind, bringing her meat three times a week and leaving undisturbed her store of bibs.

'I'm glad,' he said, 'that you women are free.'

He left her and turned into a church. A service was going on with quite a large congregation, mostly peasants. A melancholy passionate service. Religion was a refuge from the Dictatorship of the Proletariat. Priests in vestments and with long hair were chanting prayers; little candle flames lighting the darkness, and incense rising. The voices of the priests were dim like echoes, and the congregation curiously quiet; curiously still. Wraithby found their stillness hopeful; even exhilarating. It suggested that even general ideas spent themselves at last and were nothing.

The priests moved down amongst the congregation, swinging censers; their faces battered and frail; people kneeling and crossing themselves before them. They had been purified by suffering. Their spirits had been strengthened and made to burn steadily by it. They had proved strong enough to keep intact a link with the past. When they passed near him, Wraithby, unbelieving, knelt and gratefully received their blessing.

The future seemed empty to Wraithby. It was easy to burn up the past; but not so easy to face a future lacking everything that had given the past substance. Even for him; a person of no importance; a nobody, the patterns he'd made and unmade in his mind meant something. They'd at least filled up a certain space. They'd at least given him an occupation. Now, he thought, my occupation's gone. Ambition stirred painfully in the emptiness he'd made inside himself; and with adolescent morbidity he began to long to die.

To die! he would whisper to himself. To cease upon the midnight with no pain! feeling that this Dictatorship of the Proletariat, this promised land, this general idea, was everywhere; in
his own soul. Layer upon layer of chaos folding one on the other
like petals, he thought; and at the very core, myself; a chaos. The
future was a sweep of grey time to him because he had seen the
reality whose distorted shadow had been his past.

Before leaving Moscow he went to say goodbye to Blythe; an
Englishman who'd come to live in Moscow with his wife and
three children. He worked in a factory. Skin was drawn so tightly
over his face that it was like a skull. His expression was mean and
unpleasant. Wraithby liked and respected him more than anyone
else he'd met in Russia.

'I thought you'd be going soon,' Blythe said enviously; bitterly.

'Would you like to go, then?'

'I can't go, so the question doesn't arise.'

Wraithby knew that Blythe had no foreign money, and that he'd
been somehow persuaded to take Soviet nationality. He also knew
that the family was starving since Blythe only earned two
hundred roubles a month and got very little besides bread on his
ration card.

'I'm here for good.'

'I've got a little money. I'll lend you enough to get you back to
England.'

'What'd I do then?' Blythe asked, his voice angry and bitter. His
face was scarred with the fight to get the money that he'd had to
carry on all his life. The need for money had dried up his skin and
pulled it tightly over his face.

'Do you wish you hadn't come?'

'I don't know whether I wish I hadn't come or not; but I admit
to feeling angry about the lies that brought me here. Articles in a
magazine by Bernard Shaw; on glossy paper; illustrated. An aunt
sent them to me.'

He looked round at his room; in a basement and with one small
window.

'I wish,' he went on, 'that he could be made to come and live here,
and change his money into roubles, and take Soviet nationality.'

'It's a ghastly business, isn't it?'

'Ghastly failure. Ghastly misunderstanding. Ghastly betrayal.
But I don't mind that. To me the thing's justified because of its
beginnings. Because for a little while the masses stirred, became
coherent, dominant. What had to happen, happened; and nothing

46

can ever alter the fact that it happened, or that, in happening, it made the world different. All the same, when I think of that absurd, vain, rich old man letting himself be gulled; accepting the betrayal; spreading it in his magazine articles, and fetching us here to starve, I long for the same thing to happen in England if only so that he and his like might suffer the same fate they've suffered here.'

Wraithby knew the streets in Salford where Blythe had grown up. He knew the newspapers he'd read and the unemployment exchange where he'd waited, and the co-operative stores where he'd bought food, and the men he'd voted for.

'It never did happen really,' he said. 'It was a betrayal, a fraud, from the beginning. Do you remember how, when Trotsky and the others went to negotiate the Treaty of Brest Litovsk, they took with them six workers and six peasants? The six workers and peasants were given rooms and meals. They just stayed there and took no part in the negotiations. They were just a façade; a sham. It's been like that the whole way through.'

'Perhaps so,' Blythe said. 'But I don't think so. I think there was a moment, very short, very soon passed, when Lenin and his miserable crew were servants, not masters. That moment **was** the most important so far in the history of the human race.'

Blythe walked along with Wraithby. They paused in the Red Square. 'You know more about this business than anyone else,' Wraithby said. 'I mean how it works and what it means to people. If you came back to England you could write about it. After all, you haven't looked at the thing. You've suffered it.'

'I'd never write about it,' Blythe said. 'I'd have to attack it; and I'd never do that.' He pointed to Lenin's tomb. 'You can't understand what I felt when I saw them standing there, and the Red Army filing past, and the aeroplanes overhead, and the great procession, and the tanks and armoured cars.'

'I think I can. You mean it was you standing there.'

'Exactly.'

'That's the difference. I didn't see myself standing there.'

'Besides,' Blythe said, 'they'd never give me a passport out.'

Blythe went home; and Wraithby continued walking round the Red Square by himself. Two peasants and a child were huddled under a doorway. Soldiers with fixed bayonets were on guard outside Lenin's tomb. Suddenly he noticed a change in the wind that was blowing against his face. It was touched with warmth. It was fragrant. Suddenly spring had begun. The frozen river would thaw, and sun make the earth bare; then green. Thus it had happened a million times before. Thus it would happen a million times again. Nothing could prevent this process taking place – the sudden, unexpected coming of spring. Wraithby took in great breaths of the warm fragrant air.

[1934]

Why I Am Not A Pacifist

I want to try and explain why I am not a pacifist. There are three main brands of pacifism: (i) Pacifism like Tolstoy's, arising out of a conviction that taking life is in all circumstances sinful; (ii) Pacifism like Gandhi's arising out of a conviction that passive resistance is at once the only justifiable and only effective weapon to employ in resisting oppression, and (iii) Pacifism like Bertrand Russell's arising out of a conviction that fighting is never worth while. Of course these three brands of pacifism seldom exist in a pure form. The pacifism of most pacifists partakes of all three.

The belief that life is so sacred a flame that it must never be put out has been carried to its logical conclusion in the Hindu doctrine of *Ahimsa*, whose most exalted devotees claim to live without eating, since to eat is to kill. Once Tolstoy saw a mosquito crawling over Chertkov's bald head, and brought his hand down on it with a loud smack, leaving a little red patch on that serene pate. He then began to laugh uproariously, but Chertkov looked grave. 'You've taken life,' he said with ponderous reproachfulness, and Tolstoy's face fell, and he was gloomy and silent for the rest of the evening.

Ahimsa, except in the case of the aforementioned devotees who can live without eating, means becoming like Chertkov – that is a crank, who strains after an unattainable logicality, and becomes in consequence unhappy, or a bore, or absurd, and often all three. Life is infinitely sacred, and yet blood must be shed, if only a nut's blood to make a nut-cutlet; in the same way that God has counted the hairs of each individual head and knows when each sparrow falls to the ground, and yet men and sparrows are both like grass in His sight, today growing and tomorrow cast into the oven.

There remains the possibility that human life is in a category

48

of its own. Ought I, I ask myself, to make up my mind never under any circumstances to kill a man, though becoming reconciled to killing the 'mice and rats and such small deer' which were Poor Tom's fare? It is tempting to answer, yes. Killing is an acquired taste, and I should much prefer to leave it to others on the pretext that it ought not to be necessary. Besides, killing presupposes the possibility of being killed, and that is also an acquired taste.

Unfortunately, however, I cannot hide from myself the fact that the readiness of others to kill brings me advantages which I have not so far seen my way to forgo. I can sit here quietly writing what I like without fear of molestation only because those who might interfere with me, whether foreigners or my fellow-countrymen, know that they would risk being killed by doing so. There are, for instance, books on my shelves that Hitler or Stalin would not allow to remain there if Sussex happened to be within his jurisdiction. If Hitler's or Stalin's disapproval of my books is a matter of indifference to me it is because I know an armed force exists to prevent either from attempting to totalitarianize the village of Whatlington. I can even, with a passport in my pocket, go without trepidation into the very zone of terror of their secret police. My passport protects me because it is backed up by poison gas, tanks and bombing planes. In the USSR I noticed that Letts and Lithuanians and Esthonians were almost as afraid of the GPU as Soviet citizens, since their passports had no more sub-stantial backing than diplomatic protests. Again, though I have few possessions, I have some which I wish to keep and which others may well covet. Why does a passing tramp's covetous glance at my typewriter give me no disquiet? – because there are constables trained to use a truncheon with effect, and able in the last resort to invoke the aid of guns and bayonets.

If I am to continue to enjoy this security I cannot reasonably despise the means whereby it is achieved. Otherwise I am like those demagogues who refer contemptuously to the voters who make them eminent. If I believed that the soldier who killed in defence of his and my country, or the sailor patrolling the coasts within which I live, was performing a shameful act, I should first dispense with their protection – that is, renounce my nationality; then renounce the possessions they enable me to keep. Only then, naked on the naked earth, should I be in a position to preach the abomination of all warfare, and to pledge myself never to take up arms. Perhaps I ought to be naked on the naked earth. Until I am, however, it is hypocrisy for me to dissociate myself from arma-ments which enforce domestic order and prevent invasion, and so enable me, within limits, to live my life in my own way.

As long as I remain an Englishman I must stand or fall with England. I may believe that England's history is at least as ignoble as any other country's, that the Empire has been nefariously acquired, that in England as elsewhere the Few prey cruelly on the Many and charlatanry flourishes, that in the last troubled twenty years England has played a confused and sometimes contemptible part; but I have to ask myself – 'Am I prepared, given all this, still to be English?' If yes, then I must take the rough with the smooth; if no, then I must forgo whatever advantages accrue to me through being an Englishman. In peace my English citizenship brings me benefits, in war responsibilities. I cannot have one without the other. A husband who deserts his wife when she is in difficulties, even though he thinks they are of her own making, is despicable. He has enjoyed his wife's companionship when things go well, and then, when they go ill, asserts his moral right to go his own way.

If at this time England were defeated and the Empire disrupted, whatever the circumstances, it would, I believe, be a great calamity; therefore I have no alternative but to be prepared, if the necessity arises, to play my part in preventing such a defeat. I compare the state of affairs in England with the state of affairs in Germany, the USSR and Italy, and conquest by any of those Powers seems to me worse than death. Their gods are the most evil that have ever been set up, a denial of whatever in life is of any account; and I know that they despise weakness, that they are impervious to moral gestures, that each cherishes dreams of world domination, trains its youth to believe that war is splendid and hatred necessary, and has shown again and again its indifference to all considerations except expediency. Knowing this I cannot pretend that a League of Nations, or any pact or agreement or moral gesture whatsoever, is likely to curb their megalomaniacal impulses. I must envisage the possibility of having to choose between going down before them or resisting. I choose to resist in the certain knowledge that it is the lesser of two evils.

As for passive resistance as a weapon, Gandhi has shown that it can sometimes be used with effect, though even he has admitted that its use in India led to outbreaks of violence, and that it failed to achieve its object because of the moral delinquency of his followers. In any case, it is a form of coercion, a sort of spiritual blockade, entailing often as much hardship and suffering as a physical one. 'Do what I want you to,' Gandhi said in effect to the Government of India, 'or I shall instruct my followers to make it impossible for you to govern. There will be no revenue, no law courts, no children at school or students at the universities.' If he had succeeded in bringing about an administrative breakdown there would have been as much suffering, destruction and even death as if he had raised an army to fight for his cause. Morally, I can see little difference between lying down in an enemy's way to obstruct him, and pushing him into a different path. In both cases I am forcing him against his will to do what I want. Even when Gandhi limits his coercive measures to a fast unto death, it is still coercion. His death in such circumstances would lead to popular discontent, and therefore, he calculates, the Government must yield. A less eminent person's starving would not lead to popular discontent, and so would be ineffectual. It is not that a, in Mr Gandhi's eyes, satanic administration is to be made to see the error of its ways by the noble spectacle of self-imposed suffering, but made to yield through fear of the consequences if it can be held responsible for a national leader's death.

If passive resistance was up to a point effective in India, it was because of the, by comparison with other governments, astonishing squeamishness of the Government of India. Would passive resistance have helped the Abyssinians against Italy? Would it have helped the Kronstadt rebels when the Red Army mowed them down for demanding free speech, a secret ballot, freedom of the press, and other such trifles, or German Jews slaughtered and tormented for being Jews? Would it be any help to us if, to redeem the toiling masses or to establish the supremacy of the Nordic race, a totalitarian steam-roller gave a lurch in our direction?

Better, some say, to be defeated, because when we have been defeated often enough we shall settle down to a quiet Scandinavian life. Germany was defeated, but did not so settle down. Russia has been defeated as often as the most ardent defeatist could wish, and the result is not amiable agrarians co-operatively marketing plump pigs and butter, neither menaced nor menacing, but the parent Totalitarian State, armed to the teeth and preaching the blessedness of civil war, financing and sending emissaries everywhere, for instance, to Spain, to promote this blessedness.

I like not, as Falstaff would say, such grinning defeats.

Another kind of pacifism, scarcely worth considering it is so foolish, is that of the pacifist who objects to international war but approves of class war. In England he advocates disarmament and swoons with horror at the very word 'conscription'; the rattle of tanks across the Red Square, the drone of aeroplanes over it, exalt his spirit. He signs letters pleading for the preservation of civil liberties, and quotes the Sermon of the Mount against bishops who insist that it is possible to be a Christian and take up arms; Lenin, compared with whom Mussolini is a cooing dove, is his hero, and the Comintern's railings against 'Bourgeois Democracy', and insistence that classes exist to war against one another until the most numerous has consumed all the others, is as music in his ears. When it is a matter of killing a foreign enemy he pleads his conscience and goes to prison, when it is a matter of killing kulaks he sharpens his knife.

Killing is evil, and war is a senseless, terrible calamity. Like many other human activities it reflects, not the divine, but the beast in Man. As a rash manifests measles war manifests mass hysteria and hate. I might pledge myself to take every care to avoid becoming infected with measles, but it would be absurd as well as dishonest to pledge myself never to have a rash. War is but one aspect of the whole horror of human behaviour. It cannot be isolated. It belongs to Evil, which, like Good, is one and indivisible.

> Religious canons, civil laws are cruel;
> Then what should war be?

The Stock Exchange is a manifestation of greed, but greed would not be abolished by abolishing the Stock Exchange. Nor should I help matters, but only delude myself, by taking a pledge never to participate in Stock Exchange deals while continuing to belong to a society in which greed is admitted to be the mainspring of effort. So it is with war. Power and authority are honoured, weakness despised; and there is no virtue or sense in forswearing one consequence among many of the hunger for power and authority therefore set up. If every man and woman in the world sincerely pledged themselves not to fight, there would still be war as long as there was hate in their hearts; and if there was no hate in their hearts war would cease without any pledges needing to be taken. Even that is not the last word, because when hate is made into a religion, as in Marxism and Nazism, and propagated as such, it may have to be combated with its own weapons.

As a social being I am implicated in much besides war that is evil, senseless and calamitous. I sit here warm and others are cold, I sit here fed and others are hungry, I sit here unafraid and others are terrorized. To live at all I must constantly do violence to the values I know to be true. If I flee to the remotest wilderness, live in a walled prison like a bird in a cage, I am still part of a society whose values are false. There is no escape, except in the promise that with God all things are possible. I shudder to think of the cruelty, injustice, charlatanry, self-interest masquerading as altruism, around me, of the slaughter and destruction that are being prepared; shudder when I look into my own heart and see it all there too; shudder again when I remember that since the beginning of time it has been so, and that the very protests made against its being so have provided scope for frustration to find a vent, vanity to spread itself, appetite for power to be satisfied, and exploitation to be organized anew and more drastically. I shudder the more because I know that protests must be empty, revolutions empty, counter-revolutions empty, barbarism empty; that what alone is not empty is the soul's obscure longing, that this longing never has and never can be satisfied within the confines of Time (where I must live, perhaps kill or be killed, get money, indulge or extinguish my appetites), and that yet it is the whole substance of living.

[1936]

Moscow Farewell

When an official in the Soviet Foreign Office bade me goodbye, he said: 'You know, I feel that coming here has saved you from nihilism. It has given you something positive to believe in.'

'It has,' I agreed. 'It has made me believe in civilization.'

'You mean capitalism,' he said.

'No,' I insisted: 'civilization.'

Ever after I have been wondering whether that too, like the Dictatorship of the Proletariat, was a piece of humbug. It is easy to talk big about civilization, but is there such a thing? When the dead leaves are pulled off, is there anything living, real, left? In Russia, it seemed clear that there was. The emptiness of that country, its joylessness, its ghastly pageantry, its denial of every spiritual value, its bestial arrogance, its overwhelming vulgarity, the trivial hopes and vanities of its rulers, made the world outside seem, by contrast, happy and civilized. Now I am outside, myself, I wonder. Wonder as I turn over the pages of newspapers, and look at queues outside unemployment exchanges, and hear the claptrap of politicians, and see how grim, unnecessarily grim, life is for most of my fellow countrymen, and how at every moment of their waking life all that is basest in them, cheapest, is stirred up to make them buy this or that, think this or that, feel this or that. Wonder as I walk about the streets of London pursued by posters outside cinemas, and genteel radio voices, and placards: 'Mother who starved for her children – pictures', and miners singing hymns for pennies. Who can help wondering?

Yet, I believe there is such a thing as civilization. I believe that, in this country at least, underneath the confused babble of slogans and salesmanship and egotism struggling to assert itself, to make itself heard, noticed, civilized values exist. They exist precariously, threatened from two sides. Two currents of disintegration threaten to engulf them. A free-loving, sunbathing, birth-controlling, intouring attack comes from the Left; and a loutish, swaggering, God-Save-The-King attack comes from the Right; while in between is a no-man's-land full of echoes and shadows, of bleating noises as of sheep on a distant hillside. In view of so dangerous and confused an alignment of forces, who, I repeat, can help wondering?

What are these threatened civilized values? – Essentially, a sense that the real significance of life is inward and not outward, that the problems it poses are at once too sublime and too terrible to be solved by the application of any formula, that the individual is immensely precious and immensely important, and, at the same time, as a grain of sand on the seashore, that he cannot be treated in the mass, steam-rollered out of existence, without his life losing all dignity, all that makes it worth anything to him, that the past and the present and the future are one, and that men have their roots in the past, so that to destroy the past means destroying men. Too, that no civilized people in any circumstances delegate to one man or group of men a right to act for them, think for them, be them, that qualitative standards are more important than quantitative. All that is great in human history has come from such an attitude to life, all that is contemptible from its opposite. The eradication of even the memory of its ever having existed is the avowed object of most governments in Europe today. If we, too, turn our backs on it, then the world may settle down to an unbroken period of Dictatorships of the Proletariat, of Leaders, of Brain Trusts, and other such mob tyrants.

Whom God Hath Joined

Whispers overflowed the corridor outside the little County Court. Lawyers were in the corridor in wig and gown and at ease, and their clients, apprehensive, wearing their best clothes. A policeman with a waxed moustache and with ribbons on his tunic walked up and down shouting, 'Silence!' Where he was the whispering died down, only when he had moved on to swell again. The lawyers nonchalantly looked over their briefs in consultation with their clients, fingering little battered photographs, letters, hotel bills, and rehearsing evidence like a theatrical producer with an inexperienced nervous actor.

In the Court the Judge took his place, aged and in red, lean and wrinkled, his shrivelled fingers playing with a pencil, his tired eyes patient. A Clerk in black, most respectable, called out the first case to be heard and administered the oath to the first witness. This witness, a plump blonde lady with a powdery face, and with artificial fruit in her hat, held the Bible gingerly and, like a faint weary echo, whispered the Clerk's confident words after him, handing the Bible back with relief when its purpose was served. The Judge settled to listen, and a lawyer began:

'You are the proprietor of the . . . Hotel in . . . ?'

'Yes,' cautiously, as though fearful of making a damaging admission.

A photograph was passed up to the witness-box. It was a seaside snapshot of a woman on a cardboard elephant.

'You know the woman in that photograph?'

'Yes, she stayed a week at my hotel.'

'Alone?'

'With a man.'

'And they shared a room?'

'And a bed. They signed the register as man and wife.'

(Was there rapture in the double bed, long-awaited passion eagerly enjoyed? Or only momentary appetite? Was the week unforgettable as a wedding day, or already almost forgotten? Would even this sombre reminder of it make their hearts quicken, or seem as unsavoury as a glass of wine left unfinished in the evening and removed in the morning to lay breakfast? The Court was not interested in such questions. They did not arise.)

'Was this,' pointing to a stocky man holding his overcoat and hat, 'the man she stayed with?'

The witness shook her head emphatically, and the man holding his overcoat and hat blushed and looked down on the ground as though ashamed of being thus repudiated.

'That's all.'

Now the man holding his overcoat and hat went into the witness-box and took the oath. Unexpectedly, he bent down and kissed the Bible before handing it back.

'You are the husband of the woman in that photograph?'

'Yes.'

Four or five questions extracted from him the substance of his marriage, like the substance of a life on a tombstone – born on such a day, died on such a day, Rest in Peace. He answered meekly, his voice only quavering when the lawyer asked him, 'Was the marriage a happy one?'

'Oh, yes,' he answered, holding his overcoat and hat, 'it was happy.'

(Rapture for him, too, long ago; plans made and intimacies accorded, working and sleeping and eating while his hair thinned and his teeth fell out and his skin dried and wrinkled, until this unexpected moment when, after bending down and kissing the Bible as he had so often bent down and kissed his wife, he announced to an aged Judge in red and a respectable Clerk in black, to a few rows of lawyers and their clients, to a gallery of Public, that his marriage had been happy.)

The Judge wearily nodded; the decree was granted. Wondering, the man put on his hat and overcoat and went home.

Thus it proceeded through the morning. Witness after witness went into the witness-box – private detectives glib with the oath from long familiarity; hotel and lodging-house keepers grudging their evidence, husbands and wives, some stolid, some sorrowful and some distracted; children even who described their parents' adultery, and servants their master's and mistress's. The Clerk's intonation of the oath did not lose its zest however many times he repeated it. Only a slight hoarseness came into his voice. The Judge continued to loll resignedly in his seat, wearily nodding at the completion of each case, like a schoolmaster with a turbulent class on a summer afternoon giving permission to a boy to go to the lavatory.

The lawyers, ruddy and swollen under their wigs, black suits under black gowns, earned their fees and went away to lunch, a particular case momentarily interesting them, as items of news do a news-editor, and then forgotten. So much adultery they needed. Was there enough? – weighing it out – barely enough, or plenty? More adultery! – shaking their heads – 'It won't do. There's not enough adultery,' or, 'I think we've got enough adultery now.' They ladled out adultery, sparing when it was short, generous when it was plentiful, making the best show they could with the adultery at their disposal.

Disappointed by proceedings so drab and monotonous, the Public went away too. Its gallery gradually emptied. There was more to excite in a newspaper or cinema than in this interminable putting the same questions and getting the same answers – 'The truth, the whole truth, and nothing but the truth, so help me God,' and then, 'I saw so and so in bed with so and so at such a place and such a time.' The staleness of morning bedrooms pervaded the Court, and a ruttish pig if one had strolled in would have evoked reverence.

Four minutes settled each case. To such small compass had passion been reduced. What a concentration of scenes, guilty assignations, indecision, corroding suspicion and shrieking hate! Perhaps at the Judgement Day whole lives may make as poor a showing, sifted of irrelevance, their shifting emotions and appetites compressed to a few bare questions. Life is full of strange consequences, as Lambeth Palace being a consequence of Calvary, or strip-tease of the Pilgrim Fathers; one of the strangest is that the play of the same impulse which brings young lambs in spring should lead to the enactment of this curious scene in a little County Court – the aged Judge in red, the respectable Clerk in black, the lawyers in their wigs and gowns measuring out adultery with practised hands, like a draper measuring out cloth.

[1937]

What Is My Life?

I ask myself continually as so many have, 'What is my life?' This question robs even newspapers of their wonder. I open them greedily like a child biting into a piece of iced cake, but the taste disappoints. This is happening, and this; there is a crisis, there may be war, or not war. Who will go to the War Office, or stay at the Office of Works? The future of Civilization depends . . . I see the Man writing the Paragraph, able to reveal or report or announce, smoking, stabbing at a typewriter, blinking anxiously through tobacco smoke at a watch-face. Momentarily, I am infected. 'God, war!' I think; or, 'God, Belisha!' or, 'God, Civilization!' trying to hold Civilization like a slippery fish. Then I think: 'Beneath the innumerable garments that were heaped on King George VI at his Coronation there was shrinking, tender flesh, and beneath this flesh a beating heart and lungs being blown up and deflated, and beneath these a Something, a Soul; and so it is with an aboriginal crawling into his mud hut or moaning prayers before a painted stone, and with Mr Hore-Belisha and me.

'At any time in the history of the world,' I think, 'there was a crisis, a war threatening or to be averted, important people becoming more important or less important or staying the same, a civilization waxing or waning; and people got excited about it, and trembled with hope and groaned with chagrin, and there were prophets to denounce and Emperors and Kings and Leaders and Presidents to be adulated, and priests to collect offerings, and revolutionaries to put down the Mighty, and poets and saints and orators; and perhaps it all signifies Progress though I cannot see it, and perhaps it all makes a pattern which will one day be clear as the Marxists say it is clear already; but this is certain – that all this happening, and all these countless people living and dying has not answered the question I ask myself continually, "What is my life?"'

Asking myself this question, I look down at my hands and limbs and feet and wonder at them. Transactions like giving a bus conductor a penny and getting a ticket in exchange seem fabulous. The ordinary functions of living, like breathing and eating and excreting and circulating the blood and lying down in the evening to sleep and waking in the morning, fill me with astonishment. I marvel at how I came to be born and at the certainty that soon I must die. 'That man,' I think, 'with his billowing neck and misty eyes and rolled umbrella and bowler hat – that man pushed his way into the world from a womb, sucked at a nipple, cried that he was come to this great stage of fools; and one day he will stop drawing his breath, his heart will stop beating, one or two will cry and close his eyes, and he will be dead.

'All I know of that man,' I think, 'is all I know of myself – that I was conceived, born and must die. He and I and all men are the same. It is inconceivable that one man should be of greater worth than another, just as it is inconceivable to a parent that one of his children should be of greater worth than another, however varied their capacities. We are all in the same situation – stretching ourselves for a little while on the earth, staring up bewildered at the sun and moon and stars and down bewildered at the ground and bewildered into our hearts, and then no more seen on the earth and soon forgotten.'

The question which Lenin said should be asked continually was not 'What is my life?' but 'Who whom?' This question means, 'Who will be the next Prime Minister?' 'Which side will win the next war?' 'Who, today poor and weak, will tomorrow be rich and strong?' 'Who are fit to be deposed and who to be exalted?' whereas 'What is my life?' means, 'Why have I and countless others exactly like me been sent to spend a few years on a small rotating planet, moving systematically round the sun, and suspended in illimitable space which is all littered with countless other suns?'

If 'Who whom?' is the vital question, trying to answer 'What is my life?' is a waste of time and energy that should be devoted to deciding 'Who whom?'; if 'What is my life?' is the vital question, 'Who whom?' does not matter much.

'Who whom?' is easy to answer. The answer is 'We them' or, in extravagant cases like for instance Napoleon or Lenin himself, 'I them.' 'What is my life?' is difficult, even impossible, to answer with any precision or certainty. The first answer that suggests itself is, 'The satisfaction of Desire.' Various alluring objectives present themselves, as enjoying sexual intercourse with that body, acquiring that fame or wealth or sanctity or importance, exercising that authority or bringing about those reforms; and the obvious way to employ a life seems to be in straining after these objectives. Ruysbroeck refers to certain Sects of the Free Spirit which flourished in his time, the fourteenth century, and which believed in 'according to Nature everything it desires'. 'For Man to be perfect,' they taught, 'it is sufficient that he follow the inclinations that God has implanted in his heart.' Blake was a Free Spirit devotee. 'He who desires but acts not breeds pestilence,' and:

> Abstinence sows sand all over
> The ruddy limbs and flaming hair:
> But Desire Gratified
> Plants fruits of life and beauty there.

Often enough the cry has been raised of a right to satisfy Desire on the ground that since Desire exists it must be intended that it should be satisfied, or that since Man is inherently good, so must his Desire be good, or, lately, that the frustration of Desire is dangerous and its satisfaction not merely a right but a duty.

The difficulty in satisfying Desire lies in its variety. I may satisfy my sexual appetite and groan over neglected ambition; I may live laboriously to become rich or famous or learned or useful, and be racked by sexual appetite; I may be prodigiously ascetic and look enviously on those apparently enjoying what I have renounced. The difficulty in satisfying Desire is that it cannot be satisfied. Indulgence, temperance and abstinence are all unsatisfying. The young indulgent Tolstoy, the middle-aged temperate Tolstoy and the old abstinent Tolstoy were equally haunted by unsatisfied Desire; and Shakespeare found Lust:

> Past reason hunted; and no sooner had,
> Past reason hated, as a swallow'd bait,
> On purpose laid to make the taker mad:
> Mad in pursuit, and in possession so;
> Had, having, and in quest to have, extreme;
> A bliss in proof, and proved, a very woe;
> Before, a joy proposed; behind, a dream.

Some go on hoping that it might be possible to satisfy Desire. If they got hold of so much money, they think, or experienced such bodily ecstasy, or wrote such a book with such sales and such reviews, or polled so many votes, they would be satisfied. Everything and everyone that is popular ministers in some way to this illusion. It is the Best-Selling formula, and with slight adaptation can be shaped into an advertisement, a Leader, a novel, a film, a revolution, a Cause, a religion, or a newspaper. Others fall back on a belief that Desire might be collectively satisfied. Individual Desire cannot be satisfied, they argue, because of Capitalism or War, or because there are too many people or too little education, or because proportional representation and the humane-killer and the metric system have not been made compulsory; therefore, abolish Capitalism and War, extend birth-control and education, make proportional representation, the humane-killer and the metric system compulsory, and lo! satisfied Desire. This is Idealism.

Pursued, Idealism also proves illusory. Corporate achievement is no more satisfying than individual; and revolutions are as disappointing as adultery and Utopias as flat as success. It is as impossible for an individual to achieve serenity through perfecting his environment as through satisfying Desire, since his environment is only a projection of his Desire. Thus trying to

60

satisfy Desire by creating a Utopia is like trying to finance a new company with debts in the hope of thereby being able to pay them off.

Besides, a Utopia presupposes a true Law, and there cannot be a true Law because Truth cannot be formulated. When it is formulated it ceases to be true, as love becomes insincere when it is formulated, for instance, in a marriage-covenant or in pre-fornicatory earnestness. Every Law is inherently false and must be repugnant to imaginative insight. Imaginatively, I know that 'Beloved, let us love one another, for love is of God' is the only commandment, but this knowledge is constantly outraged by existing formulated Law which necessarily assumes that Greed and Lust and Envy and Fear are the mainsprings of human activity; and it will always be so because Law is concerned not with truth and perfection, but with providing a means whereby greedy, lustful, envious, fearful men may live together without quite making life impossible for one another.

Thus there cannot ever be a Utopia, and there must always be a conflict between imaginative insight and the whole structure of the Law, or the Establishment, whatever its theoretical basis – Christianity, Marxism, Behaviourism, Nudism – may be. This conflict is what makes people who live more in the Imagination than the Will find the world so alien a place. What everlasting hypocrisy and charlatanry! – like *The Times*, very Establishment of very Establishment, after fulminating for years against the repressive methods of the Soviet Government, writing of 'a temporary firmer application of those methods of repression on which the Soviet experiment has wisely and successfully relied'; like all the ghastly flattery and anecdotal facetiousness which the Coronation exuded as a slug does slime to ease its way, and all the ghastly pretence about the Spanish Civil War, that it is for Democracy or for Christianity, or for the Masses or for Spain; like swarming after Authority and the swarm's sudden movements from Czar to demagogue and from demagogue to commissar, always ready to make a quick wheel; like Mr Bolitho on Edward VIII before and after and Mr Bryant on Mr Baldwin and the Archbishop of Canterbury declaiming that foxes have holes and Mr Eden's earnest hopes and the *Daily Worker*'s flaming protests and . . . oh, Establishment, Establishment!

In his interesting little book on the USSR, M. Gide insists that this horror of the Establishment, *force d'opposition*, is a measure of a writer's worth; '*un grand écrivain, un grand artiste, est essentielle-ment anticonformiste. Il navigue à contre courant.*' He complains that

Soviet writers and painters, whoever would offer any sort of comment on life, are expected to approve in all particulars of the Law under which they live and of its constant and often drastic fluctuations, and that this puts out all creative fire in them. In so far as they have imaginative insight and so are capable of commenting on life apart from its phenomena, they know that their Law, however superior they may think it to all other Laws that have ever been, is still cruel, hypocritical, approximate, unjust, a persistent and inevitable denial of the highest values, and so in approving of it they are like clergymen who convince themselves, or at least try to convince their congregations, that there is no incompatibility between Christ's teaching and prevailing social values.

M. Gide suggests that in certain circumstances great writers have not been conscious of a conflict between their imaginative insight and the contemporary Establishment, and implies that this might happen again, though he is emphatic that it has not happened in the USSR. He gives Shakespeare as an example of a writer who 'lived and wrote in fullest sympathy with the whole people'. It is difficult to read much complacency with the Elizabethan Establishment into, for instance, *Timon of Athens*, or to believe that an Elizabethan equivalent of *The Times* would have cared to publish:

Thou rascally beadle, hold thy bloody hand!
Why dost thou lash that whore? Strip thine own back;
Thou hotly lusts to use her in that kind
For which thou whipst her. The usurer hangs the cozener.
Through tatter'd clothes small vices do appear;
Robes and furr'd gowns hide all. Plate sin with gold,
And the strong lance of justice hurtless breaks;
Arm it in rags, a pigmy's straw does pierce it.

Is there then nothing? – only Desire soon found to be unsatisfiable, a Utopia that cannot be, progress that does not take place, Great Ones that ebb and flow with the moon, 'Who whom?' for ever being put and answered – that's nothing. Was the universe created, including – an infinitesimal fragment – the earth, and life planted in the earth, including – also infinitesimal – this generation of men, as this generation of men includes me – was it only to have a crop season by season of eager appetite and disappointed hope and morose satiety and envious frustration, of Truth twisted into a Law and then the Law destroyed in the name of Truth? Is that all? Is that the answer to 'What is my life?'

Dimly, spasmodically, one receives intimations that there is another answer. There are moments when life seems a whole. In some mysterious way all its diversity makes a Oneness. What seemed incompatible, as Good and Evil, Love and Hate, are no longer incompatible. Pain and disease and cruelty and arrogance lose their sting and become irrelevant, like grievances in the presence of death. Ambition no longer torments, fear no longer corrodes, lust no longer burns, indecision no longer disturbs and regrets no longer eat, eat away at the heart. There is a Oneness, and through that Oneness, peace. The difference between man and man momentarily disappears – there loosening soil, there killing, there buying and selling, there procreating, there lifting an arm in the air until it withers, there passionately speaking, there putting down words or colours or making tremulous sounds, and all Children of Men.

These moments come rarely and unexpectedly, and they are what everyone is always looking for. That man passionately accumulating money is really trying to get rich enough to buy them, that politician worming his way from office to office is really trying to get important enough to bring them in like a bill and that revolutionary to get powerful enough to command them – like God. 'Let there be Oneness!' The sensualist hopes that by burying a piece of his body in another body he will bury himself in life and no longer be separate, the scientist that he will be able to fit parts together until, lo! a Whole; the peasant rejoices at each childbirth because children are projections of himself into life's Oneness, the artist tries like a lens to focus this Oneness in a single point, and the ascetic pares away his flesh, as the sensualist makes it molten, to abolish it and have no flesh damming back Eternity. All have the same obscure longing to shed their separateness, like a lonely man in a city drifting up and down crowded streets until his being is merged in the others round him and he loses himself in them, or drinking until the walls of his loneliness melt and let in confused light.

The burden of the Self is an intolerable one. It is the burden Christian had fastened on his back, and when he was eased of it he was 'glad and lightsome'. Nietzsche tried to glory in the same burden and it drove him mad. Huxley said he would rather endure eternal torment than annihilation. He wanted to be for all time – Huxley, with mutton-chop whiskers. Perhaps God has made an exception in his case and annihilated him out of sheer weariness with him. Unless the burden of the Self is shed there can be no inward peace, only conflicting appetites, moods coming and going.

When the Self has been shed and life seen as a Oneness, then it is apparent that life is good. Seen as a Oneness life is irradiated with an inward glow of goodness as a face may be irradiated with love. The face is the same as it was before, the same features, the same restless mouth and wondering forehead, only momentarily it has an inward glow of love which transfigures it; and life is the same as it was before, too, the same ceaseless conflict within and without, the same fluctuating bewilderment, only momentarily it is transfigured by an inward glow of goodness.

Then at these moments, these so rare moments, I think: 'I, living, am part of life's Oneness. Its destiny and mine are bound up together. If it is eternal so am I; if it is good so is my life. Why should I be afraid, then? and why find each passing moment so urgent? Nothing harmful can happen to me except to lose this sense of identity with life's Oneness, to become separate, like a child walking along a street with his father and then looking up and finding himself alone. No outward circumstance can bring about this separation. Whether I am ill or well, prosperous or needy, intelligent or stupid, successful or a failure, alive or dead even, does not make any difference. As long as I partake of life's Oneness I am delivered from fear.' And in me a conviction wells up like a spring that quite apart from what happens to me or what I do or fail to do, or what happens in the corner of the earth I inhabit or the corner of Time in which I have my fleshly existence, quite apart from any material circumstance whatsoever, to live is good because life is good, and to grow old and suffer and be disappointed in every hope of sustained happiness is good because these are implicit in life, and to die at last is good because death is implicit in life, too. 'In thus living, growing old and dying,' I think, 'in common with all the multitudinous forms of life which make up its Oneness, I am unfolding a purpose, and this purpose transcends me and the circumstances of my life and yet is implicit in them, and the key to this purpose is love.'

Then at these so rare moments everything becomes momentarily comprehensible. I see a significance in trees budding and unfolding leaves and shedding them, and in an old bent man walking to and from his work, to and from his work, monotonously, and imperceptibly day by day growing more bent, and in what happens, and in my own shifting moods and emotions, in all the multifarious activities of Man, the whole range of Man's being. 'The life in me and the life outside me are the same,' I think, and see all life like flames dancing out of one fire, flaring up and flickering out continuously yet always as many, an infinite number. 'Oh accept life,' I think. 'Oh yield to it.'

How soon this vision goes, the Oneness scattering, the Self reasserting itself! The trees are just trees again monotonously unfolding and shedding their leaves; the bent old man is just a bent old man again monotonously going to and from his work, his mind dulled and his body distorted and just waiting for death to release him. Appetite resumes its insistence; I feel for money in my pocket, and look round angrily, enviously, bitterly; I flap over the pages of newspapers dreading to be left behind by events and fashions, not to know what is happening, and wonder if the vision of life's Oneness was only pretence and the shedding of the Self a device for shedding responsibilities.

I think of all the misery and injustice there is, and of how the Few prey on the Many, and of how this is sanctioned by the Law and its appendage the Church, enforced by judges, blessed by priests, and of the war that is being prepared. 'What delight,' I think, 'if this great edifice of Greed and Hypocrisy and Exploitation, this Establishment, were pulled down! How I should love to see the Rich sent empty away and the Hungry filled! How wonderful it would be if money could no more buy adulation and if the Arrogant were broken in spirit!'

I see the Establishment come tumbling down. It is razed to the ground, and there is no King or Lords Temporal and Spiritual and Financial, no Stock Exchange, no *Times*, no one man commanding another's labour or fawning on another or deceiving another to subdue him. What happens then? Then another Establishment has to be built, another King installed, more Lords created. The men who build the new Establishment are not the same men who dominated the old one, but still men – that is greedy and envious, thirsting for power and to keep it when they have it, fawning on those who command them and arrogant with those whom they command. The new Establishment takes shape, and again there are the Few preying on the Many with the sanction of a Law, again there is Greed and Hypocrisy and Exploitation entrenched.

How I should have rejoiced if I had been in Moscow in 1917! How many did rejoice there then, and of these how many rejoice now? How many have even been left alive to mourn? It must always be like this. Revolutions take place in the name of Freedom and Brotherhood, and when they have established themselves they destroy Freedom and Brotherhood, so that those who make them are invariably destroyed by them. A revolution is sometimes necessary, and, accomplished, may lead to certain desirable changes, but it cannot change values; and those who, disgusted with prevailing values, help to bring one about in the expectation that it will change them, must inevitably succumb to it.

When I ask myself, 'What is my life?' I cannot answer 'to satisfy Desire' because I know Desire is unsatisfiable; nor 'to perfect my environment' because I know my environment cannot be perfected as I cannot; nor 'to destroy the cruel Law' because I know that when one cruel Law is destroyed another always arises from its ruins. I can only answer 'to sense the Oneness of life and my participation in it', knowing that this cannot be bought with money or authority or commanded by Will, cannot be evoked by bodily ecstasy or religious exercises, not by any external means, but only from within, and that it is evoked from within only through disinterestedness, the death of the Self.

That is, the kingdom of Heaven is within. That is, Blessed are the pure in heart for they shall see God. That is, Men have souls, and the significance of their lives lies in the soul and not in what they achieve individually or collectively. No Good is so good that it is worth sacrificing a soul for; no Evil is so evil that the soul must succumb to it; no experience is so terrible that the soul cannot be enriched by it. In the soul Time and Eternity meet. It is the seat of paradox, as that to live it is necessary to die, that suffering and renunciation are more blessed than happiness and fulfilment and yet happiness and fulfilment must be sought, that life is good and death is also good, that an individual man is of as little account as grass, one day growing and the next cut down, and so precious in God's eyes that every hair of his head has been counted. In the light of Time alone these paradoxes are meaningless, in the light of Eternity alone they are meaningless; in the soul where Time and Eternity meet they are comprehensible.

[1937]

The Revolutionaries

An old man was playing a violin outside a public house. Snow was falling; it was a cold, hard, winter evening. The old man was ruddy, with grey, untidy hair and pale, amiable eyes. He played pretty tunes that stirred the drinkers passing in and out of the public house, swinging its doors and spreading its glow and warmth on to the street. As his tunes touched their hearts they felt clumsily in their pockets for pennies to give him. His music was a success and he was gratified.

In the sight of a party of young men moving restlessly down the street – young men with lean faces, whose movements were restless and eager – the old musician was vile. They saw him standing bareheaded in the cold street, playing his pretty tunes and smiling on drinkers who gave him pennies, pausing in his music to bless their charity, and they hated him. He had no place in their world; they could find no justification for him. So they took his brown violin and broke it over his head, and then threw the broken violin down in the snow.

People stared at them. It was cruel. What harm was the old man doing? – only playing a violin for pennies; only following a trade to which he had been bred; only filling a draughty street with slight music that everyone, particularly drinkers, liked. Why should his violin be broken over his head and then thrown contemptuously aside? By what right had he been treated so?

The young men were more angry than ever to see him whimpering at the door of the public house and clutching the pennies he gained that night.

The drinkers came out in a group and stood behind the old man, his champions. 'Fair play,' one of them said – he was heavy and blond; a thick, blond moustache sprawled over his mouth. 'You've broken the old man's violin. You must buy him another.' He saw a shop – violins offered for sale – money paid over a counter. It would put the thing right. Others caught up the cry. 'Yes, buy him another,' they shouted. 'Fair play. Buy him another.'

The young men were strangers. They had no link with the place. No one knew anything of them, of their homes or their wives or their children. They had moved restlessly into the street from nowhere, and suddenly, for no reason, they had broken an old man's violin over his head. The crowd standing round the old man were afraid of them. They were so restless, so desperate.

'Revolutionaries' someone whispered; and the others repeated 'revolutionaries'.

'If we are revolutionaries,' one of the young men said, 'it is for love of you.' The contempt in his voice, the hate! 'For love of you'. Might they not even then link arms with the rest, go into the warmth of the public house, give the old man another violin, and drink and listen to his music. That was an expression of love – linking arms, comradeship, drinking together; music and drink could be bought – they had money – and the street, where snow piled up steadily, be forgotten. But their love was restless and desperate like themselves. It stirred them to violence; it was lean and fanatic.

'How can we hope to explain to you?' the same young man went on bitterly. The task seemed hopeless there, before the open doors of the public house and the crowd round the whimpering old man. From time to time someone gave him a drink out of pity. 'How can we hope to make you understand our love?'

'Love,' the old man repeated. He was tipsy.

The heavy-faced drinker pushed forward. 'You must pay,' he said doggedly, 'for the violin you have broken.' One of the young men impatiently tore out his heart. 'Will that suffice?' he asked. The crowd was impressed. To tear out his heart and offer it, warm and bloody, as payment for a violin! But the heavy-faced drinker persisted. 'No,' he said. 'It has no value. Now that . . .' he pointed to a gold watch on the young man's wrist. As he pointed his face became firm. Skin drew up round his eyes; lips closed under his sprawling moustache.

The crowd fidgeted uneasily when the gold watch lay in the snow at their feet. Who should step forward and pick it up before it was covered and lost? They eyed the gold, gleaming against the white snow. It was worth more than a violin; the old man was in luck; it was generous payment. They felt kindly, almost respectful, towards the young men. Only they wanted to pick up the watch and get away from them, out of their sight. They wanted to forget their existence. One put his foot forward to mark where the watch lay. This movement encouraged the old man to crawl forward and pick up and make off with it.

One of the young men climbed on a chair and began to speak, wearily at first, then passionately. The drinkers withdrew into the public house, shutting its doors behind them; those who were not drinkers went home to their houses, shut doors, drew curtains, crouched over fires. Soon the street was empty and silent except for the young man who poured out his love in bitter, flaming words. Snow fell on his bare head, wind blew against his lean cheeks; but he was unaware of the snow and wind as he shouted his love in flaming words down an empty street.

[1937]

Faith

'What are we to make of the universe in which we find ourselves and of our own brief individual part in it?' Clearly, the question never had and never can be answered. Knowledge and belief are by their nature partial, shifting. What is known and believed today will tomorrow seem as unsubstantial as what was known and believed yesterday. That is certain. There can be no finality, and every system of thought and belief which presupposes finality must be false. We are like passengers in a train. The view interests some, others drowse in their places, or meditate or turn over the pages of books and newspapers; yet others make for the restaurant car, or look for someone on whom to cast amorous eyes; others again study the train's mechanism, calculate its speed by passing telegraph poles, complain that their places are uncomfortable, devise plans for turning out the occupants of corner seats or for acquiring a whole side to stretch out on; yet to all sometime or other occurs the thought, with a pang of bewilderment, that they do not know whence they have come or where they are going.

Different ages and civilizations and individuals formulate their bewilderment in differing ways. An aborigine formulates his bewilderment by standing a stone on end and bowing his head before it; a country vicar puts on a white surplice and dispenses morsels of bread and sips of wine; Shakespeare writes *King Lear*, an Indian Sadhu devotes the years of his manhood to rolling from Benares to Cape Comorin and back. Behind all these and innumerable other manifestations of man's unquietness lies the same passion – to find an eternal significance in life's confused circumstances, to relate the few years we spend walking about this earth to eternity.

The contemporary formulation of bewilderment is mainly

69

scientific. It takes the form of Space-Time rather than Good-Evil speculation, though the same old roles have to be filled; as, hot-gospellers like Mr H. G. Wells noisily preaching salvation by knowledge where their predecessors preached salvation by faith; as, machine-dervishes and anti-God militants and inquisitors, fundamentalists, heretics, infallible pontiffs and saints, the ever-lasting circus, but with an entire change of programme.

It is true that as science has progressed it has tended to become less not more dogmatic. Matter, it appears, has dissolved into energy, and the law of causality itself broken down. The more minutely the mechanism of the universe has been examined, the more incomprehensible it has come to seem; the more extensive has been the range of human inquiry, the more there has been revealed to inquire into. Thus it might be and often is contended that science, instead of exploding religion, is moving towards its conclusions, developing its own mysticism, driven thereto by parallel lines which persist in meeting and hitherto inviolable laws which have become ginger in the mouth.

The fact remains, however, that the effect of recent scientific discoveries has been to engender a sense that instead of the universe being a setting for human souls, each separate and precious, man is but a fragment of this universe, like a dragonfly momentarily spreading wings and then gone, having the same significance as any other piece of creation.

The evolution theory, however ill its details have been substantiated, has established a conviction that man, to quote Mr W. Macneile Dixon '. . . is merely a creature among innumerable other creatures, tribes beyond enumeration, from bacilli to elephants, inhabiting for a moment the wrinkled surface of a burnt-out star'; and as he has become aware of the minuteness of his own part in his stupendous environment, itself moving towards inevitable extinction, so he has felt less and less inclined to believe in a God who knows when each sparrow falls to the ground and has counted over the hairs of each head. All that is left to him, indeed, is to make the burnt-out star as comfortable a habitation as possible, and to that end many now exclusively bend their energies, though not with notably successful results.

Thus, however science may have altered its ground and religion modified its dogma, they remain opposed. Bishop Barnes may scoff at the miraculous and call sacramentalism magic, but if he still sees God as a father and mankind as His children he is being as unscientific as any witch doctor since this conception rests not on scientific but on imaginative or poetic truth. However powerful telescopes may become they will never be able to prove or disprove the existence of heaven; Blake reached conclusions from a grain of sand which would not have been affected had he been shown the whole vast extent of the universe, all its furniture, its beginnings and its end, and it is doubtful if Christ would have seen fit to alter any syllable in the Sermon on the Mount in the light of quantum or relativity theory or both.

This gulf between imaginative or poetic truth and scientific truth can never be bridged. It is part of man's destiny to pursue both, as it is part of his destiny to pursue both power and love knowing them to be incompatible. 'Here am I, captain of a legion of Rome,' a recently discovered inscription runs, 'who served in the Libyan desert and learns and ponders this truth – "There are in life but two things, love and power, and no one has both." ' Yet the fact remains that man's nature craves for both, and that in eschewing one or the other he does violence to himself – living in the desert on locusts and wild honey or laying up treasure for moth and rust to corrupt. Whatever he may discover about himself and his environment, however equitably and efficiently arrange his circumstances, he will still have to derive what satisfaction he may from the thought that with God all things are possible.

[1937]

Those Put In Authority Over Us

Whenever I think of the inexhaustibly interesting subject – the incidence and exercise of power – there is one incident which always comes back into mind. It was long ago, in the early thirties. I was having a drink in a café in Vienna. My companion was a free-lance journalist of sorts, and apropos of nothing and quite casually and ruminatively, he remarked, 'I sometimes wonder if I'm licking the right boots.' The early autumn evening light was fading. That pause had come between day and nightfall, when work has ended and pleasure not begun, when the evening papers have been laid aside and the morning ones are still empty dummies; when a city seems for a moment somehow still, bracing itself for the switch from the light of the sun to all the little fragmented lights which will soon come out. Into this stillness my companion's remark fell like a stone into a pond, making widening ripples. If he is still around, he has more cause to wonder now than then.

Power

People smell power as a bull smells a cow in heat.

Money

Money is the last infirmity of ignoble minds.

Time And Eternity

Materialism, now so prevalent, takes many forms. There is, for instance, the feeling that just round the corner is a Utopia made possible by an immensely increased productive capacity. The popular prophet of this sort of Materialism is Mr H. G. Wells, whose zest and naïvety transfigure each new invention into a vision of eternal bliss. There is also Marxism, professed by so many younger men-of-letters, which insists that human consciousness is conditioned by external circumstances, and that Man is washed forward from one social system to another on successive waves of class conflict as inevitably as, to a Calvinist, he is washed forward to salvation or damnation. In a general way this materialist *zeitgeist* manifests itself in a growing preoccupation with what is here and now. People want facts, not ideas, still less a faith whose only authority is subjective experience. They get inside Europe. They attend lectures on economics. Mathematics or psychology or anthropology or sociology for the millions is their meat. They judge each tree by trying to get their teeth into its fruit.

72

Such an attitude of mind presupposes that life is no more than its immediate phenomena. The past is swept forward into the present and the present into the future, and the final pile is Creation's full significance. There is no constant. There is no permanent background against which the little life of Man is played out, no seeing through a glass darkly and then face to face. Literature is an interminable serial, each age contributing its instalment, and religion only a legend cunningly devised to ensnare the simple and perpetuate injustice and inequality. Each moment is sufficient unto itself, like each edition of a newspaper with its major crisis in large type and its minor crises in smaller type. Civilization is endangered and must be defended, or a new civilization is being born and must be delivered, or the time has come when we must all fight with Nazis and Fascists and Moors for Christianity or with the Comintern for Democracy, or perish in outer darkness.

This exclusive preoccupation with what happens or has happened or will happen seems to me wholly mistaken, even from the point of view of dealing successfully with immediate problems like war and poverty. It engenders hysteria, and hysteria is of all mental states the most dangerous. It is like identifying spring with this year's crops in relation to last year's and an estimate for next year's. Besides the manifestations of spring, there is Spring, which was the same a million million years ago and will be the same a million million years hence, which is the same in arctic regions where it brings a faint thawing to everlasting snow and ice as in the tropics where almost overnight it turns the muddy earth a startling green.

It is true that Man's circumstances are continually changing. He walked, and now he flies. He was a slave, to be bought and sold, and now he works for a wage. He was scattered and is now massed in cities. He groaned under autocratic governments and now groans under democratic ones, and may tomorrow groan under a dictatorship of the proletariat. He was illiterate and now reads and writes, and may tomorrow matriculate, graduate, know everything that is to be known. It is true, too, that these changing circumstances alter his outlook, his art, his hopes, his beliefs. At the same time, it is also true that something in him remains the same. If I read the Book of Job, *King Lear*, *Wuthering Heights* and *War and Peace*, I cannot but conclude that, though the authors of these works lived in different ages and under quite different conditions, life made very much the same impression on them. They looked round them and saw what I see now, and what has always been seen – Man coming he knows not whence and going he knows not whither, possessed by thirsts that cannot be quenched, dimly conscious of unimaginable dimensions, and yet with the Self interposed like a lens between him and this vastness and concentrating it into a single fiery point.

There is Time and there is Eternity. Because we are creatures of Time, what happens from moment to moment, from century to century, seems of crucial importance; because we are creatures of Eternity these happenings seem as unsubstantial as white clouds drifting across a summer sky. Buses glide by like shadows, the black letters of newspaper headlines make a fantastic pattern, and the man outside St Martin's-in-the-Fields winding up little clockwork pigs to dance them on the pavement is wonderful to behold.

Some balance or compromise has to be found between these two moods. If life is only unreal it is melancholy. Wonder at its unreality soon gives place to bitterness of spirit. As George Fox wrote of himself before his conversion, 'I saw professors, priests and people were whole and at ease in that condition which was my misery, and they loved that which I would have got rid of.' In the same way, Tolstoy, when he first became obsessed with Eternity, had to hide away a piece of rope for fear that, his eye falling on it, he should hang himself. When flesh loses all its substance death alone seems desirable. The burden of living a shadow among shadows is too great to be endured. On the other hand, if buses and newspaper headlines and the man winding up clockwork pigs, all that happens, represent the whole significance of life, it is equally intolerable. For what does happen? I look backwards and see for individuals and societies a round as monotonous as the seasons of rising and falling hopes; I look forwards and see the same process continuing; I look into my own heart and see such a tangle of desires, such fluctuating moods, such a burning passionate egotism, that, imagine my life as I will, I know it can yield no more than momentary satisfaction.

Religion alone has been able hitherto to effect a working compromise between what happens and the irrelevance of what happens, between Time and Eternity, between flesh and spirit, which, as St Paul said, lust contrary to one another. Even when religions as embodied in institutions become depraved, as they all do and must, they still serve a purpose, since they keep alive a necessary sense of Man's littleness and at the same time of his infinite worth as one of God's creatures. If I hear a clergyman whom I despise, who I know draws his stipend from slum property, toadies to the rich and despises the poor, who is idle, ignorant, parasitic, an enemy of good causes and a friend of bad, say, 'Except a man be born again he cannot see the Kingdom of God,' it is still more invigorating than a visit to the most perfectly equipped Anti-God museum. A savage grovelling in front of a garlanded stone fills me with more awe and hope than the most powerful hydro-electric plant under the sun.

Without religion societies and individuals disintegrate into their components, arrogance and despair, as is now well seen. Time gathers them up or Eternity gathers them up. There are prophets shrieking that Creation's climax is upon us, or prophets bewailing that all is vanity; there are men struggling, breathless, after money or power or the health, wealth and happiness of mankind, and men wanting only to escape from existing at all into some fantasy or just to die. Religion alone makes the righting of wrongs seem urgent without magnifying them to fill the whole universe, alone allows of humility without subservience, determination without arrogance, and contentment without inertia. It is, in fact, the only alternative to Totalitarianism, which explains why religion and the Totalitarian State are always at war with one another.

Even if, however, it be admitted that religion is necessary and now lacking, it is not a thing like adult suffrage or ownership of the means of production that can be decreed or propagandized into existence. It depends on individuals experiencing that they and all that lives embody a principle of goodness or love, and being thereby released from fear, since if the universe and its creatures came to pass through the functioning of a principle of love, there is nothing to fear except being estranged from that principle, which no outward circumstance can bring about. Fearlessness and happiness are the same. Whatever makeshift happiness there is in sensuality or success or alcohol or abounding health comes because these give a momentary illusion of fearlessness. Fearlessness, and so happiness, that lasts comes only through a consciousness that existence was benevolently, and not malevolently or accidentally, inspired, and therefore cannot result in harm; and that its significance vastly transcends its phenomena while being implicit in them.

There have from time to time throughout history been individuals who have said approximately this. They represent the only thread of consistency running from one civilization to another, from one age to another, from one generation to another. All else has ebbed and flowed with the moon. Tyrants have risen and fallen, freedom been won and lost and won again; the mighty have been put down from their seats and the humble and meek exalted, they becoming mighty in their turn and fit also to be put down. Oh, how many times man has become free at last, and how many times enslaved for ever! How many times the wretched have looked up hopefully, and how many times bent to a new yoke! Is it a new thing to usher in everlasting peace, or to preach a crusade on which the whole future of humanity depends? And has there been everlasting peace, and have crusades settled humanity's future? One thing only is certain – that tomorrow Hitler, Stalin, Mussolini will be names, and tomorrow's injustice seem as intolerable as today's. If this certainty were all, it would not be worth living till tomorrow. It is worth living till tomorrow, not because tomorrow will see a higher standard of life than today, or more rapid locomotion, or a more equitable distribution of wealth, or more widespread facilities for education, or better housing, or more or less birth control, or war, or peace; not for any reason whatsoever except that life, being born of goodness, is good.

This, it may be urged, is all very well for those who enjoy a sufficiency of material comfort and security, but what about the others who don't? Is an unemployed man struggling to feed his family to be expected to find life good quite apart from whether he sees any prospect of improving his conditions? Or an Indian factory worker working ten or more hours a day and living in the slums of Calcutta, to consider the lilies and be comforted? In a famine, audiences wonder what the characters in *The Cherry Orchard* are worrying about since they have plenty to eat, and stokers on a ship are not so easily made serene by a sunset as the passengers are.

If it is true that living conditions can be so intolerable as to make it seem that Man does live by bread alone (I say 'if' because many who have been most aware of life's inherent goodness have spared their bodies least), it remains true none the less that the soul's hunger matters more than the body's. *The Cherry Orchard* is not less profound because the starving are unappreciative of it, and would cheerfully exchange whatever serenity it or any other work of art or Nature can give for a good meal. Nor does a sense that life is good in itself and apart from its circumstances dry up sympathy and paralyse effort for others. On the contrary, those in whom this sense is strongest have been most persistent and effective in championing the weak and helping the unfortunate. To feel that men are all children of God, and so brothers, is a more effective spur to effort on their behalf than either a personal or vicarious grievance. Envy and hatred may make revolutions, and, incidentally, counter-revolutions, too, but charity, in the thirteenth chapter of Corinthians sense, has been the mainspring of all true disinterestedness.

[1937]

Rome, Sweet Rome

The Catholic Church, which over the centuries has rightly catered for everyone and everything, has a special niche today for twentieth-century lost souls who, in the empty caverns they inhabit, take comfort from the echoing sound of sanctus bells, and benedictions, and absolutions. Rome Sweet Rome! Be you never so sinful, there's no place like Rome.

Authority In Drag

I like very much Pascal's notion – the converse of Quixotry – that judges have to be attired in robes and wigs as otherwise the threadbare nature of the justice they mete out would be too apparent for them to have authority over their courts. This applies to all forms of earthly authority, none of which can do without drag. The only effective antidote to the enchantment which, in Don Quixote's case, led to his being brought home in a wooden cage – ours will be an iron one – is the kingdom not of this world. A kind of celestial anarchy or transcendental nihilism.

Recalling The Thirties

(Malcolm Muggeridge's social history *The Thirties* was first published by Hamish Hamilton in 1940 and highly praised by, among others, George Orwell. It was reissued by Collins in 1967 with this Introduction.)

I wrote the last pages of *The Thirties* in December 1939, in a barrack hut at Ash Vale, near Aldershot. It was the depot of the Military Police, to whom at that time we, the embryonic Intelligence Corps, known then as Field Security, were attached. The surrounding scrubland country remains fixed in my mind as particularly desolate and stale, as though troops had been tramping over it for centuries past, stunting its growth and drying up its fertility. Aldershot, likewise, I recall as a place of dull streets echoing with heavy footsteps from whose sombre gloom one turned with relief into the lights and sounds and human throng of public bars.

The Military Police, especially their warrant officers, had the greatest contempt for us Field Security men. From their point of view, we were a scruffy, miscellaneous lot, who wore our uniforms awry, made a pitiful showing on the barrack square, and nonetheless gained promotion all too quickly, sprouting overnight with stripes and other insignia of rank. We had been recruited as a result of a newspaper advertisement for linguists; in England the surest way of assembling oddities and delinquents, ranging between carpet sellers from Smyrna, travel agency couriers, unfrocked clergymen, language teachers and free-lance journalists.

Seated on my barrack hut bed, one of fourteen, I scribbled out the last pages of *The Thirties*; an ageing private, clad in breeches, puttees, heavy boots and a high-necked tunic (battledress was not yet on issue), with thick combinations underneath to protect against the winter's cold. At the time, I assumed myself to be an object of some curiosity among my fellow-privates, who, as I supposed, took me to be one of those poor creatures so domestically tied that I felt bound to write interminable letters home. When I got to know them better, it turned out that they were nearly all practising or *manqué* writers themselves, and knew only too well what I was up to. With the occupational envy of the trade, they hoped, I am sure, that my zealous efforts in such unpropitious circumstances would soon falter and come to nothing. They need not have worried. I scarcely wrote another word from then on till after the war's end.

It is one of the great illusions of war that, by participating in it, one will escape from the sort of life one has hitherto lived and the sort of companionship one has hitherto found. Not so. As the great process of sorting everyone out goes on, one necessarily soon finds oneself back in one's own milieu. An egghead came I into this world, and an egghead shall I depart thence. A chance conversation in the NAAFI with a burly lance-corporal who, in my eyes, bore every mark of authentic proletarian origins, would, sure as fate, soon get round to 'The Waste Land' and Virginia Woolf. When I had been at Ash Vale for some months, and attained the acting local rank of CSM, I was instructed to meet an officer from the War Office at the local railway station, who was visiting us on some special mission. I pressed my uniform until it almost stood up of itself; I polished my belt and the crown on my sleeve until they shone like the morning sun; the toes of my boots, treated with a hot spoon, likewise gleamed. As the officer descended from a first-class railway carriage I gave him a salute clamorous enough to be heard a mile away. He nonchalantly returned it and we got into a waiting motor car; he at the back, and I in front beside the driver. As we drove along, I examined him in the driving-mirror, and seemed to find something familiar in his sensitive, intelligent, vaguely melancholy countenance. He was doing the same thing to me. The moment of recognition was mutual and instantaneous. It was Edward Crankshaw. Afterwards, he told me that my terrific salute led him to reflect that old sweats such as he supposed me to be were the backbone of the British Army. To the consternation of our driver, we began to fall about in the car in a condition of hopeless mirth at the unconscious deception we had practised on one another. I believe I never took the war, certainly not the army, quite seriously again.

Though I did not realize it at the time, no conditions could have been more appropriate for concluding a study of the thirties. As a pseudo-warrior in a still pseudo-war (my family were living near Battle, in Sussex, so that my leave-pass would be made out 'for the purpose of proceeding to Battle'; about the only British soldier, as I used to reflect, then so bent) I was ideally placed to survey the last phases of the decade which had just passed. At the time it seemed otherwise. I anticipated an impending Judgement Day, and even asked myself whether it was worth while bothering to complete a manuscript which was bound never to be published, and which in any case would almost certainly be destroyed in the holocaust from the air, long prophesied by all the experts, and expected at any moment. What I failed to realize was that Judgement Day had come and gone, unnoticed. When the holocaust belatedly occurred, it only fell upon what was already a wasteland; like the bombardment of Pompeii in the course of the Italian campaign, leaving traces of bullet marks on walls volcanically blitzed many centuries before.

However, I did finish the book; rather cursorily, as a matter of fact, and it was duly published, with, as things turned out, a certain measure of success, even though its appearance was swamped by the march of events. By that time, we had been transferred from Ash Vale to the Island of Sheppey, where we constituted the sole garrison against an anticipated *Panzer* invasion, having been issued for the purpose with steel helmets, twelve rounds of ammunition, and rifles which we never had an opportunity of firing. Our nocturnal prowlings about the coast were interrupted by the arrival of demoralized French troops, in variegated uniforms, quite bewildered, to whom we provided succour in the form of cigarettes (the one reliable currency of our time; the Fag Standard) and good cheer. I have a vague memory of marching rather absurdly at the head of a column of these battered and disheartened allies whom I had attempted to rally by means of a spirited but incoherent discourse delivered in bad bombastic French. These events also fitted in well with what I had tried to say in *The Thirties*.

Proposals were subsequently made and entertained for dealing with the forties and fifties in a similar vein. I even made a start on the forties, but whether due to indolence, other preoccupations, or the intrinsic unsuitability of the material, the result seemed unsatisfactory, and the project was abandoned. It is, I think, a fact that, whereas the thirties fell neatly into one theme, beginning with a phoney peace and ending with a phoney war, the two succeeding decades had no such clear pattern. The conduct and ostensibly victorious conclusion of the 1939-45 War under Churchill, followed by the Beveridge Era – from the stuffed lion to the stuffed sheep; then two small mice, Attlee and Truman, in labour and bringing forth a mountain in the shape of atomic raids on Hiroshima and Nagasaki; Churchill's inglorious return to power, followed by the even more inglorious interlude of Eden; the Cold War and the final emergence of the two giants, the USA and the USSR, in whose shadows the rest of us perforce lived, and live – all this was not susceptible to arrangement in ten-yearly sections, or to the kind of treatment I had attempted in *The Thirties*.

In any case, as far as I am concerned, wars, like rhetoric, their language, are exciting but not interesting, and no labour could be more tedious and unrewarding than sorting out the battles and campaigns of which they largely consist. Of all Shakespeare's plays I most dislike *Henry V*. By the same token, the Churchill cult is one in which I did not join at the time, and find even less sympathetic as the years pass, while recognizing, of course, the unique character of his services in 1940 – services whose performance required the very temperament and characteristics I find so little to my taste. This, as I am well aware, is a minority position (though not, perhaps, quite so small a minority as might be supposed), which would make the central figure of the forties as derisory as the comparable one of the thirties – Ramsay MacDonald. As I indicate in *The Thirties*, MacDonald's efforts to promote 'the peace of the worrrld' soon came to seem merely ridiculous, leading, as they did, to Neville Chamberlain's sorry and disastrous transactions at Munich. Yet both his and Chamberlain's performances, surely, pale into insignificance compared with Churchill's at Yalta, when he and the dying Roosevelt, in effect, handed over Eastern and Central Europe to the most untender mercies of Stalin, the third man of the ribald triumvirate. Such inclination as I had to expatiate, in detail and at length, upon all this, in any case expired when I read the late Chester Wilmot's masterly *The Struggle for Europe*. With an erudition and historical grasp which I could not hope to emulate, and a patience and persuasiveness quite beyond my capacity, he shows how the ostensible champions of our civilization themselves blew the trumpets which brought its already tottering walls crashing down.

The sense of being a stranger in a strange land, among childhood recollections the most intense, induced the related feeling that the whole life of action, one's own and the society's or civilization's to which one happened to belong, is theatre; a lurid melodrama or soap-opera with history for its theme. Such an attitude of mind is, of course, common enough, both among the ever increasing number of the mentally deranged with lost identities, and among mystics and religious *exaltés* – the Kierkegaards and Kafkas down to the crazier specimens like Black Moslems and Jehovah's Witnesses. Politically, its commonest manifestation is one version or another of anarchism.

As it has afflicted me, I have been unable to take completely seriously, and therefore to believe in the validity or permanence of, any form of authority. Crowns and mitres have seemed to be made of tinsel, ceremonial robes to have been hastily procured in a theatrical costumier's, what passes for great oratory to have been mugged up from the worst of Shakespeare. Feeling thus, I could not but assume that everything pertaining to this aspect of life must shortly come to an end. It was too absurd, too threadbare, too moth-eaten to endure. George Orwell similarly was liable to break off a conversation to make statements like: 'Eton's doomed', or, 'Soon there won't be any more state openings of Parliament'.

Such a disposition made one ostensibly irreverent, pessimistic, disloyal, and – the commonest accusation – destructive in attitude of mind. In the war, when I was with V Corps at Salisbury, I was turned out of a mess by the APM, a Northern Irishman named McNally who happened to be Mess President, on the ground that I talked. When I pressed him to be more specific, he refused to be drawn. 'It's just your talk,' he said. I mention this temperamental incapacity to accept the pretensions, or even the reality, of power in any of its manifestations (which, incidentally, has made me a hopeless failure as an executive, and unsatisfactory in all roles which require ardour and decision, like citizen and lover), because it obviously affects one's view of what is going on in the world and of the people who are conducting the world's affairs. If, as I often think, power is to the collectivity what sex is to the individual, then journalists like myself are, as it were, power-*voyeurs*, whose judgements will necessarily reflect our own quirks and peculiarities. We look through a keyhole at the strange contortions and capers of those who have become addicted to what Blake called 'the strongest poison ever known . . . from Caesar's laurel crown'.

Thus, for instance, the assumption throughout *The Thirties* is that the capitalist system is irretrievably doomed, and that some form of collectivist economy, whether or not called communist, is inescapable everywhere. When in the early years of the decade I surveyed the ravages of the great depression from my editorial perch in the offices of the *Manchester Guardian*, I was entirely convinced that the economic arrangements which had produced so tragic and lamentable a state of affairs were bound to be discarded for ever. In the USSR, I considered, an alternative system was in process of construction, and gave every promise of being the wave of the future. By the time I came to write *The Thirties*, a stint in Moscow as a newspaper correspondent had cured me of the latter assumption, but the former remained intact.

Well, as things have turned out the capitalist system, as amended by the agile brain of John Maynard Keynes, would seem to be in a more flourishing condition than ever before. In the USA where in theory at any rate its exigencies are the most respected and its operations the least impeded, far and away the richest, and technologically speaking the most resourceful, human community in the history of the world has come to pass. It is true that there are aspects of this prosperity, such as its ever-increasing accumulation of indebtedness, which give rise to doubts about its permanence, and that in baleful eyes like mine it can seem nothing more than a glorified trough set about with erotic squalor; a place of barbiturate sleep, benzedrine joy and vitamin well-being. Equally, it may be argued that it, too, has in reality become a collectivist society, whose rulers' nominal championship of free-enterprise economics and representative institutions is as empty as the equivalent Soviet championship of Marxist economics and People's Democracy. Even so, the fact remains that today American prosperity, and the way of life based on it, are the envy of the greater part of mankind, and the focus of most of their dreams and much of their endeavour. This is an outcome I certainly did not foresee, either on my *Guardian* editorial perch, or in my Ash Vale barrack hut.

Again, at the end of *The Thirties* a curtain falls. The so long dreaded war has begun, the assumption being that the last act of our tragedy is upon us, and that when it has been played out the stage will be darkened and the audience depart. It never so much as occurred to me that anything would be salvaged; with a kind of exaltation, which reached its height going about the streets of London in the blitz, sometimes in the company of Graham Greene, a kindred spirit, I felt I was present at the last bonfire of the last remains of our derelict civilization. Nor at the war's end, when the Nazis were defeated, and the church bells rang out, not to proclaim an invasion, but to celebrate a victory, did I suppose for a moment that the past as we had known it could ever be reconstructed. The rubble of Berlin, piled in strange heaps like a landscape in the moon, represented, as I thought, an irretrievable extinction; as the people groping about in the rubble, constructing out of it little caves for themselves, exchanging their bodies for cigarettes and tins of Spam, or just yielding them before the rough importunities of their liberators from the east, were troglodytes fated never to emerge from their twilight. Yet emerge they did, to sit in the sunshine consuming huge beakers of hot chocolate *mit Schlag*. From the rubble there sprouted a new city, many mansions, mansions of chromium and glass. Was it really a city? Or just an ingenious arrangement of lights? Even now I am not quite sure.

Be that as it may, it is an indubitable fact that when the dust and smoke of war finally cleared, there unmistakably were the props and players whose disappearance for ever I had taken for granted – a House of Commons soon restored to Honourable Members; black coats and umbrellas making their way down Whitehall as though Hitler had never existed; the Athenaeum furbished up, *The Times* coming out, even the *Almanack de Gotha* resurrected; the House of Lords, the College of Arms, Sir William Haley, all going strong, or at any rate going. What I had assumed to be the end of the performance was only, after all, an *entr'acte*; the curtain had fallen, certainly, but only to rise again, disclosing the scenery, actors and costumes just as they had been before. Actors a shade tireder, perhaps, a shade more dependent on their prompter, lines mumbled a bit and mechanically delivered, costumes crumpled and shabby in the glare of the footlights, the pace of the whole production noticeably slowed down, yet indubitably the same old play and the same old performers.

Up to a point, then, on Armistice Day I stood confuted. The public rejoicings, recalling childhood memories of an earlier version in 1918, seemed to contradict the sombre shape of things to come envisaged in *The Thirties*. There *had* been a glorious victory; this time there really was to be a new and better world, on a basis of the Four Freedoms, the Atlantic Charter and other enlightened instruments, under-written by our three men of destiny, Churchill, Roosevelt and Stalin. Where the League of Nations had failed the United Nations would succeed; with the Beveridge Plan to ensure that wartime sacrifices had not been in vain, the new dawn would surely usher in a bright day.

In the event, this mood of hope proved even more transient than on the previous occasion. Roosevelt's Four Freedoms were no more durable than Woodrow Wilson's Fourteen Points had been; the United Nations outdid the League in confusion and fatuity, and the cheques drawn on the Beveridge Plan were honoured in inflated currency. Before the 1939–45 War had long been over, the line-up for another began, with the additional horror of being against the backdrop of a mushroom cloud. The development of nuclear weapons opened up, for the first time in human history, the prospect of blowing the human race and the earth itself to smithereens. It was in a war-scarred and war-weary world, with this weird and macabre doom seemingly so near at hand, that a Welfare State was constructed to keep us all healthy, wealthy and wise for evermore. By a strange irony – stranger than any I had envisaged in *The Thirties* – a moment of unique tragedy coincided with some of the most shallow and fatuous hopes ever to be entertained by mortal men. Prosperity was to broaden down from hire-purchase payment to hire-purchase payment; the birth pill would safeguard the pursuit of happiness against all impediments, and with the Gross National Product continually expanding, a dazzling prospect of everlasting felicity opened before mankind. As the psychiatric wards went on multiplying, suicide and crime increasing, the consumption of pills-for-all-purposes mounting, there was proclaimed with ever greater fervour the coming to pass of a kingdom of heaven on earth, richer, more easeful and blissful than any hitherto known.

So now, looking back, I feel that, after all, the assumptions and prognostications of *The Thirties* were not so wide of the mark as might previously have seemed to be the case. Though we were technically among the victors in the 1939–45 War, our participation in the victory was purely nominal. It was our positively last appearance in a major role on the stage of history, as Churchill was our last international star. He and our imperial destiny expired together; at his funeral, both were interred, making of it a great national occasion. As everyone realized, consciously or unconsciously, for us as a people it was the end of such occasions. There would never be another at all comparable. So the most was made of it.

The Empire, which theoretically emerged larger and stronger than ever from the 1914–18 War, was in fact even then in an advanced state of decomposition, and went on subsequently decomposing fast. Victory in 1945 did not invalidate my observation in *The Thirties* that the sun seemed to be setting on the Empire on which it never set. Churchill proclaimed indignantly that he had not been appointed by King George VI to be his principal Secretary of State in order to preside over the dissolution of his Empire. Had he but known it, this, precisely, was to be required of him in his confused and inglorious premiership in the post-war years under George VI's daughter, Elizabeth II. Now the Empire has gone, and the Commonwealth – a holding-company formed to realize the Empire's dwindling residual assets – has almost disappeared likewise. Figures like Redeemer-Emeritus Nkrumah, Jomo Kenyatta and Dr Banda provide a perfect cast for playing out the farce to the end, until England once again blessedly exists as a small island off the coast of Europe.

Ironically enough, it is in the field of economics, where scientific accuracy is supposed to prevail, that prognostications, mine included, have proved particularly fallacious. With great joy I described in *The Thirties* how MacDonald formed his National Government to 'save the Pound', which then was permitted to slither off the gold standard. God save our gracious Pound! Yet the economies which MacDonald went to such pains to institute with a view to persuading New York bankers that we were still credit worthy would scarcely have sufficed to finance for a single day the war which broke out in 1939, and continued for some five years, without evidently reducing us to bankruptcy. For most of my lifetime we have been living, economically speaking, in the red, to the accompaniment of dire warnings from bankers, financiers, and, between elections, from politicians, while all the while, to the outward eye, growing ever more prosperous. How this has come about, and what will be the outcome, I have no idea. MacDonald was fond of saying, with great emphasis, that you cannot put a quart into a pint-pot. It seems that you can. He was likewise given to remarking that we must cut our coats according to our cloth. Apparently, we are under no such necessity.

'They ever must believe a lie who see with, not through, the eye,' Blake wrote. It was, for me, a key-thought when I was writing *The Thirties*, though then, of course, television had not provided a third eye for us to see with; one, moreover, which cannot be seen through, however hard the seer tries. Blake's saying has gone on echoing in my mind ever since. Such lies believed! Never, surely, has there been credulity like it. African witch-doctors and makers of love-potions must look with sick envy at the impositions of our advertisers and psychiatrists, reflecting that their clientele, though black savages, would never for an instant countenance deception so gross and palpable. When people cease to believe in God, G. K. Chesterton has pointed out, they do not then believe in nothing, but – what is far more dangerous – in anything. The Christian religion requires us only to believe in certain specific dogma and supernatural happenings like miracles; the religion of Science which has succeeded it, as I indicated in *The Thirties* bestows its *imprimatur* upon any proposition, however nonsensical, which can be stated in terms of the requisite statistical-scientific mumbo-jumbo. Thus a condition of moral, intellectual and spiritual confusion has been created in which, not only faith, but meaning itself, has disappeared.

86

I well remember how, seated on my bed in my Ash Vale barrack hut, with a pencil in my hand and paper before me, striving to finish *The Thirties*, one phrase intruded itself into all my thoughts and deliberations – 'Lost in the darkness of change'. It seemed to sum up my, and everyone else's, situation. We were lost; like children trying to extricate some familiar shape or sound out of the darkness which had fallen. All we knew was that when the darkness lifted a new landscape with new contours would be revealed. Meanwhile, we had to reconcile ourselves to living in darkness. *Fiat Nox!* – it was our fate, and must be accepted.

The phrase seems to me as valid now as it did in 1940. We are still lost in the darkness of change. If anything, the darkness is more impenetrable than it was then. The difference, as far as I am concerned, is that now I find more compensations in such a plight. In times of bright light one is so easily dazzled. How readily one might have accepted, in stabler and more vainglorious circumstances, the pretensions of power, the certainties of authority, the false sense of security generated by seeming permanence. As it is, one accepts nothing. One is driven back upon those other certainties, propounded in darkness but shining with their own bright inward light, which relate, not to any conceivable human situation, favourable or unfavourable, mighty or decrepit, but to the deserts of vast eternity which lie beyond our shifting human history. There, in all humility, I venture to cast my eye, intent upon a land that is very far off, and in search of truth which is not for yesterday or today or tomorrow, but for all time.

Ciano And Mussolini

(In 1947 Muggeridge edited an English version of the Diary which Count Galeazzo Ciano, Mussolini's Minister of Foreign Affairs from 1936 to 1943, had kept and somehow managed to smuggle out of prison cell 27 of the Verona Gaol just prior to his execution. In 1948 Muggeridge edited a second volume of Ciano's diplomatic papers. This biographical sketch of Ciano and Mussolini is from his Introduction to Ciano's Diary.)

Of all the documents which have come out of the 1939–45 War and the events which led up to it, Count Galeazzo Ciano's Diary is the most interesting, and will probably prove in the end the most useful to historians. I can imagine some future Gibbon, or even Lytton Strachey, coming upon it with a gasp of delight. This is because Ciano, like Boswell, was too vain to hide the true workings of his mind and the true character of his aspirations, and too foolish to be aware of how completely he was giving himself and those about whom he wrote away. If he had been cleverer, his Diary would have been worse. Day by day he recorded his thoughts, hopes, conversations, all that had happened to him, against the background of his inordinate vanity, and in the end, waiting in a prison cell at Verona to be taken out and shot, engineered the publication of what he had written in the fond hope that thereby he would revenge himself on his father-in-law and former patron, Mussolini.

What he achieved actually was to provide the world with one more record, incomparable in its naïvety, of how futile a pursuit is power, and how certainly those who pursue it become enmeshed in their own deceits and stratagems. For this at least he deserves gratitude. In exposing Mussolini he perforce exposed himself, and all who take the path they followed. Without knowing it, he presented Mussolini as Macbeth, with Hitler for the Horrid Sisters. Duce he was, but the promise of yet greater things to come proved irresistible. Like Macbeth, he struggled sometimes against its seduction, but in the end succumbed, as many others did, to the Führer's fearful certainty.

It is not his account of the play which makes his Diary so valuable, but his revelation of the character of the players and of their relationships with one another. They formed, indeed, a remarkable and grotesque company – Mussolini, the central figure, with his alternating moods of sensible doubt and fatuous confidence, his affectionate contempt for his Italians and contemptuous respect for his German associates, his passion to emulate Hitler's military successes and participate in the loot they procured, combined with a passion almost equally strong to see Hitler humiliated and his plans frustrated; the little King, Victor Emmanuel, up to Mussolini's downfall, continuing precariously on his throne because the Duce could see no convenient way of getting rid of him, managing even from time to time to administer shrewd little blows, annoyances, to his tormentor; Ciano himself, a quite ludicrous personage, full of ludicrous contradictions, strutting his hour or two on the stage in Mussolini's shadow, aping his very appearance, and then, full of self-righteousness, writing the last self-righteous sentences in his Diary before being executed; and then Hitler, whose phosphorescent presence held them all in awe even though his turgid sentences sent them to sleep, whose will was felt even when his purposes were challenged, in whose destiny they had inescapably involved themselves like little meteors caught in the system of a larger planet blazing through space to inevitable destruction.

Galeazzo Ciano was born at Leghorn on 18 March 1903. His father, Costanzo Ciano, served with distinction in the Italian Navy in the 1914–18 War. There are frequent respectful references to him in the Diary, and there is no reason to suppose that Ciano's elaborately depicted grief at his death was not authentic. According to Ciano, Mussolini had decided to nominate Costanzo Ciano as his successor. The family was rich but far from aristocratic. On this point Ciano is misleading, and frequently implies that it was distasteful for an aristocrat like himself to mix with parvenus like Ribbentrop and even Mussolini. He and his wife Edda, Mussolini's daughter, take counsel together on one occasion as to whether it would be tactful to tell the Duce that in fact the English are not in the habit of wearing dinner-jackets for tea. Mussolini, he implies, could scarcely be expected to know about so nice a point in polite behaviour, but at the same time he did not want to hurt his father-in-law's feelings and parade his own superior upbringing by drawing it to his attention.

Costanzo Ciano associated himself with the Fascist movement in the very early days, and when Mussolini became head of the Italian Government was promoted to Admiral, ennobled, and made Minister of Communications. In this office he was presented with, and took full advantage of, opportunities for enriching himself. He became enormously rich, and served as President of the Fascist Chamber of Deputies, one of those hand-picked, obedient legislatures designed to give an air of democratic respectability to totalitarian regimes which the fall of the Axis and the triumph of the Four Freedoms and Atlantic Charter have only served to multiply.

Galeazzo Ciano studied law in Rome, and tried his hand, not very successfully, at dramatic and art criticism. His aspirations as a young man were literary, and he produced, among other writings, a version of *Hamlet* which attempted to portray the Prince of Denmark as a particularly sanguine individual. This ingenious and ambitious project was a failure. Ciano's cheerful *Hamlet* was booed off the stage, and his creator decided to follow his father's advice and enter the diplomatic service. At this time he was far from sharing Costanzo's enthusiasm for Fascism, and perhaps if his play had been more successful he might have pursued literature and liberalism instead of embarking upon what turned out to be a dazzling career as a Fascist.

After a series of minor diplomatic posts in South America, China, and at the Vatican, Ciano married Edda Mussolini, and thenceforth, not surprisingly, his advancement was rapid. The marriage, despite its obvious usefulness to the groom, may have been based on an element of mutual esteem. Ciano's references to Edda are rare and mostly disapproving, but there is no reason to doubt the genuineness of his affection for his children. In his last Diary entry he refers to his 'wife, who in my hours of sorrow has revealed herself as a strong, sure and faithful companion'. They did not see a great deal of one another, and in that strange, vulgar, Balzacian period when Mussolini ruled in Rome, dazzled the obsequious and shocked the respectable by their mutual and separate extravagances.

Ciano's first appearance on the international stage was as a member of the Italian Delegation at the World Economic Conference in London in 1933, presided over by Ramsay MacDonald, who was already approaching his final incoherent decrepitude, and at which two voices much to be heard thereafter also made their international debut – Hitler's through Hugenberg, and Roosevelt's through Raymond Moley. Two years later Ciano became Under-Secretary for Press and Propaganda, then a member of the Fascist Grand Council, and the following year, at the age of thirty-three, Minister for Foreign Affairs.

Ciano himself was genuinely opposed to Italian participation in the war. At the same time, like Mussolini, Ciano was dazzled by the prospect of illimitable loot which Hitler's military successes held out. Like Mussolini, too, against his better judgement, he found it difficult at times not to believe that the Führer must succeed. In any case, his fortunes were bound up with those of his father-in-law whom he invariably obeyed whatever doubts he may have nourished about the wisdom of his conduct. If the Nazis had won instead of losing, it would not have been very difficult for him to represent himself as having from the first foreseen their victory and the advantages which Italy might derive from it. His Diary would not have needed so very much revision to present that moral. If, thanks to a Nazi victory, Ciano had been granted the 'quiet old age' he had hoped for to transform the raw material of his Diary into an Autobiography we may be sure that his theme would have been Mussolini's prescience and his own brilliant execution of the Duce's policy.

In other words, Ciano had no policy, any more than Mussolini had. He and the Duce were totally unprincipled. His doubts about the wisdom of Italian participation in the war were based on fears, which Mussolini except in occasional moments of lucidity was too far gone in megalomania to share, of the inadequacy of Italy's armed forces. His doubts along with all record of them would have disappeared with victory as surely as they were confirmed by defeat. He, too, played only to win, and no other consideration weighed with him. If his last appeal to history, his expectation that 'an honest testimonial to the truth in this sad world may well be useful in bringing relief to the innocent and striking at those who are responsible', is human and therefore in its way touching, it is no more so than the convicted criminal who in all sincerity proclaims his good intentions when he is beyond hope of clemency.

It was this opportunism of the Fascist regime which made the efforts of Chamberlain and Halifax to come to terms with it so futile. As the Diary shows, every attempt they made to be reasonable and considerate was interpreted as weakness, and only confirmed Mussolini in his conviction that all strength and resolution lay on the German side. After a conversation with Chamberlain he complained to Ciano that Chamberlain bore little resemblance to Drake, which indeed was true as far as it went. Goering, from the Duce's point of view, produced a much nearer approximation to an Elizabethan adventurer than the British Prime Minister. Appeasement in this case, as it always will, only made war more certain. Those who exercise authority irresponsibly suffer from the disability that they cannot understand authority in any other terms; no traffic is possible with them except in terms of power. Inability to understand this has already cost the world most dearly, and may yet cost it more dearly still.

The great quality of Ciano's Diary, however, is not that it demonstrates such principles, often enough demonstrated but never learned, or that it goes over once again the now wearisome tale of Europe's progress to rubble and despair, but that it records the mental processes, sudden rages, lechery and sentimentality, flashes of insight, inconceivable stupidities, ingenuousness and shrewdness of the buffoon who for a quarter of a century imposed himself on the Italian people, and for the greater part of that time on Europe, as a considerable statesman. No picture of Mussolini hitherto available has come near to this one for verisimilitude. It is more denigratory than the most savage and hysterical attacks of his detractors, and more sympathetic than the most adulatory biographies of his admirers. Whoever at any time is interested in Mussolini will turn to Ciano. There the man is in all his folly and humanity.

He was in his way a prodigy – as Ciano shows, a revolutionary who became a dictator without ever ceasing to be a revolutionary, an adventurer who made good without ever ceasing to be an adventurer, so coarse that his closest associates were sometimes shocked, so sensitive that an obscure newspaper attack would make him want to go to war. As his astonishing career moved to its close he more and more reverted to the attitude of mind of his youth. His loathing of the Monarchy, of the rich and the respectable, of the Church and especially of the Vatican, would have done credit to any shabby anarchist thumping his soap box at Hyde Park Corner. Characteristically, he explained away the scandal of his association with Clara Petacci and her disreputable and corrupt family by saying that such things were regarded as normal at the time of the Borgias. There was no consistency in him, no constancy even in his perfidy and self-dramatization. The strange confusion of his mind and emotions was reflected in the confusion of his directions to Ciano. Contrary to the generally held opinion, no one could have been less resolute or unwavering than he. From day to day his intentions varied – now he would go to war and now he would not, now he would march with Germany and now he would double-cross Hitler and promote Germany's ruin. He was utterly unstable and incalculable.

It was his relations with Germany which provided the torment of his later years and brought about his final ruin. From the moment that he first met Hitler in Venice in 1934, when the carefully assembled crowds cried 'Long live the Duce!' and quite ignored the Führer in his belted mackintosh, until his humiliating rescue from his own people by the Sicherheitsdienst ten years later, the Führer haunted him. It was the Germans' strength that impressed and maddened him, especially by contrast with his own countrymen, who obstinately resisted becoming martial however much he bellowed at them and made them goose-step, do what he absurdly called the '*passo Romano*', under his window. Though he sought comfort by assuring himself that he was cleverer than Hitler, he knew that his position was incomparably the weaker. He had to do everything by the exercise of his wits, whereas, as he often enviously reflected, Hitler had the massive weight of German strength behind him, and had no Victor Emmanuel or Vatican to plague him. That he got as far as he did is the measure both of the sharpness of his wits and of the feebleness of his assailants. We think of him now strung up by the feet in the market-place at Milan with his Clara beside him and an enraged crowd spitting and kicking and hurling insults at him, and conveniently forget that at the time of the Munich Pact he was spoken of most respectfully by many who now would wish their words forgotten, and that at different times he won the approval of Winston Churchill and Bernard Shaw, not to mention Rabindranath Tagore.

Having attached himself to Hitler, Mussolini's position became increasingly subservient and humiliating. He was left in ignorance of the Führer's purposes; when he decided to undertake a military adventure on his own account and attack Greece, it was a miserable fiasco, and he had to appeal to Hitler for help; at his much advertised meetings with the Führer his position became increasingly that of a subordinate receiving instructions from his superior officer. At one of these meetings he rather pathetically made it a condition that he should not be expected to eat with his German associates. He did not want them to see that he was on a diet and could only eat slops, for fear that they should laugh at him and think of him as a weakling. In attaching himself to Hitler he encompassed his own and his country's ruin, and sometimes knew that it was so, and yet saw no way of retracting. Whenever he had almost decided to reverse his course some new turn of events would make him change his mind, until at last no retraction was possible, until at last there was no flying hence nor tarrying here.

Looked at in the light of subsequent events Mussolini's vacillation, so intimately and faithfully described by Ciano, seems unaccountable. Why did he not see the consequences of what he was doing, the absurd figure he was cutting? one wonders, as Ciano himself doubtless bitterly wondered, too, in his Verona cell as he looked over the pages of his Diary for the last time. Yet at the time how should Mussolini have known? He also was entangled in events beyond his control which shaped him rather than being shaped by him; he also became eminent only because there existed in his heart a confusion which matched the confusion without. A disintegrating civilization racing like the Gadarene swine to destruction was personified in him, in his arrogance and cupidity and shifting purposes and vanity and folly. For a little while he led the rush, and then was trampled underfoot, others struggling to the fore to be first over the cliff.

[1947]

Humility

I discussed with a friend the other evening whether the virtue of humility is to be found among the eminent. He mentioned Attlee, but I thought that in his case it was a matter of modesty – by no means the same as humility. We decided that none of the present political leaders could be credited with this particular virtue; in some ways the most important of all, being, as I think, the essential condition for all virtue. Nor could we then and there call to mind a suitable candidate in the past. Afterwards I looked up an extract from a speech by Lincoln that I like very much, and which seems to me a true expression of humility in one of the greatest of men:

> I have been selected to fill an important office for a brief period, and am now, in your eyes, invested with an influence which will soon pass away; but should my administration prove to be a very wicked one, or what is more probable, a very foolish one, if you, the people are true to yourselves and the Constitution, there is but little harm I can do, thank God.

Taking Sides

If I accept, as millions of other Western Europeans do, that America is destined to be the mainstay of freedom in this midtwentieth century world, it does not follow that American institutions are perfect, that Americans are invariably well-behaved, or that the American way of life is flawless. It only means that in one of the most terrible conflicts in human history, I have chosen my side, as all will have to choose sooner or later, and propose to stick by the side I have chosen through thick and thin, hoping to have sufficient courage not to lose heart, sufficient sense not to allow myself to be confused or deflected from this purpose, and sufficient faith in the civilization to which I belong, and in the religion on which that civilization is based, to follow Bunyan's advice and endure the hazards and humiliations of the way because of the worth of the destination.

94

Webb And Webb

(Malcolm Muggeridge's stormy association with the British Broadcasting Corporation began with his first broadcast on 30 May 1948. A repeat, scheduled for 21 June, was cancelled under pressure from Lady Simon, wife of the then Chairman of the BBC, who objected to its critical flavour.)

All through her long and interesting life Beatrice Webb regularly kept a Diary. However tired or otherwise occupied she might be, she managed to find time to jot down in her illegible handwriting what she had been doing, whom she had seen, her most secret thoughts and hopes and fears. She normally slept badly – so the most convenient time was in the very early morning – sitting up in bed in the grey light of dawn, and, as she wrote, wearing, I imagine, that look of puzzlement, of earnest endeavour, which so became her. About her there was always something innocent and ardent. She was more like a nun than a suffragette – Saint Teresa rather than Margaret Bondfield or Mrs Pankhurst.

When she died in her 86th year she had filled a large number of manuscript volumes. She was exceedingly candid in her judgements, particularly of people, and decided that much of her journal would be suitable for publication only after a lapse of years. One volume, dealing with her early life, was published in 1926, with the title *My Apprenticeship*. It describes her circumstances before her marriage to Sidney Webb, when she was young and rich and attractive. It explains why she didn't make a 'good marriage' in the worldly sense, like her sisters, the other Miss Potters, but decided to become Webb's partner in virtue and devote her life to a study of what are called 'social problems'.

A sequel to *My Apprenticeship* has now been posthumously published, called *Our Partnership*. Mrs Webb worked on the manuscript herself for a number of years, but had still not put it into final shape when she died in 1943. What still remained to be done has been undertaken with care and discretion by Margaret Cole, who recently produced an interesting biography of Mrs Webb, and Barbara Drake, one of Mrs Webb's many nieces. As in *My Apprenticeship*, extracts from her journal are interwoven with a narrative of the events with which the extracts deal. The period covered is from 1892 to 1911, the first years of the famous Webb Partnership.

Mrs Webb writes with unusual lucidity, and even charm; but neither the extracts from her journal, nor her own descriptive passages, adequately convey the curious character of this remarkable Partnership, and of the household in which it operated. The two partners were, at once, so ill-assorted, and, intellectually, so perfectly attuned to one another. Their manner of expressing themselves was so different, and what they had to say so identical. The routine whereby they lived was so immutable; they themselves were so unusual. An indescribably bizarre effect was produced – rather like when the clown, Grock, used to take a minute violin out of a large case and play exquisitely upon it.

The identification of the Webbs was inward, and found expression in their joint endeavour. Outwardly, they were in striking contrast. She was tall and elegant; he short and plump. Her own description of him in *Our Partnership* could scarcely be bettered:

With his big head, bulgy eyes, bushy moustaches and square-cut short beard (it is this latter feature which gained him the name of 'Nannie' in the House of Commons), small but rotund body, tapering arms and legs and diminutive hands and feet, he lends himself to the cubist treatment of the ridiculous. These ill-looks, however, are not represented in photographs; for the photographer always selects the profile or half-face. Taken in profile, with the disproportion between head and legs corrected by the falsified photographic perspective, he is not only remarkable but attractive in appearance. The massive head, covered with thick wavy hair, the broad finely-moulded forehead, large kindly grey eyes, imposing Roman nose together with the aforementioned bushy imperial, would look well on a coin!

The day's routine began with an austere breakfast at 7.30. Mrs Webb's personal habits were rigidly abstemious. Again and again in her journal she refers to the necessity for a moderate diet and the avoidance of intoxicants. Her partner accepted a similar abstemiousness, though perhaps not altogether willingly. Her guests were provided with better fare, and sometimes, as they pleasurably munched their bacon and egg, she would appear and stride up and down, keeping up a running conversation as the meal proceeded.

Through the morning the Partnership operated. The two partners sat at the same table, conducting their interminable joint researches. Their habit of working together was so engrained that it is probably impossible now to disentangle the contribution of each. By contrast with Mrs Webb's journal, their massive works on the History of Trade Unionism, on the Consumers' Co-operative Movement and English Local Government, are written with an excruciating dullness. Thus it is reasonable to deduce that he rather than she did most of the actual writing of them.

At lunch the Partnership emerged for general conversation. This, too, was an unforgettable performance. One would begin an anecdote and the other take it up and then relinquish it for the first to bring it to completion. Views were always expressed collectively, with the royal pronoun 'We'. It was like a singer and an accompanist so used to appearing together that the slightest variation in the voice immediately found expression in the playing, and vice versa. The characters Altiora and Oscar Bailey in H. G. Wells's *The New Machiavelli* were intended to, and indeed do faithfully, portray the Webbs.

There is an admirable description in this novel of how a conversation with them proceeded:

'We have read your book,' each began – as though it had been a joint function. 'And we consider . . .'

'Yes,' I protested, 'I think . . .'

That was a secondary matter.

They did not consider, said Altiora, raising her voice and going right over me, that I had allowed sufficiently for the inevitable development of an official administrative class in the modern state.

'Nor for its importance,' echoed Oscar.

That, they explained in a sort of chorus, was the cardinal idea of their lives, what they were up to, what they stood for. 'We want to suggest to you,' they said – and I found this was a stock opening of theirs – 'that from the mere necessities of convenience elected bodies must avail themselves more and more of the services of expert officials. We have that very much in mind. The more complicated and technical affairs become, the less confidence will the elected official have in himself. We want to suggest that these expert officials must necessarily develop into a new class and a very powerful class in the community. We want to organize that. It may be *the* power of the future. They will necessarily have to have very much of a common training. We consider ourselves as amateur unpaid precursors of such a class...'

Though any subject was open to discussion, the Partnership only pronounced itself, as a Partnership, on matters which came within its terms of reference. These terms, Mrs Webb explains, did not include art or literature or religion or philosophy, but only the nature, origins and purpose of the social structure. For instance, on the subject of the novels of D. H. Lawrence, the partners might have views in their separate capacities, but such views were unofficial and private. The Partnership only had views after due thought and consideration of all the relevant facts. Once formed, the Partnership's views changed rarely, though with constant repetition before different audiences they did, like a coral reef, slowly increase in bulk and elaboration.

The period of general talk after lunch was followed by exercise, usually a walk. In her later years Mrs Webb found it more convenient to lie down in the afternoon, but she still insisted that Sidney should exercise. He, however, was liable to employ what might well be described as Fabian tactics, and go only as far as the nearest convenient haystack, where he, too, would have a nap. This mild deception was made plausible by hurrying over the return journey, and thus appearing breathless enough to have been for a long ramble. After tea, the Partnership again became operative, its two members disappearing until just before dinner. In the evening there was more talk until Mrs Webb gave the signal for retirement to bed.

This austere and painstaking existence, followed over many years, inevitably produced an exceptional output. By their writings and activities the Webbs unquestionably had an outstanding influence on the political thinking and administrative institutions of their times. They devised a method of research, which was subsequently much emulated, and were largely responsible for the establishment of that cradle of Labour Cabinet Ministers, the London School of Economics, and of an organ for expounding their political theories – the *New Statesman*. In the early years of their marriage, as *Our Partnership* shows, they were deeply involved both in LCC and national politics. They both served on various commissions of inquiry, she, notably, on the Royal Commission on the Poor Law, and acted as unofficial advisers to many eminent politicians. He was a Cabinet Minister in two Labour Governments, and their last years were devoted to advertising what they considered to be the merits of the Soviet regime and constitution. 'Old people,' Mrs Webb once remarked, 'take to pets, and mine is the USSR.' A tabby or a pekingese she might have found easier to handle, and certainly better house-trained, but her bold and passionate nature demanded a deeper solace than such domestic pets could provide. She had a portrait of Lenin lighted from below which she used to show with pride to her visitors. He was the last of a long line of heroes, beginning with Joseph Chamberlain, and including Arthur Balfour.

Mrs Webb believed that it was her account in her journal of the Partnership's manifold activities which would constitute its major interest to posterity. True it is that whoever wishes to investigate, for instance, the early development of public education in London, and the activities of the Poor Law Commission, will necessarily turn to her journal. Her judgements of eminent contemporaries, however, though less calm and dispassionate in temper, may well have a more enduring interest. She sums up individuals vividly, and with at times a pleasing acidity. Dr Dalton she describes as 'a subtle, wily man with a certain peculiar charm for those who are not put off by his mannerisms'. Mr Churchill, she writes, though a rhetorician, 'has a hard temperament, with the American's capacity for the quick appreciation and rapid execution of new ideas, whilst hardly comprehending the philosophy beneath them. But I rather liked the man . . .' Asquith 'eats and drinks too much and lives in a too enervating social atmosphere', and Balfour is a 'a man of extraordinary grace of mind and body – delighting in all that is beautiful and distinguished – music, literature, philosophy, religious feeling and moral disinterested-ness, aloof from all the greed and grime of common human nature. But a strange paradox as Prime Minister of a great Empire! I doubt whether even foreign affairs interest him; for all economic and social questions, I gather, he has an utter loathing.'

When she was thinking about human beings she was liable to forget the Partnership and its objectives, and to react in the light of her own intuition and tastes. Thus, she liked Balfour just because he was charming and attentive to her, in spite of the fact that, from the point of view of the Partnership, he was dross. Between her private inclinations and the exigencies of the Partner-ship there was a conflict which she never succeeded in resolving. In those early morning hours, when the journal was being written, and Sidney was happily snoring, she allowed herself to be a mere woman, given to illogical preferences and dislikes, pursuing her own fancies and forming her own human judgements. Then she could confess that 'secure in the possession of an attractive garment', she would very much have liked to 'parade herself' at Lady Wimborne's, Mr Balfour's and the Duchess of Sutherland's evening parties: and that the interminable sessions of the Poor Law Commission were often a bore. This was not the Partnership speaking. The Partnership in its social relations, as in all others, was strictly utilitarian.

This sensitive and essentially bewildered woman forced herself from a sense of duty to adopt an ungainly and uncongenial way of life. In her there took place a struggle which reflected a larger struggle taking place in the society to which she belonged. It was the struggle between a preoccupation with the phenomena of life and a longing to reach beyond them at life's significance. It was, had she but known it, herself versus the Partnership.

In her journal she describes rather touchingly how, when her spirit was troubled, she used to walk along the Embankment from Grosvenor Road, where the Partnership was installed, to Westminster Abbey for evening service. The singing and the prayers made her tranquil again. This was a private, not a joint enterprise. Her partner felt no need for what he called, with sibilant disapproval, 'religious exercises'. He was liable even to manifest a slight impatience when such matters were raised, since they were not on the Partnership agenda, and had no evident bearing on the work in hand. 'The subject,' she writes, 'bores Sidney as leading nowhere and as not capable of what he considers valid discussion – exactly as he dislikes discussing what train you will go by before he has got hold of the Bradshaw.'

She was a truly remarkable person, although like Wells's Altiora Bailey it could perhaps fairly be said of her that 'her soul was bony, and at the base of her was a vanity gaunt and greedy'. There was as Wells pointed out, a 'dreadful aptness' in her being called Donna Quixote with Sidney for her Sancho Panza. Like the Knight of the Woeful Countenance, she did truly desire to champion the downtrodden and oppressed, and protect the weak against the oppression of the strong. Only, again like the Knight, she lost contact with reality. Where he mistook windmills for giants and squalid inns for majestic castles, she mistook statistics and blue books for wisdom, and diligence for virtue. Like him she finished up enmeshed in her own self-deception, adulating a regime which bore as little relation to the Fabian Good Life as Dulcinea del Toboso to the Mistress of Don Quixote's dreams.

[1948]

The Art Of Non-Conforming

If I were to write, as I have sometimes thought I might, the Confessions of a Non-Conforming Man, they would begin with an assertion that the mid-twentieth century, far from being a period of enlightenment, has been notable for credulity and servility to a quite exceptional degree. It would be necessary, I should go on, to go back at least to the Dark Ages to find a generation of men so given over to destruction, superstition, and every variety of obscurantism. Over large parts of the world the institution of slavery has been re-established in a particularly cruel and callous form. At the same time, huge areas, formerly dependencies of Britain and other West European countries, are rapidly and evidently falling into chaos and ruin. Two atrocious wars have laid waste and impoverished Western civilization, whose leaders have been constantly outwitted, and whose assets, moral as well as material, have been recklessly squandered. At the same time, amidst these horrors, and confronted at every turn with evidence of his own ineptitude, Twentieth Century Man has continued to pin his hopes on the untenable and obsolete doctrine of progress, convinced, apparently, that with him the life process has attained its apogee. So ludicrous a spectacle has rarely, if ever, been seen on earth.

Questioning, thus, the basic assumptions of the age, the Non-Conforming Man cannot but find its pretensions particularly derisory. Ironically, ignorance seems to grow with education and freedom seems to decay to the accompaniment of protestations of devotion to its cause. Charlatanry, he observes, flourishes as perhaps never before, and decay of belief in a deity, or in any transcendental concept whatsoever, leaves, not a vacuum, but a capacity and a readiness to believe in anything, however non-sensical. He notes that established pundits, in such circumstances, grow ever more fatuous in their assertions, and dictatorships ever more unbridled in the cruelties and lies whereby they maintain themselves in existence. Nor can he hide a smile when, for instance, the absurd Webbs are sanctified for detecting a 'new civilization' in the Kremlin's cruel empire; when a new dawn is seen in the eerie light which atomic explosions put into the sky; when the outworn and outmoded conclusions of a Karl Marx provide a dogma, and the partial, and mostly superficial conclusions of a Sigmund Freud have, like Marx in the field of history and economics, been furbished up into a philosophy of life which they were in no wise intended to become; above all when, while mental homes, slave labour camps, and psychoanalysts' waiting rooms alike fill to overflowing, partisans of all parties and exponents of all ideologies vie with one another in proclaiming the coming to pass of the most forward-looking, peace-loving, humane, prosperous, and enlightened era the world has ever known.

Civilization presupposes the integrity and inviolability of each separate human being, and it is contemporary neobarbarisms like Fascism, Nazism, and Communism, which have sought to destroy the individual in favour of the collectivity. Institutional Christianity, even when least practised, has clung to the concept of separate souls, all infinitely and equally precious in the eyes of a Creator, who has numbered the hairs on each head, and who knows when each sparrow falls to the ground. By contrast, the materialists, the power-worshippers, the demon-demagogues of our time, insist that individual men and women are of no account, and have no destiny of their own to work out apart from mankind's.

Against such a trend, the impulse not to conform constitutes a kind of resistance movement, whose practitioners, as the claims of collectivism augment, are liable to be forced to become *maquisards*, living cautiously on the fringes of society, and only occasionally and discreetly disclosing their true attitude of mind. Yet how important, how necessary they are! Without them, collective assumptions may pass unchallenged, and there may be no one to puncture the pretensions of established authority.

The Gadarene swine raced as a herd for the cliff over which they were to hurl themselves to annihilation, but Bunyan's Pilgrim proceeded alone, or at most with one companion, along the difficult way from the City of Destruction to the Delectable Mountains. The basic failure of our time, future historians may well decide, has lain in the too ready acceptance of current orthodoxies, whether through fear of being suspected of rebelliousness and consequently punished, or just as a result of succumbing to mass persuasion. The independent, non-conforming mind is visibly becoming rarer. Conformity is more and more the order of the day, inevitably bringing with it that subservience to prevailing fashions of thought, values and behaviour, which prepares the way for – to use the sombre expression originated by Belloc more than four decades ago – the Servile State.

To a civilized and free mind any enforced orthodoxy must be abhorrent. It is inconceivable that the last word should ever be said about anything, or that history should ever reach any sort of finality. Non-conforming is a recognition that Man and all his works are inherently imperfect, and therefore susceptible to criticism, if not ridicule. It is tremendously invigorating, adding a quite special spice to life. As a habit of mind, it is greatly to be recommended.

We know from the past that mass or mob judgements have nearly always been mistaken. As Hitler and other demagogues have abundantly shown, unhappily the democratic process can be perverted to bring about the opposite – enslavement – by means of substituting collective judgements for the summation of individual judgements on which true democracy must ever rest. True democracy, in fact, requires a non-conforming citizenry. Its worst and most dangerous propensity is the impulse to conform. The greatest and most enduring achievements have been due to individual skills and insight. Why, then, should we suppose it to be otherwise today? Shakespeare, rightly, always made the mob ignoble, cruel and unstable. His mobs laud a Coriolanus or a Caesar one moment, and shout for his blood the next. On Golgotha, likewise, the mob easily forgot the first Palm Sunday, and called for the release of Barrabas, obediently echoing the cry: 'Crucify him! Crucify him!' In such circumstances, the temptation to conform is very great indeed. Even one of the Apostles, Saint Peter, succumbed to it.

Nor is it only on dramatic occasions that this temptation presents itself. In, for instance, matters of taste it is constantly operative – whether to follow inertly a prevailing popular fashion, or, what is even more insidious, to go along with some dreary little *avant-garde* coterie, irrespective of one's personal judgement or predilection. Yet what exhilaration, what a sense of life's salty tang, when the decision not to conform is taken! What a wonderful sense of freedom on becoming released from the necessity of repeating, let alone believing, the vast rubric of the Century of the Common Man. It is like driving monotonously along a turnpike road, mile after weary mile, and then suddenly realizing that all around are expanses of a delicious and varied countryside to which access is readily available.

Jonathan Swift, a Non-Conforming Man if ever there was one, devised his own epitaph, which was to be set forth on black marble, 'in large letters, deeply cut and strongly gilded'. It was to say to any traveller who visited his tomb in St Patrick's Cathedral, Dublin, that Swift was now lying where 'his furious indignation can no longer lacerate his heart' (*ubi saeva indignatio ulterius cor lacerare nequit*), and that the traveller should seek to 'imitate, if he can, this strenuous defender of manly liberty' (*imitare si poteris strenuum pro virili libertate vindicem*). The words are immensely touching when one thinks of their writer's splendid attainments, and of the many disappointments which befell him. By the time the epitaph came to be used, his furious indignation had become insupportable. In his last years, poor Swift was mad. It is a danger which besets the non-conforming temperament, liable, as it is, to set up internal stresses and strains. In the same way that slum children, removed to the English countryside to get them away from the blitz, moaned and groaned for the pavements, the noise, the teeming squalor of the streets whence they had come, so individual morale can collapse in withdrawal from that spiritual slum, the collectivity.

Another danger of a like nature is exemplified in the character of Don Quixote, whose creator, Cervantes, like ourselves, lived in a period of deep social change calculated to disconcert and bewilder. Don Quixote made the fatal error of taking flight from reality. His refusal to conform with a *zeitgeist*, and an environment to him both incomprehensible and distasteful, led him to withdraw into a past which he deluded himself into believing was still extant. Absurdly accoutred in rusty armour, and mounted on his scraggy nag, Rosinante, he rode forth into his own fantasy, with disastrous consequences to himself and to others. It is not difficult to think of his equivalents today – those lean-faced humanitarians, for instance, who still believe, with Rousseau, despite all the evidence to the contrary, that human beings are naturally good, and have only to be left to their own devices to create an earthly paradise.

If, however, the Non-Conforming Man may become enraged, as in the case of Swift, or fall into undue eccentricity, as with Don Quixote, or even into despair and madness – like Nietzsche, at his best he exemplifies true sanity. A good example is Paulinus, who, aware that Roman civilization had collapsed, chose to tend a particular shrine, to keep alive one clear lamp amidst gathering darkness. His serenity when his world was falling to pieces around him finds expression in his writings, and is a source of comfort and inspiration still. This is non-conforming at its very best – a refusal to be swept along by contemporary follies and vain hopes; likewise, a refusal to surrender to the terror and hopelessness generated when human societies and institutions take on unfamiliar shapes, and emit strange sounds, like furniture in a child's bedroom when the light has been put out. A Non-Conforming

Man today is in a very similar case to Paulinus. He, too, has seen the treasures of civilization sacked, and, what is worse, perverted, and the barbarians sweep forward in a seemingly irresistible rush; he, too, has come to doubt the applicability to contemporary circumstances of the values, beliefs and loyalties which guided the conduct of his forebears; he, too, has been disconcerted and appalled by the apparently limitless capacity of his contemporaries to be deluded, and to content themselves with bread and circuses when their very existence is threatened. And he, too, must choose his shrine, must light his lamp, and keep it burning.

There is one last aspect of non-conforming which, naturally, appeals to me personally. Non-conforming is the basis, the very fount, of all humour. A totally conformist society never laughs – laughter itself being a kind of criticism, an expression of the immense disparity between human aspiration and human performance. As such, it is intolerable to all orthodoxy-enforcers, from Torquemada to Stalin.

The circus clown is made to look different from his fellow-performers. He falls over, he stands on his head, he grimaces and rides absurd bicycles. Yet what would a circus be without him? How especially the children would miss him, however daring the trapeze artists, however majestic the lion-tamer! It is worth noting, too, that Shakespeare's fools are given some of his most sagacious and poetic lines. The non-conforming Fool proved, in the end, King Lear's most tender, understanding, and faithful friend, when all the conformists had abandoned him to his fate.

[1953]

Journalism

The only fun of journalism is that it puts you in contact with the eminent without being under the necessity to admire them or take them seriously. It is the ideal profession for those who find power fascinating and its exercise abhorrent.

Farewell To Freedom?

A favourite exercise of mine is to try and imagine how this strange time will look to some historian viewing it across subsequent centuries. By then our civilization, like the many others which have gone before it, will have disappeared, leaving only traces in stone or in the written word for scholars to decipher. The conflicts which torment us will all have been resolved – for everything here on earth must be resolved at last. It is a fair assumption, I think, that these conflicts, in the eyes of my historian, will seem in retrospect as unreal, as unnecessary and as ruinous as do to us the religious wars which in their day also led to much bloodshed, vast destruction and human suffering, as well as to a huge outpouring of words.

How will it all look to him – some Gibbon, rather than a Macaulay or Carlyle, of the remote future, urbane and detached, more curious than zealous, more eager to understand and to explain than to justify and to acclaim? How will he see this age through which we are living – this age of inane hope and inane despair, with its pretentious dreams of enduring human felicity and its equally pretentious nightmares of ultimate destruction, not only of the earth, but of the very solar system of which the earth is a part?

Looking, as historians must, for some general trend, some guiding principle, he cannot but reach the conclusion, it seems to me, that this was pre-eminently the age of the elevation of the State and the obliteration of the individuals who compose it. Hobbes's Great Leviathan, he will say, swallowed up more and more, until, at last, there was nothing but the Leviathan, splashing about, supreme, and occasionally diverting itself by ejecting gushes of muddy water. We all know how this has come to pass on the other side of the Iron Curtain. And we are all, I suppose, more or less in agreement in abhorring the resultant form of society, with its rigidly and cruelly enforced orthodoxy, its abolition of all individual human rights, its exaltation and adulation of power as such, and its contemptuous dismissal of all save materialist values. American Senators and Labour Members of Parliament vie with one another in proclaiming, with their hands on their hearts, their detestation of such totalitarianism in all its manifestations.

Heaven knows, it would be easy enough for me to show, with

reference to the Soviet, the Nazi and kindred regimes, that the individual shrinks as the power of government grows. In those societies the State has become everything and the individual nothing. His political rights extend no further than assenting to whatever the State may decree. His only duty is to think and believe as he is told; his only fulfilment to put at the disposal of those set in authority over him whatever skills, intelligence and energy he may possess. Nonconformity is a crime most drastically punished, and to think at all on his own account is dangerous.

All this is too obvious to need any exposition. Only the more imbecile type of fellow-traveller – some poor, deluded Dean of Canterbury or forlorn millionaire – will bother to deny that the Soviet State, far from withering away in accordance with the Marxist prophecy, has grown ever more powerful, until today it dominates everything and everyone, meticulously and relentlessly supervises the whole economic, cultural, ideological, yes, and spiritual life of the peoples over whom it has acquired control. It is the individual who has withered away.

So far, as I have said, we might all agree, and, if matters were left there, part comfortably convinced that such are the unhappy Slave Societies of our time, in contrast to the free ones to which we have the good fortune to belong. A few observations about Western values would provide a suitable conclusion. Ah, those Western values – like inflated currency without an adequate gold backing; pieces of paper tastefully designed and marked with immense sums, but purchasing ever less; blared out from the transmitters, thundered from platforms, tapped out on leader-writers' typewriters, absorbed along with cigar smoke and brandy when my lords, ladies and gentlemen, your excellencies and your graces have all been prayed for silence. Ah, those Western values!

It is not at all my intention to add my little bleat to this unconscionable braying. I want to look, not over the Iron Curtain, but at our side of it. How about the Free World which we are supposed to be defending? What about our much-boosted Free Societies? How does the trend go in them as between government and the governed? Let me say at once that I am personally convinced that in these so-called Free Societies of ours the same drift towards servitude is apparent as in the Slave Societies across the Curtain. In them, too, that great Leviathan, the State, is waxing ever fatter, and all the little fishes, ourselves, are tending to find our way into its dark, cavernous stomach.

When I was living in Moscow in the early thirties I used to have a recurrent fancy that the scene there, to me so unutterably hateful – the grey unsmiling figures padding about the grey unsmiling streets, like the terrible picture by Van Gogh of prisoners being exercised in a courtyard – would inevitably reproduce itself elsewhere, until, at last, it was everywhere. Was my fancy, I have often subsequently wondered, so wide of the mark? Is not enslavement (which means the shedding, through fear, or inertia, or cowardice, or weariness, of the burden of individuality) spreading like a plague, a horrible contagion, through the whole world?

Let me take the case of my own country, England, and begin with its sovereign assembly, the House of Commons, supposed to be the guardian of the liberties and rights of us ordinary citizens, who every so often are called upon to re-elect it. How does the individual MP stand in relation to the Party Machine of which he is a part? Ill, it must be admitted. I read in the newspapers the other day how in Finland, where voting in the legislature is by pressing a button, a number of members were reprimanded for going off to carouse during a parliamentary session, having left matchsticks wedged in their voting buttons so that they continuously registered aye votes. This practice might well be adopted in the House of Commons. It would make no difference.

No objective observer of the English scene, I submit, could possibly fail to agree that, as far as Parliament is concerned, the individual Member has become submerged in the Party Machine. Indeed, the institution would work better, more expeditiously, if, following Mr Balfour's well-known directions, poodles replaced humans on all save the Front Benches – Mr Attlee's poodles and Sir Winston's poodles trotting obediently through the division lobbies, or dozing in the Chamber, tongues hanging indolently out, while their masters orate.

Now let us take a look at the other great watchdog of liberty, the Free Press, in whose *maquis*, like many another ideological straggler, I have lived, not, I confess, without amusement and some profit, during the last quarter of a century. Here, surely, is a little reserve for the individual cleared amidst the collectivist jungle. I fear not. The Press, too, in my opinion, is increasingly becoming more a purveyor of orthodoxy than an expression of individual views. The State which in a variety of ways, ranging between subtle pressure and persuasion and unabashed handouts, feeds it with 'news', is able more and more to call its tune. The Press, too, in my opinion, is in process of succumbing to the collectivist *zeitgeist*. At its obsequies the mutes are public relations officers, and the service is read by an ordained Minister of Information, with massed choirs provided by the British Broadcasting Corporation.

You will forgive me if, in regard to this matter of what the late Dr Goebbels called the *Gleichgeschaltung* of the Press, I refer briefly to some rather curious recent experiences of my own. As you will perhaps have heard, some eighteen months ago I became Editor of an allegedly humorous weekly magazine whose remoter origins were strongly 'Radical', and whose considerable reputation, in the nineteenth century at any rate, derived from its practice of commenting harshly, satirically, and quite irreverently, upon public personalities and affairs.

It was an attractive and alluring project to try to revive this tradition, which had lapsed in the timid twilit inter-war years, when the English middle and upper classes had tried to interpose the figure of Christopher Robin between them and Hitler. The result, however, was electric. Angry letters poured in accusing me, among other things, of being a Fascist, a Communist, an atheist, a bigot, an Americanophil, a republican, an anarchist, yes, and even a Bevanite. Even when the possible truth, or at any rate plausibility, of a particular comment was admitted, it was condemned as being in the worst taste. The Italians would be hurt, the French would be grieved, Dr Malan would be upset, Mr Malenkov would harden his heart, Anglo-American relations would suffer; Sir Beverley Baxter would be made so indignant that it might bring on an apoplectic stroke. In fact, I was being 'unhelpful'.

Do you see what I'm getting at? The exercise of a free, independent judgement is so out of keeping with the contemporary climate that it requires some explanation. Like a tumour or cancerous growth it can only exist at all as a result of some abnormal condition capable of a simple diagnosis. If one is against Senator McCarthy one must be for Professor Lattimore; if one considers that Dr Malan is vainly and foolishly trying to set the clock back one must necessarily believe that Pandit Nehru is the champion of Western civilization; if one happens to have formed the opinion that Mr Eden is making the same ruinous mistake that Neville Chamberlain made – of supposing that peace can be negotiated with those whose philosophy and programme of action presupposes the absence of peace – it can only be because one is bent on promoting a war. It is in this passion for thinking in terms of categories that I detect the clearest and most ominous symptom of the subordination of the individual to the collectivity.

A voluntary uniformity, no less than an imposed one, prepares the way for servitude.

It is, of course, true that a potent factor in generating such an attitude of mind has been, as far as England is concerned, the British Broadcasting Corporation, which, through its close association with government, has necessarily become a mouthpiece of current orthodoxy and a powerful instrument on the side of the State in subduing the individual. The anguished cries of elderly peers in opposing a recent rather pitiable measure aimed at instituting commercial television in competition with the BBC, strongly recalled the yapping of decrepit sheep dogs when they are trying to round up a recalcitrant herd.

The late Mrs Sidney Webb had a, to me, infinitely repugnant way of referring to 'Man as Consumer' and 'Man as Producer'. These two roles have undergone great changes since her time, partly, it must be admitted, as a result of her and her consort's efforts. In England, as you all know, certain basic industries have been brought under direct government control, and the Labour Party is pledged (though with a marked lack of enthusiasm compared with earlier times when its programme was young and in the spring) to extend this process more or less indefinitely. Thus, on present showing, the day will come when, without any revolutionary upheaval, the State will own and direct the whole national economy, and virtually the whole population will be, in effect, State employees.

This may or may not lead to greater security, prosperity, efficiency and other beneficent ends. I am not here concerned with that. I am concerned, however, to point out that such a development cannot but, in my opinion, result in the diminution, and final obliteration, of the individual as we know him today. Regarding ourselves, for a moment, in Mrs Webb's two distasteful categories – as consumers, freedom lies in being able to consume what we will and how we will, to eat grass like Nebuchadnezzar, to be naked as the naked earth like St Francis of Assisi, or to seek the splendours of a Borgia; as producers, freedom lies in being able to work much or little, at what we will when we will, to be our own masters or accept the mastership of others.

These, you may say, are sentimental or obsolete notions, of no more relevance now than was Rousseau's Noble Savage in his day. Very well. But what is neither sentimental nor obsolete is to point out that relations between the individual and the State always have, and always will, be governed by the division of power between them. Habeas Corpus, as we all know, was designed to provide protection against arbitrary arrest and imprisonment. But what is the worth of Habeas Corpus if he for whom it provides protection is already employed by the State, housed by the State, insured by the State, conditioned by the State to think, and evaluate what is going on in the world, as the State wishes? The Corpus is duly produced to show just cause for its detention, but is it alive? How if Habeas Corpus becomes Habeas Cadaver? Where's the protection then?

The State, in fact, is the greatest of all tyrants, the ultimate tyrant. Kings can be executed, oligarchies can be broken up, millionaires can be despoiled of their money, Popes can be defied and heresies persisted in, but the State is, in principle, ourselves, and how can we put down ourselves? We who are the Leviathan cannot slay it. To try to do so is suicide, not rebellion. Just as, under Roman law the suicide of a slave was punishable with the most horrible penalties, which were visited upon his living relations as well as his dead carcass, on the ground that, by killing himself, a slave robbed his master, so, as the power of the State grows, rebellion against it in word or deed, or even criticism of it, comes to be accounted the ultimate offence.

A recurrent nightmare, with me, is that in our inimitable English way we are allowing a servile State to come to pass of itself without our noticing it; that one morning I shall wake up and find that, with the Monarchy still extant, Honourable and Right Honourable Members still meeting in Westminster, *The Times* and the *Manchester Guardian*, the *New Statesman* and the *Spectator* and *Punch* still regularly appearing, cricket still being played at Lords, and the BBC still providing its daily offering from 'Bright and Early' to 'Goodnight everyone, goodnight', we have nevertheless become a totalitarian society. In this nightmare it seems clear that all the faceless men, the men without opinions, have been posted in key positions for a bloodless take-over, and that no one is prepared to join a Resistance Movement in defence of freedom because no one remembers what freedom means. The walls of Jericho fell down, not because the trumpet blast was strong but because the walls themselves were crumbling. People, that is to say, are never enslaved unless they have become slaves already. They swim into the Great Leviathan's mouth; he does not need to chase them.

I have drawn my illustrations from my own country because that is the one I know. I would, however, venture to point out that during the three years that I worked as a correspondent in Washington it seemed to me that there, too, government was gaining and the individual losing; that, as it were, there was a rush of blood to the Capital, with consequent anaemia elsewhere. Has not, I ask myself, a dangerous passion for uniformity and conformity become apparent likewise even on this side of the Atlantic, providing an outward and visible manifestation of an inward and invisible desire to get into the Leviathan's belly, which is warm and secure, but dark and confined?

May I, in conclusion, go back to the future historian with whom I began? He will not only note of this age that it was signalized by the elevation of the State and the obliteration of the individual; he will also wonder why. And this is the explanation I believe he will hit on. The Christian religion, he will contend, for two thousand years persuaded Western man that he existed as one of a human family whose father was in Heaven. As in a family, each individual was separately and particularly loved.

It followed from this that each individual soul was infinitely precious in its separate individuality. Men might go to war in regiments, but they attained salvation one by one. Bunyan's Pilgrim found companions along his way, but the trumpets, when they blew for him on the other side, blew for him alone. The most sacred, the most inviolable thing on earth was a human soul, any and every one, whether it inhabited the flesh of rich or poor, clever or foolish, well or sick. Thus, to incorporate a man in a herd, and to put him under the necessity of following the herd's destiny, was to destroy the purpose of his being. He was himself or he was nothing. Of the herd, the fearful image stands for ever – the Gadarene swine rushing to destruction.

The liberties which we prize, or at any rate praise, my historian will contend, were born, not in Westminster, nor even in Philadelphia, but on the shores of Galilee. They are implicit in the Christian faith, and were that faith to perish, they would perish with it, quite irrespective of any apparatus of law and of military force which might exist to sustain and safeguard them. Our civilization derives from the Christian religion, and will end with it, and neither H-bombs, nor wealth, nor humane laws, nor equitable societies will suffice to shore it up. My favourite of all images is Plato's, of the man in the cellar who yet by craning his neck could see the light of day and figures passing by like shadows. The light he could glimpse was his freedom. Without it he is in darkness indeed – a slave, nothing.

[1954]

Lord Beaverbrook

There are few more diverting, or for that matter more beneficial, experiences in life than being attacked by one of Lord Beaverbrook's newspapers. This has so far happened to me twice, and I found the second occasion (in connection with an article I wrote called 'Royal Soap Opera') even more enjoyable than the first. Apart from anything else, the attack ensured for the article in question a far wider circulation than it would otherwise have enjoyed. I am still getting press cuttings and letters from remote parts of the world, the great majority of which express general concurrence with the observations I made. For this, too, I owe Lord Beaverbrook thanks. There is a widespread tendency to believe that whenever his newspapers take up a strong position about anyone or anything the opposite must be true – a consequence, perhaps, of their insistence right up to September 1939, that there would be no war.

It is, of course, true that the pleasure of being attacked by a Beaverbrook newspaper is greater for those who, like myself, have been employed on one of them. We know just how the job is done. Like gastronomes, we not only savour the delicious flavour of a favourite dish; we are also familiar with the recipe, the components, the cooking. In our mind's eye we see the chosen scribe being briefed, watch him as he thumbs over the envelope of cuttings, enter into his efforts to instil into his writing a malignity which he does not necessarily share; go with him to take the resultant copy to the editor, and then perhaps, if the occasion is considered important enough, hear it read over to Lord Beaverbrook himself, who may be far away – sunning himself in the Midi or the Caribbean – but never so far away that he will overlook short-measure in the presentation of his vendettas.

Lord Beaverbrook is, indeed, expert at conducting vendettas by remote control. The telephone, the telegraph, above all the force of his curious personality, suffice to maintain his direction when his physical presence is lacking. Long years of practice have conditioned those who receive his instructions to follow them almost before they are given. They are his men. Like perfect dancing partners, they know instinctively when the pace or the step is going to be changed. Their very voices are liable to contain an echo of his harsh Canadian accent; their relationship with him is almost mystical in its perfect and complete identification. I once heard one of the more vivacious of his writers asked which section of the vast readership of the Beaverbrook newspapers he particularly aimed at in his articles. 'I write,' he said majestically (and it seemed to me an historic pronouncement which thoroughly deserved to be recorded), 'for one little old reader – Lord Beaverbrook.'

The fact is that Lord Beaverbrook has used the powerful publicity machine he has created entirely to pander to his own personal whims. Other press lords have at any rate imagined themselves to be supporting and attacking causes, admiring and denigrating individuals, in the public interest. He is just an imp, always prepared to adjust public positions in the light of private quarrels. Campaigns, when he has conducted them, have been – like Empire Free Trade which entertained the thirties – too nonsensical to merit serious consideration. Leader-writers, however obedient, are hard put to it to construct any sort of meaning out of his meandering and inconsequential directives. The telephone rings, an awed operator says who is there, and the thick, oddly modulated voice launches upon a singular news commentary. Such, at least, was what used to happen in my time. The problem of translating this commentary into ostensible sense seemed at one moment so oppressive that a tape recorder was installed. Thereby our master's words could be listened to again and again in order that their full import (such as it was) might be grasped. Unhappily, the practice was soon abandoned, and the recordings, alas, destroyed. What would I not give to have one of them in my possession now. No party need ever be dull with so bizarre an entertainment available as playing it over would provide.

Just imagine having to advocate, for instance, an ever closer and more impregnable alliance with the United States, and, at the same time, the calling home of British forces in Europe as well as our withdrawal from the United Nations; the refusal of all dollar aid, and, at the same time, 'freeing' the pound, the strengthening of the sterling area, and larger purchases in Canada; the abandonment of purchase tax, and, at the same time, higher wages, a check on inflation, and the removal of all controls; the maintenance of our position in the Middle East, Malaya and throughout the colonial territories, and, at the same time, a cut in the period of national service and a large reduction in national expenditure. It is a tough assignment. The wit of Voltaire, the dialectical ingenuity of G. B. Shaw and the wisdom of Aristotle would scarcely, all combined, suffice to extract a cogent argument from propositions so strange and so contradictory. Yet the job is somehow done. The little editorial paragraphs duly appear, still studded with 'For why?' – a favourite expression of their only begetter.

If, as I have said, it is decidedly pleasurable to be, even momentarily and unimportantly, attacked by a Beaverbrook newspaper, it is also a comfort. Those who in the past have been similarly attacked have invariably thriven, and vice versa. What did not Stanley Baldwin owe to the Beaverbrook press for the savage onslaughts which maintained him as leader of the Conservative Party when his inadequacy as Prime Minister became ever more apparent and his situation ever more precarious? And Brendan Bracken? After being hailed in the Beaverbrook press as the greatest First Lord of the Admiralty of modern times, he sank, politically speaking, without trace, to emerge in the City as a viscount who had never bothered to take his seat in the House of Lords. Where are those Members of Parliament and others who earned lavish praise for 'speaking up for the Empire'? – all forgotten, whereas Lord Mountbatten, who disposed of an empire, and who has been continuously abused in the Beaverbrook press, goes from strength to strength. It is difficult to think of a single case in which abuse has not proved beneficial and praise ruinous. Lord Beaverbrook's rancour is like the Dead Sea – so salty that, thrown into it, you cannot sink.

By what process is the victim decided upon, and by what means is the order to attack transmitted? These are mysteries. All that can be said is that in the office of a Beaverbrook newspaper it is always known that such a name is better not mentioned, that such another requires adulation, and that in the case of such another obloquy will be rewarding. From tiny gossip spite to editorial fulminations, the whole apparatus is brought into use to give proprietorial satisfaction; kicks, pats on the back and small twists and teases faithfully follow the little old reader's latest whims and fancies. The baton is lifted, the orchestra strikes up, and lo! the music thunders or trills or lilts as the conductor wills, each instrument, large and small, noisy and quavering, playing its allotted part.

Journalistically, it must be admitted, it has all been a very great success. However preposterous the contention or unfair the assault, Lord Beaverbrook's journalistic flair was impeccable. Now, even in this respect, there are intimations of failing powers. Perhaps the clearest is the degree to which he himself is nowadays featured in the columns of his own newspapers. The last infirmity of a newspaper proprietor is, surely, to make his own news. Mentions of Lord Beaverbrook have of late been growing ever more frequent in the *Daily Express*, the *Evening Standard* and the *Sunday Express* – references to him laboriously and sometimes fatuously quoted from other newspapers and magazines; extracts from his *Success*, a contemporary Samuel Smiles, which has, it is safe to say, been more serialized, quoted from, commented upon and generally worked over by Lord Beaverbrook's minions than any other work, with the possible exception of the Bible; news stories of sorts fabricated out of some public utterance of his, whose exclusivity no other newspaper is likely to challenge or begrudge; often told tales of his early experiences in journalism, and so on. The little old reader, it would seem, now not only wants his newspapers written for him, but also wants them written about him. An old man's vanity is overlaying the impishness which, however maliciously and inconsequentially it might express itself, at least had the merit of being journalistically viable.

Another curious enterprise in which he has been engaged is to sponsor and subsequently boost biographical works which involve an account of his own political activities. Thus there was Frank Owen's Lloyd George and Robert Blake's Bonar Law, in both of which the Beaverbrook touch is clearly discernible. To have, as it were, his own apologia written by another hand and in the context of another theme was an ingenious but characteristic notion. If he could only acquire the Churchill papers as he did the Lloyd George and Bonar Law ones, the record would be almost watertight. This, however, might be difficult, if not impossible.

How, I have often asked myself, has such a man succeeded in playing such a part in his times? I suppose the short answer is money, in which, however his other loyalties and enthusiasms may have fluctuated, he has consistently believed. Money has been his instrument. It has borne him along. He tells himself constantly in his own newspapers that its pursuit is valid still, and that the old who have become rich inherit the earth. Does he really believe it? It would be a cruel but not inept fate for the little old reader to be taken in at last by what was written to please him.

[1955]

Fact And Fantasy

As available factual material becomes more plentiful, so does its unreliability become more marked. What is known about everyone and everything gets ever more abundant and ever more misleading. The documentation is terrific. Newspapers, magazines, old newsreels, memoirs, biographies, recorded sound and television broadcasts – there is no end to the available material. Yet what credence can be placed in any of it? In this vast orchestra every instrument has its own score. *The Times* practises one sort of deception, the *Daily Express* another, the BBC another. Statesmen like Lloyd George, Churchill and Eden produce what purport to be first-hand accounts of contemporary events which are in reality only self-justifications. It is easier to know what happened centuries ago than what happened yesterday; in the one case, a paucity of information is the difficulty; in the other, a too great plenitude, conflicting and, for the most part, dubious. I used to derive comfort from the thought that paper normally falls into dust in half a century or so. Alas, microfilm now prevents this deliverance.

In his social history of the forties and fifties (*The New Look*, Secker and Warburg, 1963) Mr Harry Hopkins writes: 'And then, in the new year, came an event which, in an instant, somehow transformed the whole quality of the situation, seemed for a moment to sweep away the last remaining certitude – and then to restore them all.' The event in question was the death of King George VI. 'The news spread swiftly from mouth to mouth in unbelieving whispers,' Mr Hopkins goes on. 'The muffled bells began to toll.' 'A great hush, a sabbath stillness,' wrote a witness, 'descended on the City.' I remember the occasion well. I was walking along the Strand in the direction of Fleet Street and the City. There was no hush that I could discern; no unbelieving whispers passed in my hearing. The early editions of the evening papers had banner headlines announcing the King's death. That was all. No face I saw, no remark made to me, intimated a last remaining certitude swept away. Now, who is reporting this incident correctly, Mr Hopkins or me? There is no means of knowing. No doubt his version is nearer than mine to tele – or editorial – truth. All who have written editorials know the splendid sweep of sentences tapped out on a typewriter about how the people of this country will never for one moment countenance . . . how they repudiate with indignation any suggestion that . . . how they mourn the passing of . . . ; just as all who have sat before microphones know the weird and awful sensation of hearing one's own voice as though it were someone else's blowing bromides like bubbles into the air. All this stuff remains on the record; the cuttings, boy, the cuttings! Sometimes, going through an envelope of them, I have come across some particularly fatuous observation which was vaguely familiar. Now where had I heard that before? What idiot perpetrated it? Then a light breaks. The perpetrator was myself. Like a parched desert traveller, I was drinking my own urine.

In Defence Of Bad Taste

Since I became editor of *Punch* some four years ago I have received a great many abusive letters, nearly all of which accuse me of having been guilty of bad taste. Most of these letters come from what are euphemistically called 'good homes' – from retired generals and admirals and clergymen who have long been accustomed to regard humour as a sedative rather than a stimulant. The fact that subsequent events have in most cases borne out the essential justice of the comments to which exception was taken constitutes no excuse for having perpetrated them. As with libel, truth is not a defence. Indeed, it would appear, if anything, to add to rather than extenuate the crime.

Thus, for instance, when *Punch* published a cartoon showing a decrepit Sir Winston Churchill with a caption indicating that it was high time he relinquished the premiership, obloquy was heaped on my head. I had been cruel, ungrateful, disrespectful, unworthy of the great traditions of the venerable magazine I so unworthily edited. Few now (possibly not even Sir Beverley Baxter) would care to dispute that Sir Winston damaged his own splendid reputation, his party's longer-term interests, as well as his country's standing in the world, by clinging too long to office. This, however, in no wise mitigates my offence in having prematurely drawn attention to what was, or should have been, obvious enough. Nor was it the slightest use pointing out that it was a concern for Sir Winston's reputation, not a desire to belittle it, that led me to feel so strongly that the time had come for him to make his bow and leave the public stage. There are occasions, as C. P. Scott, the famous editor of the *Manchester Guardian*, once wrote to me, 'when truth should be economized'. This was one of them. To be too profligate with truth is, *ipso facto*, to be guilty of bad taste.

I was likewise abused for a whole series of comments, written as well as graphic, drawing attention to Sir Anthony Eden's evident inadequacy as a national leader at this time. It is almost inconceivable that anyone, objectively surveying the melancholy consequences of his twenty-one months of office, could fail now to admit that events have only too tragically confirmed such a view of Sir Anthony. Yet I do not find letters pouring in to withdraw, let alone to apologize for, the previous strictures. On the contrary, the eminent (including, alas, some advertisers) continue to frown. Good taste required that, like Sir Anthony's colleagues in his government, I should go through the motions of believing in his wisdom and efficiency despite the overwhelming weight of evidence to the contrary. In such circumstances, bad taste, surely, becomes a virtue.

Again, the invitation to Marshal Bulganin and Mr Khrushchev to come as official guests to this country seemed to me misguided and undignified. I said so, in *Punch* and elsewhere, with some emphasis. Imagine my astonishment when highly respectable and affluent persons (whom Bulganin and Khrushchev would assuredly regard as fit only for the tumbrel) wrote to complain that I had once more been guilty of execrable taste. The canons of polite behaviour required that no mention should be made of the ferocious insults with which our guests had lambasted us and everything we stood for in the world during a recent tour of India and Burma, or of the murderous practices and treacheries whereby they had managed to survive through the Stalin era – to whose enormities Mr Khrushchev himself has so vividly testified.

It is one of the many ironies of trying to bring out a humorous magazine that what actually happens is so vastly funnier than what can be imagined. For sheer comicality nothing could have exceeded a letter I received from a Church dignitary, rebuking me in indignant terms for having been rude to the heads of the most brutal and most irreligious state so far known on earth. I might, from the manner of his address, have been casting aspersions upon some archdeacon's impeccable widow rather than upon two gangsters compared with whom Tamburlaine the Great and Genghis Khan were mere beginners.

Perhaps the best example of all of this confusion between honest comment and bad taste is provided by the consequences of any observation, other than purely adulatory, about the monarchy as an institution and about members of the royal family as individuals. Thus when the abortive romance between Princess Margaret and Group Captain Townsend was being publicly and tediously expounded, I ventured to suggest that the monarchy, if it was to survive, could not afford to be conducted in terms of a royal soap opera. This, too, failed to please.

Yet far from any disparagement of the monarchy being intended, my motive was to draw attention to the possibility that this precious institution would be endangered if its purely personal aspects came to take precedence over its symbolism. Undue adulation, with its inevitable accompaniment, undue curiosity, could ultimately bring it into disrepute more effectively than the most astute and energetic attacks upon it; the tendency to make of royalty an *ersatz* religion, not republicanism, endangered its future. An unwholesomely adulatory atmosphere might lead members of the royal family to lose their heads, not, indeed, physically, as Charles I lost his on the executioner's block, but with consequences scarcely less calamitous.

Until quite recently such considerations would have appeared perfectly legitimate. Queen Victoria was publicly and harshly criticized for her insistence, after the Prince Consort's death, on living in strict retirement. No one (except the Queen) considered this to be in bad taste. It was accepted as fair comment. The fact that it could be made without giving rise to accusations of bad taste was a measure of the strength of the monarchical institution, of the degree to which it was taken for granted. Today like comment would be considered in execrable taste.

This, it seems to me, is because the assumptions on which our institutions and values are based have come to seem so dubious that any questioning of their validity appears indefensible and intolerable. In other words, accusations of bad taste are in reality no more than a means of evading disagreeable truths, a smoke screen to protect a tottering citadel from assaults which it has little hope of being able to withstand. To the Scribes and Pharisees the Christian Gospel as preached by its Originator appeared in the worst possible taste. So, to the Christian Church, did St Francis of Assisi's exaltation of poverty and contemptuous disregard for the acquisition of property. So, to the ecclesiastical authorities of his time, did John Bunyan's insistence on preaching to the poor rather than seeking favours and preferment from the influential and the rich.

In our own time, Sir Winston Churchill was freely and venomously condemned for having the bad taste to draw attention to the disastrous defeat suffered by Neville Chamberlain at the Munich Conference, and to the ominous scale of German re-armament in the years before the outbreak of the 1939–45 War. His bad taste was such that the British Broadcasting Corporation (arbiter *par excellence* in this field) refused to allow him access to its microphones, while that temple of respectability and conformism, the Albert Hall, was denied him when he wished to hold a meeting there to protest against Chamberlain's appeasement policy.

For my own part, then, I should like to start a Society for the Preservation of Bad Taste, which has lately fallen into a sad decline. A Swift or a Hogarth, even a Max Beerbohm, would find it difficult today to get his work published, while comments in early issues of *Punch* on members of the royal family, on eminent politicians like Disraeli, and on cherished institutions like the Established Church, the Athenaeum Club and the Brigade of Guards, would induce a fit of apoplexy in present-day readers, and make them think of me as, by comparison with the then incumbent, a monument of respectability and conformity. Even the mealy-mouthed *Times* was once a veritable scold, with scant respect for those set in authority over us, before whom it now so consistently grovels.

Doubtless the change is due to the increasing sense of insecurity that has afflicted society in recent decades. Rabelais, though a cleric, was allowed to ridicule monasticism with impunity. He lived in an age of faith, and his contemporaries were not made uneasy by ridicule of the institutions that enshrined it. None of them, anyway, are on record as having accused him of bad taste, whereas today the faintest suggestion that gaiters are not necess-arily synonymous with perfect probity enrages the faithful.

Why, I was astonished to find that a not altogether favourable review of Kwame Nkrumah's lately published autobiography, and some not wholly sanguine observations on the translation of the Gold Coast colony into independent Ghana, called down on my head another torrent of abuse as being in the worst possible taste. How disgraceful, it was contended in yet one more batch of angry letters, to poke fun at Dr Nkrumah who had so brilliantly and so courageously led his country to its deserved independence; who with his own hands had pulled down the Union Jack, replacing it with Ghana's own flag of red, yellow and brown, and who had been honoured on this joyous and momentous occasion by the presence of the Duchess of Kent, Mr R. A. Butler, not to mention Mr Jagan from what is still known as British Guiana.

Surely his finest hour deserved something better than ridicule, something more constructive than criticism.

To suggest otherwise was to be guilty of shocking taste. Yet was it? All social assumptions and institutions, as history shows, require constant checking if they are to be maintained in a healthy condition. And how can they be checked except by the exercise of what passes for bad taste? The principle of *lèse majesté* was one of the factors that prepared the French monarchy for destruction. In the famous story of the Vain Emperor the situation is saved by the impertinent small boy, who shouts out that the Emperor is naked, and not, as he has persuaded himself and the rest of his subjects, clothed in exquisitely spun cloth. If no one dares to mention the Emperor's true condition for fear of being accused of bad taste, he will go shivering on his way to perdition.

Kings and prime ministers, all who, in Shakespeare's majestic phrase, are 'drest in a little brief authority', are, after all, but men. It is highly desirable that this obvious, and in its way reassuring, circumstance should be drawn attention to from time to time. And one of the most effective ways of drawing attention to it is ridicule, which is notoriously and necessarily in bad taste. The grinning, unsightly gargoyles that stand below Salisbury Cathedral's exquisite steeple, in underlining its inadequacy, heighten its sublimity. They represent, on the part of their medieval creators, a deliberate gesture of bad taste, which, in relation to the rest of the edifice, adds to its glory.

The trouble is that, when authority is faltering, there is a natural tendency to bolster it up by means of taboos, one of the more effective of which is this concept of bad taste. Those who objected most strongly to the suggestion that Sir Winston Churchill was becoming unfit to direct his country's affairs were precisely the ones who in their hearts most doubted his capacity to continue in office, just as those who were equally insistent in the pre-war years that he should not replace Chamberlain (they were largely the same people) were secretly or subconsciously most doubtful about the efficacy of trying to placate Hitler and Mussolini.

By the same token, there was a tell-tale plaintive note in complaints about suggestions that Sir Anthony Eden was too meandering, sick and subject to hysteria to provide decisive leadership – 'Poor man, he's doing his best; why add to his difficulties?' Incidentally, it is one of the more bizarre notions of this age that newspapers and magazines exist to help rather than hinder governments. Their historic function is to provide a minefield over which politicians and administrators must proceed warily and at their own risk. They are, in fact, repositories of bad taste or nothing.

In the case of comments upon morals and religion, the same difficulties arise. A recent issue of *Punch* applied itself to satirizing the highly indecent exploitation of sex for commercial purposes. Our target was the everlasting, and often decidedly inappropriate, use of cheesecake to stimulate sales. Again the cry of bad taste was raised; again letters poured in bewailing the fact that a magazine of hitherto unsullied reputation should lend itself to so unbecoming a theme. Could absurdity be carried further? It was as though the great satirical draughtsman Hogarth should have been accused of encouraging drunkenness, gambling and other vices because, in his *Rake's Progress*, he demonstrated their disastrous consequences. As for religion – the mere suggestion that it encompasses laughter, along with all the other blessings bestowed upon human life, both shocks and enrages. When Miss Dorothy Sayers, with fine and pious mockery, demonstrated in the pages of *Punch* how materialism had come to usurp the imagery and idiom of faith:

> The day that Nature gave is ending
> The hand of Man turns on the light;
> We praise thee, Progress, for defending
> Our nerves against the dreadful night

vicarages, rectories and cathedral closes rose up in their wrath.

For myself, despite these gruelling experiences, I remain impenitently a champion of bad taste. If I had a banner, that should be inscribed thereon; if I had a race horse, that should be its name. Life without bad taste would be, for me, pallid and flavourless.

[1957]

Collected Speeches

Volumes of past orations and addresses, however apposite or impressive at the time, soon hang like flags on a windless day. Such volumes seem to me to be, in terms equally of content and style, just about the last rinsings of all human endeavour in the field of composition.

Pursuit Of Happiness (*International*) Inc.

For the past six months I have been more or less on the move; constantly fastening and unfastening seat-belts, descending upon patterns of lights, living briefly in hotel rooms, mooning about unfamiliar streets, looking forlornly at passing landscapes out of railway carriage windows, driving through interminable dust, embarking upon brief intimacies and satisfying momentary curiosities. Thus seen, the world is small, compact and uniform. Indeed, it may be said with truth that everywhere is becoming noticeably like everywhere else, and that everyone tends to want what everyone else wants. This induces a tremendous momentum towards uniformity which makes the yells and howls of nationalism and racialism and ideological conflict singularly irrelevant and absurd. The overwhelming impression one has is, not of the discord, but of the almost total unanimity which prevails. For the first time in history the great majority of the world's inhabitants have identical desires.

Thirty-five years ago, when I first went to India (to the part which is now Kerala and Communist, but was then Travancore, and a rather well-governed Indian state), this was not so. There was a great diversity of desires. What a Travancore Brahmin wanted was not by any means identical with what, say, a Leeds wool manufacturer wanted, or an Alexandrian cotton broker, or a Kansas City real estate man. They all wanted to be rich, of course, but their manner of life, if they became rich, varied enormously. Now they build the same houses, install the same refrigerators and other amenities, have the same motor cars, acquire the same girls, and meet together on their travels at the same hotels.

Moreover, most of the human race were not in those days in a position to have any concrete desires at all. They had to make do with transcendental ones. An Indian or Chinese peasant, toiling away – what did he look to have, except, with luck, the barest sufficiency? Now, they have come to feel that they also are entitled to get in on the mid-twentieth century act. Fruit machines and the jackpot's yield are for them, too. The Russian Revolution, and, of course, still more immediately, the Chinese Revolution, presented the possibility, and the American cinema displayed the prizes. I remember in that distant time asking a government official who had come from the North-West Frontier whether there was any talk there of Communism, and he said, No, there wasn't, but everyone seemed to have heard of Lenin Sahib. Again, I remember at one of those huge Hindu festivals, when hundreds and hundreds of thousands of nondescript Indians assemble on a river bank, noting a cinema show in a tent (some ancient, foolish film, with ladies in evening dress, and elegant dinner tables, and motor cars driving up to massive doorways) and how utterly rapt the packed audience were at this spectacle of a life so infinitely remote from theirs, and now made actual at their festival. Even then there seemed some sort of connection between the two things – interest in Lenin Sahib and the screened splendour.

This increasing uniformity of the world, brought about by uniformity of desire, is obscured by seemingly contrary tendencies. Thus Russians and their satellites and the Chinese are supposed to want Communism; Americans and their satellites are supposed to want freedom. We Western Europeans are supposed to prize our Christian civilization, and to want to join ourselves together, under the auspices of M. Spaak and General Norstad, to revive and defend it. As for the Indians – Pandit Nehru and his colleagues try with increasing difficulty to convince themselves that what they want is British-type welfare and parliamentary democracy. I find the present Indian governing class who are engaged in this impossible pursuit infinitely touching and appealing. They are the last survivors to make jokes about the rivalry between Oxford and Cambridge, and indulge in whimsical matrimonial asides, and dredge up faint echoes of the London School of Economics when it was young and in the spring. Their political talk has the sweet, musty flavour of old Hansards; in New Delhi there is a street that is for ever Bouverie, and the air is full of the Home Service in its true Reithean purity. The only Englishmen left in the world, I sometimes think, are Indians.

Very few Russians, Chinese and satellite peoples really want Communism; very few Americans really want freedom; very few Western Europeans really care much about Christian or any other civilization; very few Indians really want welfare and parliamentary democracy. What they all want, and what practically everyone else really wants, is what the Americans have got – six lanes of large motor cars streaming powerfully into and out of gleaming cities; neon lights flashing, and juke boxes sounding, and skyscrapers rising, storey upon storey, into the sky. Driving at night into the town of Athens, Ohio (pop. 3450) four bright coloured signs stood out in the darkness – 'Gas', 'Drugs', 'Beauty', 'Food'. Here, I thought, is the ultimate, the *logos* of our time, presented in sublime simplicity. It was like a vision in which suddenly all the complexity of life is reduced to one single inescapable proposition. These signs could have shone forth as clearly in Athens, Greece, as in Athens, Ohio. They belonged as aptly to Turkestan or Sind or Kamchatka. All the world loves Lucy.

In the light of this uniformity of current desires, the ostensible present is a museum, to go round eagerly or listlessly according to one's temperament. Some of the curators are, it is true, excessively insistent, to the point of imagining, and trying to convince their conducted parties, that the exhibits have still contemporary validity – for instance de Gaulle, rumbling through the residue of a colonial empire with some vague notion of integrating it with a visibly disintegrating France; or, for that matter, our man, Harold Macmillan, trimming up his moustache for television appearances, and momentarily conveying the impression that by sending troops to sustain an unsustainable regime in Jordan he has somehow asserted something, achieved something.

Such efforts, however, are largely unconvincing. The conflicts which seem to be dividing the world are like television or radio shows for which it is increasingly difficult to find the requisite studio audience. The Cold War itself has no more reality than the wars between the Big-enders and the Little-enders in *Gulliver's Travels*. It is about nothing. The very words which express it are becoming, on both sides, emptier and emptier, more and more turgid, laboured and tedious. By contrast, whenever one of the huge motor cars used by the United States embassy in Moscow stops, it is at once surrounded by a little crowd of awed admirers. So would a sputnik be if it were on show in New York. There are, properly speaking, no Communists, no capitalists, no Catholics, no Protestants, no black men, no Asians, no Europeans, no Right, no Left, and no Centre, none of the categories which have to be assumed to sustain the Cold War and all its ancillary strife and argument. There is only a vast and omnipresent longing for Gas, for Beauty, for Drugs and for Food.

It may be, of course, that before this longing is satisfied (as it could be), the world will get blown to pieces. If so, the cause will be, not the divisions among mankind, but their unanimity – a unanimity which they failed to express in their way of life. The atomic explosion will be but an outward and visible manifestation of an inward and invisible schizophrenia between desires which are unanimous and wills which are divided.

History has decreed one world, as is manifested by the characteristic inventions of our time, which are all calculated to eliminate material circumstances and ideas and beliefs fostering separateness, whether in individuals or communities – like jet planes, which abolish distance, and television, which abolishes thought, and the *Reader's Digest*, which abolishes despair, and, therefore, faith, and atomic fission, which makes unity the only alternative to extinction. Either history will have its way, or there will be no more history. The world (pop. 2000 m) must, like Athens, Ohio, hang out its four signs – 'Gas', 'Drugs', 'Beauty', 'Food' – or cease to exist.

[1958]

Eisenhower

I watched Eisenhower on television just before Macmillan's arrival. He looked like some kindly Church Elder reading out a sermon in so benevolent and unemphatic a manner that even references to the wrath of God or the Day of Judgement lost their sting. He tackled the sentences in terms of words rather than of meaning. The effort of just reading seemed to exhaust all his energies, leaving none to convey or even grasp, what was signified. It was a touching, if pitiable, performance.

America

The great puzzle about America to me has always been the contrast between its amazing economic vitality and its cumbersome government and administration. Senatorial minds moved so slowly, and the traffic so fast; there was so much energy and initiative in factories and offices and farms, so little in the State Department. Never has this contrast been so marked as it is today, when, to all intents and purposes, there is no government. Everything's at sea except the fleet, Horace Walpole dolefully remarked. In America everything seems to work except the administration.

Harold Ross And The New Yorker

Harold Ross, founder and first editor of the *New Yorker*, died in December 1951, aged 59. Since then, various attempts have been made to provide an account of this extraordinary man. None seemed quite to tell one what one wanted to know. Now James Thurber has, in his own inimitable way, done the job. His *The Years with Ross* (Hamish Hamilton) is perceptive, humorous and sentimental. Out of it there emerges the authentic Ross. One puts the book down feeling one has met, been exasperated, enchanted, stimulated by the most original figure to be produced by American journalism in this century. Mr DeWitt Wallace invented the *Reader's Digest*, certainly, upon which now, as was once said to be the case with the British Empire, the sun never sets. Mr Henry Luce has given the world *Time*, *Life*, and *Fortune* – all, particularly the first, substantial achievements, but representing only another way of toasting the posties or posting the toasties. Ross's *New Yorker* was something quite new. It is part of American social history. I can see those bound volumes proudly standing on the shelves of reference libraries, and being taken down by everyone who wants to write, in whatever *genre*, about Ross's time. They are an enduring monument.

I first came across the *New Yorker* in the early thirties, and became an immediate addict. Then, for a while, I was faintly concerned in *Night and Day*, a rather pitiable effort to copy the *New Yorker* on this side of the Atlantic. I was going to add that copying, especially in journalism, is invariably disastrous when I recalled that, in point of fact, Ross began by copying – of all things – *Punch*. His first numbers, as Thurber points out, were quite deplorable. Then, suddenly, it got going, and became for some years the most brilliant magazine of our time, with contributors (including, of course, Thurber himself) who have become household words in such parts of the world left where people still like and are permitted to laugh, and occasionally break off from televiewing to have a go at the printed word. This, alas, is a diminishing territory.

Ross had the great advantage, in an editor, of being largely illiterate. This meant that he wanted everything explained, and refused to pass a sentence not wholly comprehensible to him. It also meant that he instinctively distrusted pretentious, mannered writing, and, in matters of taste, followed his flair rather than any conformist (or anti-conformist) system. Literate editors can be charming, but they seldom read what goes into the publications they edit, except, sometimes, their own contributions. Ross interminably mulled over proofs, covering them with queries which must have pained contributors. He never quite knew what he wanted – another great advantage in an editor. It prevented the magazine from having too defined a shape. Journalism always has to be experimental. A good editor goes tapping his way along, like a blind man. Each issue, as it was to Ross, is part of a process which has no beginning and no end. It is utterly unsatisfactory except in so far as it provides the possibility of bringing out another issue.

Again, Ross had a deep, instinctive and quite irrational detestation of the magazine's business management. Raoul Fleischmann, who heroically financed the *New Yorker* in its precarious beginnings, once said, according to Thurber, that he could never make out whether Ross hated him for having the money to do this, or for being such a fool as to put money into a magazine edited by Ross. Probably both. There has to be war between the business management and the editorial department. Only by this means can an essential equilibrium between them be maintained. If peace breaks out, the editorial department is bound sooner or later to become subservient to the business management, which is utterly disastrous. This has happened to a lot of publications in our time. When an editor stops grinding his teeth over the spectacle of the advertising manager returning blithely from an expense-account luncheon with shreds of smoked salmon at the corners of his mouth, he will soon, you may be sure, be wringing his hands over hints and directives coming from that quarter which he dare not ignore.

In the conduct of his own department, Ross was haunted by a dream of order which he never could realize. This, too, was a good sign. Editors should aspire after order, but it is fatal if they achieve it. He was always trying to find a man who would sit at 'a Central Desk . . . a dedicated genius, out of technology by mysticism, effortlessly controlling and co-ordinating editorial personnel, contributors, office boys, cranks and other visitors, manuscripts, proofs, cartoons, captions, covers, fiction, poetry and facts, and bringing forth each Thursday a magazine at once funny, journalistically sound and flawless. This dehumanized figure, disguised as a man, was a goal only in the sense that the mechanical rabbit of a whippet track is a quarry. Ross's mind was always filled with dreams of precision and efficiency beyond attainment, but exciting to contemplate.' Thurber himself did a stint at being the man in question, with, as one might suppose, the most bizarre consequences. He was one of many. They came and went, but, happily, there never was a Central Desk; only Ross.

A consequence of this system, or rather pursuit of an unrealizable system, was a lot of sometimes rather brutal firing of people. The staff turnover was terrific. Once, Thurber relates, a member of Ross's staff who was spending the evening with him ventured to ask him how he was getting along on the *New Yorker*. Ross thereupon fired him. Then, seized with panic contrition, he said that he would also fire Peter Arno; got him on the telephone, and told him he was fired. By this time it was 2 a.m. Arno, having been awakened by Ross's telephone call, bawled him out. And that was the end of the matter. I agree that it was hard on the man who was fired. Even so, I find this episode both humorous and touching. It shows in Ross a certain divine irresponsibility. He first fires a man for irritating him by asking how he is doing on the *New Yorker*, and then, to compensate, tries to fire his most valuable contributor.

It also has to be remembered that, however eccentric his methods of recruiting and getting rid of staff, he succeeded in gathering round him the most brilliant collection of writers and artists perhaps ever assembled, and in getting out of them their best work. Here again, he proceeded by flair rather than rule. For instance, it took him months to appreciate the charm and wit of Thurber's own drawing. He was always feeling his way, groping; but, by virtue of a unique editorial genius, groping in the right direction. He contributed, Thurber writes of him, 'something that had not happened before in his country, or anywhere else, to literature, comedy, and journalism, and he was leaving behind him an imposing monument. He had got his frail weekly off the rocky shoals of 1925, and piloted it into safe harbour through depression and recession, World War II, and the even greater perils of the McCarthy era. His good ship stood up all the way. He sometimes threatened to quit, and he was at least twice threatened with being fired, but he kept on going like a bullet-torn battle flag, and nobody captured his colours and nobody silenced his drums.'

Of course, editing a humorous magazine is a very specialized business. No one who has not experienced it can imagine the agony of looking over piles of roughs to decide whether or not they are funny; of going through manuscripts which in one mood strike one as uproariously funny, and in another as abysmally woebegone. On the *New Yorker* under Ross they selected drawings on Tuesday afternoons. 'Ross,' Thurber writes, 'rarely laughed outright at anything. His face would light up, or his torso would undergo a spasm of amusement, but he was not at the art meeting for pleasure. Selecting drawings was a serious business, a part of the week's drudgery, and the back of his mind ever held the premonition that nothing was going to be funny.'

His own sense of humour seems to have been somewhat tenuous. Quite often jokes had to be explained to him, which must have been very painful for one and all. Also, he was terrified that some phallic reference would escape his eye and get into the magazine. He was much troubled by Thurber's famous drawing of a nude female figure on a bookcase, about whom a man is saying to a visitor: 'That's my first wife up there, and this is the *present* Mrs Harris.' He telephoned Thurber in the country to know whether the woman on the bookcase was alive, or stuffed, or just dead.

'She has to be alive,' Thurber told him. 'My doctor says a dead woman couldn't support herself on all-fours, and my taxidermist says you can't stuff a woman.'

'Then goddam it,' Ross roared back, 'what's she doing naked in the house of her former husband and his second wife?'

As I was reading *The Years with Ross*, I kept looking back at the photograph of Ross at the beginning. His face is a curious mixture of innocence and sophistication, of wry laughter and puzzled anguish – a dry, twisted, irritable, kindly face such as you still find around in New York. What an egg he hatched out! How improbable the whole project must have seemed when he originated it! Yet it came off, and today, under the careful editorship of his successor (who was also, in his last years, his trusted lieutenant), William Shawn, his magazine goes marching on, lush and fat and profitable. It is not so sparkling, not so dry, as it was under Ross. Nor is America. Fond of a glass and of a game of crap, jingling dollar pieces in his pocket, shouting 'Goddam!' and other expletives, troubled by ulcers, puzzling and bellowing and pushing his way along, he is an image of the America which produced him and to which he belonged – an image now made delightfully explicit by Thurber.

[1959]

Who Betrays Whom?

Accusations of treason have been heard in our time more vociferously, I should suppose, than ever before in history. Treason is a contemporary obsession, perhaps, because there are so few loyalties, and those so imprecise. The impotent are obsessed with sex, the sick with health, and the disloyal with treachery. We were born citizens of national states, for the preservation of which oceans of blood have been shed, only to find in the end that they were historically obsolescent, if not already obsolete. As nationalism has increasingly become an irrelevance, so it has been the more stridently, ubiquitously and bloodthirstily asserted. Even a theoretically internationalist system like Marxist Communism has succumbed to the prevailing temper. The Soviet Fatherland ate up its own Comintern, and the great majority of those who founded it died at its hands, self-confessed traitors to the very state they had brought into existence.

William Joyce sent to the gallows for disloyalty to a passport he had acquired by fraud. The tens of thousands of French collaborationists butchered for accepting the legality of Marshal Pétain's government, and failing to transfer their allegiance in time to General de Gaulle, who had himself been convicted in his own country of treason. Each newly fabricated state, from ancient Bohemia to newest Ghana, ejecting along its troubled course successive puffs of treasonable exhaust. A whole new, grisly vocabulary coming into usage; words like 'liquidation', 'purge', 'brain-washing', and the corresponding cant of 'freedom', embodied in empty and portentous 'covenants', 'charters' and other solemnly meaningless declarations and instruments!

One might go on and on. The subject is vast, confused and painful, and yet somehow inescapable. Camus, Mauriac, Sartre, Whitaker Chambers, Rebecca West, and many another have struggled with it, achieving, however, no more than a momentary clarification of their own uncertainties. The Christian martyrs could sing and shout for joy as the damp faggots packed round them caught fire, and the flames reached in their direction. They saw heaven's glory shine, or thought they did. But what of the thud of a body in a cellar, with only the memory of a bogus confession to give the squalid scene any meaning? What of the atrocious pantomimes put on by a Senator Joseph McCarthy, by Nuremberg learned counsel and honourable judges? What of the vast outpouring of words spoken in judgement, and of horrors masquerading as justice, which have haunted our time? Who betrays whom? The sentences have been pronounced and executed, but the crime remains obscure in an all-pervading fog of guilt.

A sober and illuminating study of this tangled question was produced by Dr Margret Boveri in *Treason in the Twentieth Century* (Macdonald). This is a rare and profound book, which shines throughout with a true nobility of spirit. It is also, as far as I can judge, well translated from the original German. Dr Boveri's approach is neither arrogant nor opinionated. She writes of a world catastrophe; not of one which has befallen this or that people, adherents of this or that faith or ideology, but one which has stricken all mankind. It is our particular inward tragedy, of which the mushroom cloud is but an outward and visible manifestation, and the Cold War an inaccurate projection which fails to convey the tragedy's true lineaments.

I know nothing of Dr Boveri except what can be deduced from her book. She is German and a journalist who during the war years was working abroad as a foreign correspondent but made periodical visits to Germany. She was obviously against the Nazis to the point of being in close contact with various Resistance circles. (Counterfeit words like 'Resistance' are alas, unavoidable; moral fall-out which destroys the soul and mind as actual fall-out does the flesh and bones. Who does not wince today at the thought of being 'liberated'? Or turn away in disgust from 'human rights' as adumbrated by UNESCO and other worthies? For whom the 'Freedom Bell' tolls has surely lost his freedom.) At the same time, it is clear that Dr Boveri was not at open odds with the Nazis; not at any rate to the point of being *persona non grata*. She appears to have been able to come and go unhindered. This absence of a sense of martyrdom, actual or *manqué*, has been an advantage in writing her book. Treason is, by its nature, a subject which cannot be objectively tackled by those whose bodies or souls bear traitors' scars upon them or who are ashamed of not bearing such scars. It is part of the great merit of *Treason in the Twentieth Century* that its author does not intrude her own views, or seek to imply any heroism, or lack of it, on her own part. Her position would seem to be, in a general way, Christian rather than 'liberal' or 'progressive', and to lead her to regard with disappointment and distaste both Dr Adenauer's *Wunderwirtschaft* and Herr Ulbricht's *Hungerwirtschaft*.

Dr Boveri first makes a preliminary analysis of the changes in the concept of treason from the high tide of Christendom, when, as she sees it, there was no treason, only heresy, to the present day, when there is no heresy, only treason. Loyalty to a deity, and to a divinely anointed monarch, came naturally to those to whom the deity in question was their father in heaven. When the unity of Christendom was shattered by the Reformation, heresy began to go out and treason to come in; still more so when the French Revolution abolished God and His viceroy on earth, the King, substituting for them the sovereign people owing allegiance only to themselves. It was but a short step from the sovereign people to the sovereign state, to which alone loyalty was due.

What, if we search our hearts, does this amount to today? Loyalty to the Inland Revenue Department, or the Board of Trade? Loyalty to shadowy occupants of Government and Opposition Benches and the pale words they utter in sham parliamentary battles? Or to a paste-board monarchy? What, die for Dimbleby! For the pay pause, the balance of trade, and the National debt! For Saint Chatterley and Merry Bingo! Swear an oath of allegiance to the Great Deterrent, and nourish with martyrs' blood the rotting edifice of a Welfare Church! Are we to swear to read the truth, the whole truth, and nothing but the truth, so help us Beaverbrook?

In the 1914–18 War it was possible to mobilize a still extant loyalty, though many and diverse hands were put to the task, from Rupert Brooke to Horatio Bottomley. It was also necessary to reinforce the mere achievement of victory with numerous high-sounding war aims, chief among which was the abolition of future wars. Even then there was the ticklish case of Casement's treason, buttressed up by the irrelevant circumstance of his homosexuality. Though he was duly hanged, his guilt was far from being universally accepted. The 1939–45 War presented a far tougher proposition, particularly as the ostensible aims of the previous war remained dramatically unrealized. It took the Germans in the Channel ports, and the full rhetorical range of Churchill's fervid oratory, to get the nation engaged at all. The French never were engaged, nor any of the other Western European countries whose national anthems were added, one after the other, to the BBC's lugubrious repertoire.

Now the question of loyalty and treason became complicated indeed. The simple pattern of a Western, with Good Guys and Bad Guys, was shattered, to be replaced by a confused Kafka situation; a shifting phantasmagoria of charge and counter-charge, in which everyone sat in judgement on everyone else, and judges and accused were constantly changing places. It is with this situation, and its subsequent developments in relation to the Cold War, that Dr Boveri is primarily concerned. She rightly leaves out of the account both the Nuremberg Trials and the various treason trials which have been mounted in the USSR and the Soviet satellite countries. These, after all, were only macabre fantasies, in which revenge masqueraded as justice, and political assassination arrayed itself in the trappings of a court of law. The Nuremberg Trials were the more odious only because, in their conduct and setting, they more closely approximated to a serious judicial procedure. Let us hope that mankind will sometime recover sufficient equanimity to get a laugh out of the spectacle of English and American judges sitting alongside Soviet ones, and solemnly pronouncing Germans guilty of the use of forced labour and of the partition of Poland.

Dr Boveri, surveying the landscape of treason, begins with collaboration, a crime never heard of before our time. She considers in some detail the cases of Quisling in Norway, King Leopold of Belgium, and of Marshal Pétain, Admiral Darlan and Pierre Laval in France. All these men have been held up to obloquy, though probably few nowadays would care to have to repeat the abuse which was levelled at them in the heat of their defections. Surveying, as Dr Boveri does, in detachment and charity what they did, and the motives which actuated them, it is difficult not to conclude that they were rather victims of circumstances, as Mikolajczyk, one of their number, put it at his trial, leaves caught up in a hurricane of history, than miscreants. Even Laval, an unedifying figure at the best of times, was essentially a politician who miscalculated rather than a traitor in any hitherto accepted sense. Such miscalculations normally lead, at worst, to resignation and retirement from the public stage. In England they usually take their perpetrators to the House of Lords. They were considered in Laval's case to amount to treason, and led to the scaffold. 'La trahison,' Talleyrand said, 'c'est une question du temps.' With the collaborators, the timing was hopelessly at fault. They made the fatal error of backing the losing side, and in consequence came to grief. If the cards had fallen the other way, they would have been the patriots, and those who convicted them the traitors.

France provided the classic example of collaboration. No one who witnessed what happened is likely ever to forget it. The grotesquely crowded prisons, the utter confusion in the Palais de Justice, the shaving of heads and the sinister executions all over the country, without any attempt at legality, and providing the possibility, of which full advantage was taken, to work off private grudges and to settle long-standing ideological disputes. Above all, the atmosphere of fear and hysteria, with a whole nation's corporate sense of guilt and cowardice finding expression in individual malignancy. The police stations were full of denunciations by Frenchmen of Frenchmen addressed to the occupation authorities, and soon received a further deluge, addressed this time to the liberation authorities. Only the police themselves and the prison warders remained the same. They continued to round up and guard collaborators as formerly they had *maquisards*. The traitors changed, but not their jailors.

Actually, of course, apart from an insignificant minority in the Resistance networks, the whole population had, to a greater or lesser extent, collaborated. If they were to continue to support their families, they had no choice but to collaborate. Individuals have their loyalties to life as well as to collectivities and the shifting authority they generate. The barber who shaved the occupying forces, the waiter who served them, the prostitutes who slept with them, the bank employees who cashed their cheques; all who, in whatever manner and to whatever degree, kept Vichy France going, could plausibly be charged with collaboration. As it was impossible to indict everyone as a traitor, scapegoats were chosen, haphazardly, vindictively, and summarily disposed of. It was a grisly, pitiable and shameful business.

My own small part in it all was as a liaison officer with the French *Services Spéciaux*. I had the task of trying to protect some of those who had worked for us during the occupation, and whose clandestinity and usefulness had required them to seem to be on good terms with the occupation and Vichy authorities – now, of course, a highly suspicious circumstance. Many, alas, were soon beyond protection. Having risked their lives to promote France's liberation, they were struck down by the liberators. One incident sticks out in my mind amidst the confusion and perturbation of visiting prisons, pleading with ostensibly juridical bodies which, in the circumstances then prevailing, had neither dignity nor sense, and physically removing individuals in danger of molestation to a place of safety.

There was a certain Lafond, a French gangster of whom the Germans had made use, as they often did of such types, in return allowing him to enrich himself. Many, understandably, were on the watch for him when all his German protectors were removed from the scene, and he was soon caught, and handed over to the French police. Their fear was that, under their decidedly rough treatment, he might in despair commit suicide, thereby depriving

Parisians of the enjoyable spectacle of his trial and inevitable death sentence. To keep some hope alive in him, he was encouraged to believe that a possibility existed of his being handed over to the Anglo-American forces. In order to encourage this hope I had to see him, and listen with seeming sympathy to his account of how his heart had been all along with the Allied cause. Like practically everyone else in Paris at that time, he claimed to have hidden escaping RAF officers. I used to reflect that if all these allegedly hidden officers had really existed, the RAF would have been so enormous that we should easily have won the war long since. As a final proof of his innocence of any taint of treason, Lafond insisted that the only woman he had ever truly loved was a lady in Hull, to whom he had managed to send food parcels through the Swiss Red Cross. Thus Lafond, an avowed and common-or-garden criminal, managed to persuade himself, or at least tried to persuade me, that he was enmeshed in the same intricate web of divided loyalties as Pétain and Laval. If Lafond, then who not? Needless to say, he was in due course guillotined, and there were none, except perhaps the lady in Hull, to regret his passing.

Charges and countercharges of collaboration continued for long to be heard. Poor deaf old Maurras thundered away from the dock, as he had for years in the columns of the *Action Française*. It all proved nothing, and settled nothing. De Gaulle's final judgement was the best, or at any rate the best expressed, as so many of his judgements have been. In appealing for the amnesty of 50,000 political prisoners, he said of Pétain: 'It was necessary to condemn him because his person symbolized the capitulation. But now there is just an old man in a fortress who once did great things for France. Is he to die without ever seeing a tree again, a flower or a friend?' Would that the whole sad, profitless business could have been wound up everywhere on such a note.

Dr Boveri's next category of traitors is the propagandist who engages his voice and powers of persuasion in the service of an enemy. The invention of radio has greatly extended the potentialities of this sort of treason. No doubt in the course of time television will further extend them. We shall see as well as hear our future Haw-Haws. The examples cited by Dr Boveri are William Joyce, Ezra Pound, Knut Hamsun, and numerous lesser figures like 'Tokyo Rose'. Of Joyce, thanks to Dame Rebecca West's brilliant and penetrating study, we already have a clear picture. He was intellectually convinced of the desirability of a Nazi victory, as Klaus Fuchs was of the desirability of the Russians having atomic bombs. In their cases, unlike the collaborationists, a course of action was freely embarked on. They were not propelled into it by circumstances beyond their control, unless, indeed, honestly held opinions may be regarded as such. Here again, if the Nazis had won the war, Joyce would have been vindicated, and all the equivalent enemy aliens who worked for the Anglo-American propaganda services would have been condemned with equal plausibility as traitors.

Just because he is a poet and writer of note, the case of Pound (as also that of Hamsun) stands apart from the others. Anyone who is familiar with Pound's pre-war writings will know that in a somewhat incoherent, but still stridently impressive manner, he stood against the way things were going. He was not prepared to accept the New Deal as an adequate answer to twentieth-century dilemmas, or Roosevelt as an authentic saviour. His opinions, however abhorrent they might seem, were accepted as valid until he expounded them from Rome after his country was at war with Italy. Then they became treason. His offence, like Bunyan's, lay, not in his beliefs, but in his inconvenient propagation of them.

To avoid avowedly punishing Pound for what, in their mystique of life, is virtuous behaviour, the Americans decided he must be mad, and incarcerated him in a state asylum. A rather similar attitude, interestingly enough, was taken to the poet Blake when he ran into trouble with the authorities for making a complimentary remark in public about Napoleon. He, too, was considered mad, though, fortunately for him, in those pre-psychiatric days there was no question of putting him into an institution. Pound has now been released. Yet if he was mad before, he is mad still. It is not he who had changed, but the climate of opinion. As the Cold War intensifies, we may yet see him elected to the Senate.

The longest and most interesting section of Dr Boveri's book is devoted to a study of the individuals and clandestine organizations in Germany which sought, with increasing fervour as the war proceeded and began to look like being irretrievably lost, to bring down Hitler and disrupt the Third Reich. Little was known of all this at the time. With singular moral obtuseness, Churchill and Roosevelt refused to take any account of it, and, in order to ingratiate themselves with Stalin, or perhaps because they really considered unconditional surrender to be a suitable war aim, declined to make any differentiation between one German and another. They fell into the same gutterthinking as any assertive, beer-flushed warrant officer, who, between throwing one dart and another, pontificates about the only good German being a dead one. This has cost us dearly in the post-war years, and the bill is still far from being settled. Stalin asked nothing better than that the drafters of the Atlantic Charter should be identified with such an attitude. It was an enormous help to him in acquiring his European empire, and in suppressing any possible resistance among the populations he took over.

As Dr Boveri indicates, among the dissident Germans there were two main groups – the Nazi-named *Rote Kapelle*, Socialist-Communist in outlook, and the Kreisau Circle, which mainly comprised Conservative Germans, though including some, like the priest, Father Alfred Delp, whose ideas for Germany's future by no means merely consisted of a reconstruction of the pre-Nazi, if not pre-Weimar, past. Most of them, in any case, by the time the war ended, had been caught by the Gestapo and executed. The German Resistance not only failed, for instance in the attempt on Hitler's life on 20 July 1944. Its members were largely obliterated. The question of whether they are to be regarded as traitors or heroes remains unsettled to this day.

Some of them, like Stauffenberg, had been ardent Nazis in their time. Most like Von Trott and Von Hassell, continued almost to the end ostensibly to co-operate with the Nazi regime. What can be said of them is that, sooner or later, they came to realize that Nazism was not just a German aberration, but a destructive force directed against what remained of European civilization and of Christendom. As the egregious Dr Schacht put it in his inimitable way: 'We have fallen into the hands of criminals. How could I have imagined such a thing?' How indeed? Belatedly, incompetently and ineffectually an attempt was made inside Germany to destroy these criminals. The treason of those concerned in it was clear enough to Himmler. It remains an open question to this day in the Federal Republic. What is far more extraordinary is that a similar doubt existed, and still for that matter exists, among those outside Germany who were likewise bent on overthrowing the Nazi regime.

Churchill and Roosevelt would not admit that the treasonable activities of anti-Nazi Germans, directed against the Third Reich, could possibly be reputable or useful, though acceptance of Soviet pretensions to being peace and freedom-loving presented no difficulty. Future historians, if there are any to interest themselves in our strange times, will surely note this as a truly ironical circumstance. In any case, Dr Adenauer and Herr Ulbricht have, between them, put paid to the hopes of any of the Kreisau Circle and the *Rote Kapelle* who survived Germany's 'Liberation'.

There remains a last category of traitor – the spy. Since the beginning of time there have been spies, some purely mercenary, and others ready to run the grave risks involved to promote a cause. A case in point were the Jesuits who served Spain in the time of Queen Elizabeth I. Spies are, generally speaking, traitors to the governments against which they operate, and patriots to those they serve. Double agents manage to be both simultaneously, and can hope to be awarded an OBE and an Iron Cross or Order of Lenin. It may be observed, however, that a Fuchs, a Nunn May or a Donald Maclean today is not the object of the same universal condemnation as heretofore. There are those who question the validity of the ideological spy's condemnation, and ask themselves whether the services he renders to the regime of his choice should not take precedence over the loyalty he ostensibly owes to the country of his birth or nationality. Thus even espionage, which might seem the simplest and clearest of all forms of treason, has come to be as ethically indistinct as the others. History is largely the propaganda of the victor and will record traitors as patriots if their side wins, and vice versa.

This landscape of treason is, indeed, a shadowy and troubled limbo, or no-man's-land, between a way of life which is passing and one which is coming to pass. Or perhaps none is coming to pass. Perhaps the pursuit of happiness will end in extinction, which would be a fitting outcome of so foolish a pursuit. The landscape is full of spiritually displaced persons, who, having no homeland, have no allegiances; for whom, therefore, loyalty and treason are alike meaningless concepts. I remember years ago in India a missionary doctor telling me that, when he asked his patients whether their bowels had moved, they answered, with the profound and savage irony of the very poor: 'How should our bowels move when we have had nothing to eat?' In the same way, how can we betray or be betrayed?

[1962]

Oratory

It is true that US Senators were capable of lofty oratory on their own account. Listening to them, one cried out, adapting a famous saying usually attributed to Voltaire, that one agreed with everything they said, but would die to defend one's right not to hear it.

Whitman

I have long been of the opinion that Walt Whitman, rather than Thomas Jefferson, George Washington or Abraham Lincoln, is the true originator of contemporary America, and I try to read everything I can lay hands on about this bearded, narcissistic old charlatan-pederast, who wrote adulatory reviews of his own works under a pseudonym, and paid for a national tomb to be constructed while sponging on others for his housing and sustenance. Imagine my delight, then, at receiving a magnificently printed and produced volume of his *Specimen Days* (Godine) the first complete edition of his autobiographical jottings to appear since the original publication in 1882. A truly wonderful book to read and to possess. Whitman was an early devotee of the camera, that instrument of moral destruction more deadly in its consequences than nuclear weapons. Many photographs of and connected with him are finely reproduced, including a remarkable assortment of him in old age, when his vanity had swollen to monstrous proportions. There is also the famous butterfly portrait, which appeared as a frontispiece to *Leaves of Grass*; it shows Whitman looking tenderly at a butterfly perched on his finger. Among his effects there was found the cardboard butterfly specially fitted with the wire loop which was used for this photograph.

The New Statesman And I

My father was an original subscriber to the *New Statesman*, and I have a vivid memory of it lying on the doormat in our small suburban house in South Croydon. I doubt if I ever tried to read it as a child. If I did, nothing remains in my mind of its early contents. What I remember from these days is its physical appearance and texture; heavy block-type and rather thick paper, unsuitable for lighting fires, but suitable for making improvised cigarettes. I smoked the *New Statesman* long before reading it or writing for it. My father held the paper in the highest possible esteem, more particularly the back part. Its political attitudes he might sometimes question, but its book reviews never. These were sacrosanct, being produced, as he supposed, by distinguished writers and scholars; the people on earth whom he most revered and envied. Early English socialists like my father had little veneration, and sometimes contempt, for their party leaders like MacDonald, Snowden, J. H. Thomas, Clynes and Henderson, whom they recognized as the same clay as themselves; but for men-of-letters inclined to be of their political persuasion they had a deep and unquestioning veneration. When, later, I made the acquaintance of some of these, I realized how misguided the preference for them was. Academic sycophancy and compliancy exceed all others, except perhaps for the Services. Dryden, I am sure, was thinking rather of the groves of academe than of Sir Charles Snow's corridors of power when he wrote: 'For almonds he'll cry whore to his own mother.'

The first piece of writing I ever had published was in the *New Statesman*. It was a short story about an elementary schoolmaster who (need I say it?) felt frustrated, sad and inadequate. I have not dared to look it up, but I read it about a million times when it appeared. It was, as I recall, in the sub-Chekhov manner, to which many aspiring pens then were dedicated. At the time I was living in South India, at a place named Alwaye, near the border between the states of Cochin and Travancore (now Kerala), and teaching at a Christian college there. The *New Statesman* arrived by sea mail, weeks old, and I read it by the feeble light of an oil lamp round which dead insects piled up as the evening proceeded. A certain querulousness in its attitude, particularly towards questions of British policy in India, mitigated my pleasure in its contents. Its admirable handling, however, of an episode like the adventures of Sir Leo Chiozza Money and Miss Savage in Hyde Park brought a sweet whiff of Old England to my lonely exile.

One of the sorrows of egghead life is being constantly confronted with old loyalties and enthusiasms. Back numbers of the *New Statesman* are a graveyard packed with these. Though their flesh decays and their bones whiten, their spirits go marching on. A Tynan or a Wesker rises up, bright-eyed over a Commitment or a Method which, one fondly supposed, had perished with the 1917 Club. This may account for the permanent state of irritation which characterizes so many eggheads and so much egghead enterprise. A friend has described to me how, as a youth, he saw Frederick Harrison, the famous positivist (whatever that may be), seated in a railway carriage, and reading the *New Statesman*. As he read, the veins in his forehead swelled, his hands holding the journal shook with rage, and occasionally a strangled cry broke from his lips. I know the feeling.

While in India, as befitted a *New Statesman* addict, I embarked upon a correspondence with Gandhi about birth control. Would it not be better, I asked, to concentrate on raising the standard of life of Indian workers by encouraging the spread of industry, at the same time making contraceptives available to them, rather than going on about handspinning and abstinence? Gandhi replied at length and most politely on the lines of Tolstoy and Ruskin, two major influences in his life. At the time, I felt contemptuously disposed, but now I wonder. Just because industrialism had to happen in India does not invalidate Gandhi's protests against it. One of the basest aspects of much contemporary thinking is the acceptance of what happens as right, and of any villain who establishes himself in power as thereby justified, if not glorified. As for birth control, is the colporteur of rubber goods, with a sideline in the preposterously named 'life' pills, really the best missionary we have to offer? Gandhi visited the college while I was there. Villagers poured in on foot from miles away just to look at him and take the dust off his feet. It was a curious spectacle – this little gargoyle of a man talking in measured English like any Quaker or 'ethical' Christian, with this vast, deeply respectful concourse of the poorest people in the world gathered, awed and uncomprehending, round about him.

In Manchester three years later (in 1930) I first made the acquaintance of Kingsley Martin, who was to edit the *New Statesman* for some three decades during which it throve and became increasingly famous. His own regular contributions as Critic represent a unique journalistic achievement and provide a piece of one-man social history, neither objective nor unbiased, but piquant, and, as they say along Madison Avenue, personalized. Future social historians are bound thankfully to avail themselves of it. He and I were both leader-writers on the *Guardian*, and had adjoining rooms on what was known as the Corridor; a sombre passage, as it seemed to me, through which there echoed the forgotten slogans of once good causes and the elaborately dead sentences of C. E. Montague and other past occupants. We leader-writers waited to be summoned to the presence of C. P. Scott, who, though he had retired from the editorship in favour of his son Ted, continued to direct editorial policy. One entered his office with a certain trepidation. White-bearded and ruddy, like some high-minded Falstaff, he courteously awaited one and, after a brief and not always particularly illuminating discussion on a topic of the day, sped one on one's way to editorialize thereon. KM, characteristically, but imprudently, was liable to argue with Scott, or at any rate chew nervously in his presence over some point of principle. The old fellow did not like it. At his great age, he had reached the stage in life when he wanted to believe that every controversy could be resolved into a general declaration of righteousness. Less conscientious than KM myself, I was content to accept more rudimentary and rougher guidance, putting my head into a colleague's room (not KM's) and asking, for instance: 'What's our line on corporal punishment?' to which the reply would be: 'The same as capital, only more so.' It sufficed. KM departed to the *New Statesman*, and I inherited his room along the corridor, distinguished by having a fireplace of its own. A kind of nausea came to possess me at the conclusion towards which, however one might begin, one's fingers on the typewriter keyboard seemed inexorably to move; 'It is greatly to be hoped that wiser counsels will prevail, and that moderate men of all shades of opinion will ...' What, oh! what, is greatly to be hoped? I inwardly groaned, and lined up moderate men of all shades of opinion against a wall for summary execution.

The Webbs, when I first got to know them, were very displeased with the *New Statesman* for the bizarre reason that it had attacked Ramsay MacDonald. Mrs Webb herself, with her delightful taste for malicious gossip, would tell one the most scandalous things about him, but she still considered that a journal which supported the party he led should continue to uphold his leadership. This was typical of the authoritarianism which underlay all the Webbs' thinking and led them to fall so wholeheartedly for regimes like Stalin's in the USSR and Tojo's in Japan. They liked discipline, order and obedience and deplored individual rebels like Wells and Bertrand Russell as much as they applauded rebellions once they had succeeded. There was another reason why Mrs Webb was liable to indulge in one of her short, sharp sniffs (a danger signal to all who knew her) when the *New Statesman* was mentioned. J. C. Squire, she once confided in me, had come down to Passfield when he was literary editor, and asked for a scotch and soda at teatime. Men have been awarded VCs for less audacious acts than this. Sidney was allowed two medicinal whiskies, prepared under Mrs Webb's watchful supervision and well diluted with water, in the course of the evening. Otherwise, the bottle remained inviolate. Squire's deed of reckless daring was, I am glad to say, rewarded. He got his whisky and soda, but ever afterwards Mrs Webb regarded the *New Statesman* office as a place of nameless debauchery.

I spent a good deal of the first three months of the 1939–45 War in the company of Dick Crossman, whose name, like Kingsley Martin's, is indissolubly associated with the *New Statesman*. We were incarcerated in a room at the Ministry of Information, had little to do and only the vaguest notion of what we were supposed to be doing anyway. On the door of our room was the word 'Editor', but its precise connotation we never discovered. Our boss was Robert (now Sir Robert) Fraser; not then a man to strike terror in our breasts or to stir undue zeal in our hearts. Crossman and I just talked our way through this first phase of the phoney war. Only he could have kept it going, with never a dull moment, and no exigencies of purpose or consistency to impede or spoil the flow. It was an exhilarating and unforgettable experience. Crossman went off to Woburn Abbey and I to a barrack hut at Ash Vale. It seemed a dull and silent place after his company.

Even in the war years one still saw the *New Statesman*. In the Intelligence Corps it was as much in evidence as *Sporting Life* in a cavalry regiment in the old days. The greatest and most seductive illusion of going to war is that one will thereby escape one's fate. Alas, when the dust settles and the tumult dies, there is the Home Service and *Lift Up Your Hearts* still going strong. The *New Statesman* must be part of my fate. It always turns up. The Russian censorship which impounded almost everything when I was working as a journalist in Moscow (for instance, a blameless copy of Mrs Beeton's *Household Management*) let the *New Statesman* through. I saw it the other day in the anteroom of a Scandinavian prime minister's office. Ageing Indian intellectuals tear it open when it arrives with exasperated joy. It reminds them of the good old days of the British Raj. President Kennedy, they say, keeps it by his bedside, alongside James Bond. I once saw a man reading it in a bus in Bangkok; a lady with an address in Borneo wrote to me complaining about something I had written in it, and a Chinese professor of sociology in Mukden mentioned under his breath that he occasionally ran his eye over a copy. Wherever two or more eggheads are gathered together, there is it to be found. It has, in fact, become an institution, like *Janes Fighting Ships*, or *Burke's Landed Gentry*, with an editor whose face and mannerisms are known to millions through the ubiquitous television screen, on which he has been an outstanding performer. This opens up new possibilities and new hazards. Reverting to C. P. Scott, I well remember a discussion about printing the *Guardian* in London.

He was against it, on the curious but cogent ground that, if there was a London edition, people in the South might start reading the *Guardian* instead of contenting themselves with praising it. There is always this insidious danger to guard against.

[1963]

G. K. C.

G. K. Chesterton is one of those writers for whom either too much or too little is usually claimed. Unlike some of his eminent contemporaries (Arnold Bennett, for instance), he still has devoted readers. The Father Brown stories continue, I suppose deservedly, to be popular and are endlessly reprinted in paperback. Collections of hitherto uncollected pieces from the vast body of Chesterton's journalistic writings continue to appear from time to time. These pieces are neither better nor worse than others which appeared in volumes with names like *Tremendous Trifles, All Things Considered, Alarms and Discursions*, while Chesterton was alive. They are well above the average level of their kind, and occasionally pull one up with some unexpected profundity or poignancy.

It is often contended that Chesterton wrote too much and too hastily; that his financial exigencies and polemical inclinations led him to prefer journalism to literature. This, in my opinion, is highly dubious. In the first place, I question the hard and fast distinction between the two categories of writing. Obviously, there are literary masterpieces like, say, *War and Peace* and *L'Education Sentimentale* on the one hand, and hack journalism like, say, writing editorials for the *Daily Express* or ghosting Christine Keeler's memoirs for the *News of the World* on the other. Between them lies a vast no-man's-land in which most writers, from Johnson to H. G. Wells and Shaw, have been content to forage, if not to reside. Wells, indeed, actually preferred to call himself a journalist, though in point of fact his early novels like *Kipps* and *Mr Polly* have better credentials to be regarded as imaginative literature than many more highly regarded works – *Howard's End* for instance, or *Mrs Dalloway*.

Then again, I question whether Chesterton had it in him to be much more than the journalist he was. It seems to me that periodical writing exactly suited his talents, as it did Orwell's.

They were both atrocious novelists and, on form, superb essayists. Chesterton's most notable talent was for the sudden crystallization of illuminating observations. It would be a good idea, incidentally, to make a collection of these, like La Rochefoucauld's *Maximes*. The following are chosen at random from Mr Maycock . . . 'When you break the big laws, you do not get liberty; you do not even get anarchy. You get the small laws.' 'The meanest man is immortal and the mightiest movement is temporal, not to say temporary.' 'In the whole world of things conceivable there is nothing so unmercifully hopeless as an infinity of mere facetiousness, a tyrannical nightmare of jesting.' Let me add two others which have always stuck in my mind. When Chesterton first saw the lights of Broadway he remarked that the spectacle would be marvellous if only one couldn't read. And somewhere or other he writes that when people cease to believe in a deity they do not then believe in nothing, but – what is much more calamitous – in anything. This sort of facility is used to best advantage in occasional journalism. With too portentous a presentation the charm is lost. Chesterton's flashes are like Chinese lanterns – pleasingly spread about a sprawling garden on a warm summer evening; meagre, frail and even tawdry, indoors.

Mr Frank Swinnerton has, it seems, suggested 'that it will be at least a hundred years before Chesterton's greatness is fully recognized'. Chesterton himself, with commendable modesty, was convinced that what he wrote was for the moment only: 'I would rather live now and die, from an artistic point of view, than keep aloof and write things that will remain in the world hundreds of years after my death . . . It so happens that I couldn't be immortal: but if I could, I shouldn't want to be.' One is always a little hesitant about accepting assurances of this kind, but all the same Chesterton's own estimate of his work would seem to be juster than Swinnerton's.

It is, of course, from the standpoint of a Christian, and specifically a Roman Catholic convert, that Chesterton propounds his view of life. He never tires (though a reader sometimes does) of belabouring Darwin and the pretensions of 'science'. Among contemporary liberal intellectuals he was something of an odd man out, with his passion for ritual and ceremonial, civic as well as liturgical, and with his loathing of collectivist hopes and Quaker virtues, and refusal to endorse the fatuous expectations invested in the idea of progress. He felt a deep, instinctive distaste for the way the twentieth century was going which enabled him, in his early years of pessimism, to be an impressive prophet. 'The earnest Freethinkers,' he wrote in 1905, 'need not worry themselves so much about the persecutions of the past. Before the Liberal idea is dead or triumphant, we shall see wars and persecutions the like of which the world has never seen.' Stalin, then a young man of twenty-six, and Hitler, ten years younger, were, along with others to make good his words to a fabulous degree.

It is surprising, in a way, that, when Chesterton has so often been proved right in his judgements, he should still be less seriously regarded than contemporaries like Wells and the Webbs who were almost invariably wrong. This is due partly, I think, to a certain ingrained flippancy in his whole attitude of mind, which, though acceptable to English readers, precludes them from taking him seriously. The Reformation, and a long diet of sermons, has conditioned us to associating wisdom with solemnity. I have to admit that, rereading Chesterton's autobiography, I could not myself get over a feeling that, amiable and gifted as he undoubtedly was, he was also somehow a fraud.

Perhaps it is just the enormous size of him. Those illustrations conveying his colossal bulk weigh on the text. One is oddly conscious of his physical appearance, as with Walt Whitman; a not dissimilar figure in some ways, and greatly admired by Chesterton. His get-up, with flowing cloak and wide-brimmed hat,was a kind of fancy dress from whose fastness he proclaimed the glory of the common man. Of Henley and Whistler, 'two very great men', Chesterton wrote that 'nothing strikes one so much about the attitude of both as the fact that a superb melancholy made it necessary for both to take refuge in something outside current life'. However he saw himself as a writer, he was in very much the same case, though he would not have admitted to the superb melancholy; rather, prided himself on a boisterous cheerfulness, with his macabre: 'What larks!' Yet underneath the happy Christian and happy husband, the lover of peasants, Fleet Street roistering and country inns, one senses in Chesterton a brooding, anguished, frightened spirit; a frustrated romantic, a displaced person, a letter delivered at the wrong address.

The only time I ever saw him in the flesh he was seated outside The Ship Hotel at Brighton shortly before he died. His canvas chair looked preposterously small, as did a yellow-covered thriller he was reading. It was a windy day, and I half-expected him to be carried away. Though so huge, he seemed to have no substance: more a balloon than an elephant.

It was, one feels, as a fugitive from an estate agency in Kensington rather than from Victorian agnosticism that Chesterton found his way to Rome; an awareness of the terrors of a larger stage which led him to peer down so assiduously at a toy theatre. The answer to the inadequacies and tedium of Notting Hill is surely not, as Chesterton supposed, to imagine a Napoleon there, but rather to see in that horrible, vainglorious little Corsican all the vulgarity and littleness which so detracts from human life everywhere. Likewise with the notion, to which Chesterton constantly recurred, that the monotony of familiar things and faces can be counteracted by making them seem unfamiliar. This is worked out in, for instance, *Man Alive*, in which the hero, Innocent Smith, goes on an enormous, adventurous journey in order to arrive at Clapham Common and home; breaks into his own house in order to taste the excitement of burglary, and ravishes his own wife to experience the delights of seduction – this last, incidentally, a theme which might have made the Marquis de Sade draw back appalled.

The Christian view of the matter I have always assumed to be almost the exact opposite – that going, like Satan, to and fro in the world and up and down in it is a futile proceeding because every part, Clapham Common or Tashkent, is equally illusory; that a Napoleon only projects on to a larger screen the squalid egotism of each human heart; that flesh and spirit pull in contrary directions irrespective of whose flesh. An undercurrent of uneasiness, if not anguish, in Chesterton's writing perhaps derives from an awareness of this contradiction between Christian pessimism and the obligation he felt himself to be under not to shoot the contemporary pianist.

In his play, *The Surprise*, the action is first performed by puppets in accordance with the author's wishes; then it is performed by living men and women with wills of their own, who, of course, create havoc and confusion. 'In the devil's name,' the author cries out from the wings, 'what do you think you are doing to my play? Drop it! Stop! I am coming down.' This, a superb image of the Incarnation, is Chesterton at his best. Such is the occasional yield of precious metal from the vast disorderly open-cast operations in which he engaged.

[1963]

Evelyn Waugh, R.I.P.

Waugh, as I see him, was an antique in search of a period, a snob in search of a class; above all, a mystic in search of a beatific vision. Like all failed saints (Swift, for instance) he was given to irascibility and humour – the one unedifying and the other delectable. The twentieth century, which he so hated, nonetheless moulded him, as it has all the rest of us. He too was a man of his time – avid for delights he could not enjoy, bent on journeying where he did not want to go; on fighting for causes which soon turned to dust, and burrowing into the past to mock the future. His gifts were great, his use of them estimable, his follies easily forgiven, and his death (to use Johnson's splendid memorial to Garrick) 'has eclipsed the gaity of nations, and impoverished the public stock of harmless pleasure'. May he rest in peace.

Kipling Sahib

I remember very vividly, as though it were yesterday, strolling along the Mall in Simla around six o'clock on a November evening thirty-two years ago, and thinking suddenly of Rudyard Kipling, with such intense vividness that it almost seemed he was there with me. If one had happened to believe in ghosts, his presence in that place would have been in no way surprising.

It was Anglo-India *in excelsis*, and he was the prophet, the chronicler, the poet of Anglo-India; the only one. If he were to walk anywhere, it would surely be there, on just such an evening – the distant, majestic Himalayas glowing with the light of the setting sun, and the notes of 'Colonel Bogey', played by a military band in full regalia, sounding so clearly in the crystalline mountain air from the bandstand further along the Mall. As for the passers-by, some on foot and some in rickshaws (only the Viceroy and the Commander-in-Chief were permitted to use motor-cars), they were all Kipling characters. Mrs Hauksbees in plenty, Privates Ortheris and Mulvaney, Platte, the Subaltern, any number of Hurree Babus, Colonel Creighton, monocled, and seated bolt upright in his rickshaw as though it were a Daimler,

Kims chasing one another in the golden dust. A signpost pointing nonchalantly to Tibet suggested that even the Lama might appear at any moment.

I, too, at that time was working on an Indian newspaper, as Kipling had some half century before; in his case, first the old *Civil and Military Gazette* in Lahore, and then the *Allahabad Pioneer*. There, I may add, the resemblance ended. Few any longer really believed in the Englishman's continuing destiny to rule over palm and pine; least of all me. In the fifty years since Kipling's time the British Raj he extolled had grown tired and feeble, and was soon to come to an end in great bloodshed and ignominy. Yet if posterity ever cares to know about our short-lived conquest of India, one among so many, it is from Kipling's writings alone that they may learn what it was like; from the seeming magnificence of Viceregal power and glory, down to Eurasian ticket-collectors, Babu clerks, and the urchin boy, offspring of a drunken Irish trooper who grew up amid the dust and gossip and squalor of an Indian bazaar – Kim, the embodiment of all Kipling's first fresh delight in the sights and sounds and vast diversity of that fantastic land and its diverse, fantastic people.

We English have left behind no Taj Mahal to remind the world that once we ruled over India; only a few of our old haunts like Simla – hill stations, clubs, polo grounds, and other national idiosyncrasies. If the British Raj is remembered at all, it will be because of Kipling. Artistically speaking, he is its single notable product and its only enduring memorial.

Kipling was born in India (in Bombay on 30 December 1865), a hundred years ago this month. He spent but seven of his adult years there – 1882 to 1889. Yet, as I see it, his response to India represented far and away the deepest and most formative experience of all, at any rate as far as his writings were concerned. He positively looked like an Indian (the source of the ridiculous, but widespread, rumour that he was really a Eurasian), being sallow, and supple, and maturing early for an Anglo-Saxon. He had a moustache while still a schoolboy. If he had never been to India he would have been a totally different person; perhaps some boring and pedantic don lost in the fastnesses of Eng. Lit., in which he was exceptionally well versed. Or, following a clear bent, one of those tedious maniacs about machines who insist on explaining to all and sundry how the wheels go round. I have been told, even in the Athenaeum – that haunt of seasoned bores – members were liable to flee when his bushy eyebrows and gleaming spectacles were seen entering the club, in dread of the tedium he might inflict upon them.

India, it seems to me, in one premature exotic harvest, brought out all that was most imaginative and warm and intuitive in him, and, at the same time, planted in him the proneness to adulate power and action – those two black sirens – which so often vulgarized his emotions and distorted his character, which Max Beerbohm found so offensive, and which induced him to draw a particularly cruel cartoon of Kipling. I spoke to Beerbohm about it in Rapallo a year or so before he died, and it visibly saddened him. He regretted the drawing's venom, he said, more particularly as Kipling had gone out of his way to be kind to him when he first began to write.

Still strolling along the Mall in Simla with that so vivid sense of Kipling's presence upon me, I could project my life as it then was into his when he was working as a journalist in India. The very presses (rotary in my case, flatbed in his) seeming to make their mechanical movements languidly in the sweltering heat; the Indian proof-readers chanting uncomprehendingly the stilted sentences of the next day's paper, like weird, intoning priests; the curling galleys, so limp and damp and lifeless, black rivulets of ink spreading over them like the Hoogly's delta when one made corrections; the punkahs waving to and fro in solemn uselessness, and the insects flying in dark clouds about the lamps, then falling, to pile up in high heaps of transparent holocausted dead. In such circumstances, thinking was a slow, exacting business; words had to be laboriously extracted, and arranged with the studied deliberation of a drunk counting his change. Outside, there was the incredible Indian night, so fantastically rich in texture; full of little lights and distant, tinkling sounds, and muffled chatter, and shuffling bare footsteps, and alternating whiffs of stench and fragrance which made one's heart stand still. With the paper put to bed, and the presses subsiding into stillness like a heart that stops beating, there was the club to go to; a cavernous place, smelling of cheese and cold beef, where a few mildly tipsy Sahibs in cummerbunds and white coats tried to play billiards, watched by inscrutable servants.

No one has ever described it all as Kipling did. His genius as a writer, it seems to me, found its most satisfactory expression in *Kim*. Take this famous passage about Kim and the Lama on the Grand Trunk Road; illustrated in bas relief, and, I believe, partly suggested by his father, Lockwood Kipling:

The Grand Trunk at this point was built on an embankment to

guard against winter floods from the foothills, so that one walked, as it were, a little above the country, along a stately corridor, seeing all India spread out to left and right. It was beautiful to behold the many-yoked grain and cotton wagons crawling over the country roads: one could hear their axles, complaining a mile away, coming nearer, till with shouts and yells and bad words they climbed up the steep incline and plunged on to the hard main road, carter reviling carter. It is equally beautiful to watch the people, little clumps of red and blue and pink and white and saffron, turning aside to go to their villages, dispersing and growing small by twos and threes across the level plain. Kim felt these things, though he could not give tongue to his feelings.

Kipling, fortunately, could.

Then there was the other, Sahibs' India, which Kipling also described with great skill, and even some humour, but not with the feeling that he had for Indian India. This was the India of the hill station and Mrs Hauksbee, of the cantonment and *Soldiers Three*, of government offices, and up-country administrators and visiting MPs. Kipling accepted the Raj and its mystique unquestioningly. Ideas travel on waves like sound and light; at about the same time that Kipling was working out his notion of our imperial destiny, Edward Elgar wrote his 'Imperial March' in the same vein – a musical equivalent of Kipling's writings.

Kipling was liable in some of his writing to make a hero, if not a god, of the upper-class Englishman, like young George Cottar, the hero of his short story *The Brushwood Boy*, who moves inevitably from public school to Sandhurst.

His reward was another string of athletic cups, a good-conduct sword, and, at last, Her Majesty's Commission as a subaltern in a first-class line regiment. He did not know that he bore with him from school and college a character worth much fine gold, but was pleased to find his mess so kindly. He had plenty of money of his own; his training had set the public-school mask upon his face, and had taught him how many were the 'things no fellow can do'. By virtue of the same training he kept his pores open and his mouth shut.

This excessive adulation led Kipling into transports which now seem almost imbecile. When Cottar Sahib comes on his first home leave from India:

The house took toll of him, with due regard to precedence – first the mother; then the father; then the housekeeper, who wept and praised God; and then the butler; and so on down to the under-keeper, who had been dog-boy in George's youth, and called him 'Master Georgie'.

Finally, his mother comes to tuck him up,

and they talked for a long hour, as mother and son should, if there is to be any future for our Empire.

It may be doubted, however, whether Kipling ever managed wholly to acclimatize himself to the Sahibs' India, much as he wanted to. English journalists in his day, even more than in mine, were, hierarchically speaking, of small account. At a Viceregal dinner their place was with the lowliest – among missionaries and even 'natives', as Kipling punctiliously calls Indians, who are not so far above him in rank as to be princely, nor so far below him as to be droll.

The English in India soon followed the example of the Hindus they had conquered, and instituted their own caste system, in which everyone had his due place and status expressed in terms of his salary and the decorations which fell to him. Kipling's reaction was to glamorize not only the dedicated officer or administrator who selflessly kept order and ruled in India, but also the private soldier, illiterate, blasphemous, and a rogue, but a true adventurer. Some of his best stories and verses are about these; for instance, the superb *Man Who Would Be King*, and 'Mandalay', which George Orwell told me once he considered to be about the best poem in the English language. Without going with him all the way, one can still admire its feeling, lilt and panache:

Ship me somewheres east of Suez, where the best is like the
    worst,
Where there aren't no Ten Commandments, an' a man can raise
    a thirst;
For the temple-bells are callin' an' it's there that I would be –
By the old Moulmein Pagoda, lookin' lazy at the sea –
    On the road to Mandalay,
    Where the old Flotilla lay,
    With our sick beneath the awnings when we went to Manda-
        lay!
    Oh, the road to Mandalay,

Where the flyin' fishes play,
An' the dawn comes up like thunder outer China 'crost the
Bay!

In Kipling's fragment of autobiography, *Something of Myself*, written in old age, he describes how, when he was a young man, one evening he was hissed in the Lahore Club. It was an incident which obviously made a deep impression on him. One can imagine how distressed Kipling must have been. He, the laureate of the Sahibs and their Raj, found himself in disfavour in their holy of holies – the Club, with Indian servants witnessing his discomfiture.

Whenever the imaginatively gifted turn to glorifying authority or its Janus-face, revolution, they are liable to find themselves in such predicaments. This applies just as much to a Byron as to Kipling. Byron's reputation as a man of action was saved only by his death at Missolonghi, and Lord Snow, God bless him, must now be regretting that he ever set foot in the corridors of power, as D. H. Lawrence assuredly would have regretted taking a job as a gamekeeper. Kipling's recourse was to fall back on the black mystique of action and violence. At the end of *The Light That Failed*, that truly lamentable novel, the hero, Dick Heldar, having gone blind, manages to make his way to the Sudan where he is fortunate enough to hear and smell slaughter before a stray bullet kills him. 'What luck!' he exclaims. 'What stupendous and imperial luck . . . Oh, God has been good to me!'

It was such glorifications of violence, and sometimes cruelty in his writings – in life he was, by universal consent, kindly and affectionate, especially with children – which horrified the more squeamish among Kipling's contemporaries. When Andrew Lang was shown Kipling's story *The Mark of the Beast*, written in 1890, before its author was known in England, he described it as 'poisonous stuff', and another – William Sharp – to whom the manuscript was referred, recommended the instant burning of so detestable a piece of work, and predicted that the author would die mad before the age of thirty. One sees the point. In *The Mark of the Beast* an Indian leper is savagely tortured by two Sahibs, and there is unmistakable relish in the recounting of the episode.

Kipling did not, as Sharp predicted, die before he was thirty, but he did become fabulously famous in his twenties. Part, at any rate, of his fantastic popularity was due to the faculty which he developed early in life, and which never left him, for expressing the public mood at any given moment – sometimes, as in 'The

Absent-Minded Beggar,' when it was warm-hearted and generous; sometimes, as in 'Recessional' when it was infused with a true nobility, but sometimes, too, when it was inflamed with the rage, fury, and vindictiveness of war. He declined the Poet Laureateship as he did all other public honours, but if ever there was a People's Laureate, it was he.

After I returned to England from India in 1936, I went to live in Sussex, a few miles away from Burwash and Kipling's home, Bateman's, where he settled in 1903 to spend the last thirty-three years of his life. He who was by temperament as rootless as Kim, rooted himself with singular tenacity, if not ferocity, in this place, to which he belonged no more than I did. On my own restless walks in the locality, as on the Mall in Simla, I was somehow abnormally conscious of Kipling. There must have been something mediumistic about him which made his physical presence extrude from his writings to an unusual, or even abnormal, degree. To me, at any rate, his spirit brooded palpably over that countryside which he so brilliantly evoked in his writings. Again, as in Simla, I recall with particular vividness a particular occasion; an evening in early summer by the Rother, with the grazing cows seeming to be afloat on the mist rising over the lush meadowland, heavy with sodden pasture and creamy buttercups. There I saw him – a little, dark, spectacled man, so alien a figure, and yet pulling out of the scene its quintessence, his gaze behind the thick spectacle lenses digging deep into the land itself, and excavating its very history.

A portrait of Kipling, as I see it, should be in the medieval style, with a white angel perched on one shoulder and a black devil on the other. The white angel signifies the imagination, out of which come truth and love and laughter; the black devil signifies the will, out of which come rhetoric, hate, and portentousness. Kipling was always, it seems to me, in thrall to one or other of those two demons. He found no peace in the quiet grey twilight between their two kingdoms where most of us reside.

Bateman's is a dark house with dark panelling, full of shadows, and almost overwhelmingly oppressive. I easily imagine him bent over his desk there; he so diligent and conscientious a writer. As he works the dark house enfolds him. Then he emerges, blinking short-sightedly round, evoking all those shadowy figures from the past with which he has peopled the place, and filling the air with the cries of children playing. I have the feeling that Kipling barricaded himself in this house and garden, shutting out the dangerous world, and making, as he so often did, his own prison.

All writers are split personalities; literature is a current which flows between the two poles of mysticism and action. Kipling was an extreme case. Perhaps the division was established at the very beginning of his life when he was farmed out with a highly unsympathetic evangelical lady in what he called the House of Desolation, while his parents were in Lahore. It was the common fate of the children of Anglo-Indians in those days. He described the episode in his story *Baa, Baa, Black Sheep*, and referred to it again with undiminished bitterness in his fragment of auto-biography, *Something of Myself*. One naturally thinks of Dickens's self-pity in *David Copperfield*; but as Edmund Wilson has pointed out, David at least bites Mr Murdstone, and ultimately runs away. Kipling, I think characteristically, came to terms with his tormentor.

As I have said, it is his memories of India which seem to stir most infallibly the imaginative side of him. Take the case of *Without Benefit of Clergy*. This marvellous story is about a love affair between a Sahib and an Indian girl, who initially has been bought by him for money. Subsequently he falls in love with her, and she bears him a son. To the mother's and his infinite grief the child dies, and then the mother dies in a cholera epidemic, and the Sahib goes disconsolately away muttering to himself: 'Oh, you brute! You utter brute!' One may ask oneself why, in the circumstances, the Sahib's grief should take so self-condemnatory a form. Is it, perhaps, because the story relates to some actual experience? After he left for England at the age of twenty-four, Kipling, though an inveterate traveller, visited India only once again, for a few days.

Most of Kipling's love scenes are, to put it mildly, unconvincing, ranging between atrocious sentimentality and, in his verses called 'The Mary Gloster,' such worldly-wise observations as the self-made millionaire, Sir Anthony Gloster, addressed to his wife:

An a man 'e must go with a woman, as
    you *could* not understand;
But I never talked 'em secrets. I paid 'em out o'hand . . .
I'm sick of the hired women. I'll kiss my girl on her lips!
I'll be content with my fountain. I'll drink from my own well,
And the wife of my youth shall charm me – an' the rest
    can go to Hell!

Perhaps fortunately, Lady Gloster was already in heaven, where Sir Anthony was shortly to join her. Thus, her response to this piece of gallantry, if any, is not recorded.

Kipling himself managed to see some of the action he so admired in the South African war, when for the first time England came up against a tough opponent after a series of easy victories against Tibetans, Zulus, and other relatively speaking unarmed fuzzy-wuzzies. Prior to this, Kipling's idea of war was largely based on the Indian North-West Frontier; a romantic, but not very dangerous style of fighting which, contrary to Sahib mystique, came to an abrupt end when India achieved independence. Though few recognized it at the time, least of all Kipling, the South African war marked the beginning of the decline of the British Empire, and of the cause of imperialism so dear to him.

In South Africa Kipling made the acquaintance of Cecil Rhodes, and they became, in a manner of speaking, friends. They would sit together in silence for long periods of time, with Rhodes's huge body stretched out on a sofa; then, twisting and turning, he would ask: 'What am I trying to say, Ruddy?' Ruddy might well have retaliated by asking Rhodes: 'What am I trying to do, Cecil?' They make, it seems to me a perfect pair – the tubercular giant who became a millionaire on the diamond fields before he was twenty, and the little short-sighted poet who became world famous at about the same age.

'What's your dream?' was a question Rhodes was fond of putting. What was Kipling's dream, I wonder? Certainly not worldly success. He was a singularly unworldly and ungrasping man, genuinely reticent, and much more personally identified with the bazaar urchin Kim and the junglechild Mowgli than with the captains and the kings, who as he observes in 'Recessional' must infallibly depart. His cousin Stanley Baldwin (their mothers and the wife of Burne-Jones were sisters, the daughters of a dissenting minister from the Highlands, named MacDonald) became Prime Minister, but Kipling would never accept any office or distinction at his hands. He once rather surprised a friend (who described the episode to me) by saying that, after all, he did have a trinket, and went upstairs to fetch it. It turned out to be a Croix de Guerre which a French soldier had sent him in the 1914-18 War for safe-keeping. The soldier was killed, and Kipling was characteristically generous to his family. He kept the Croix de Guerre intact in the careful wrapping in which it had been sent to him.

In India, when Kipling was there, power was symbolized by the British Raj, and he bowed down before it. Yet in his masterpiece,

Kim, the Lama, with his unwordly passion to escape from the Wheel of Life, is the dominant figure, and even Kim finds himself poised between his service to the Raj and to the Lama. Moreover, Kipling's veneration for authority as such by no means extended to what we nowadays call the Establishment. He despised, with increasing bitterness, the conduct of affairs under his cousin's premiership; his poem, 'Gehazi', about Lord Reading, then Lord Chief Justice, is among the most scorching in the language:

> Stand up, stand up, Gehazi,
> Draw close thy robe and go,
> Gehazi, Judge in Israel,
> A leper white as snow!

He lived to see Gehazi-Reading become Viceroy of India, which must have given a great impetus to the mounting gloom about the prospects for England and the Empire which clouded his latter years. I see him at Bateman's when, as often happened, sleep eluded him, and, as he put it, the night got into his head, shutting him out from the city of sleep, until Policeman Day, that inexorable drill sergeant, came to collect the wakeful like himself:

> Over the edge of the purple down,
> Where the single lamplight gleams,
> Know ye the road to the Merciful Town
> That is hard by the Sea of Dreams –
> Where the poor may lay their wrongs away,
> And the sick may forget to weep?
> But we – pity us! Oh, pity us!
> We wakeful; ah, pity us! –
> We must go back with Policeman Day –
> Back from the City of Sleep!

It has always seemed extraordinary to me that this enchanting fancy, which Kipling, even as a young man, felt deeply, should have been incorporated in a story as otherwise commonplace as *The Brushwood Boy*. Yet there it is, the dream which came to the Brushwood Boy to solace him in moments of desolation when the breathless Indian night seemed to suffocate him; a dream more real than life, also dreamed in identical terms by the woman he was to marry before they had made each other's acquaintance. Their mutual recognition when they met in the flesh made them realize that love exists before it comes to pass, as it goes on existing after its mortal span is over. Again, at the end of *Kim*, the Lama finds his river which frees from all human sin, and is offered the chance to escape from the Wheel of Life; his thoughts and hopes at that time reach beyond the world of the will which so much of Kipling's work sets out to glorify. The old Lama wrenches himself back from his vision of joy and eternity and returns to this world to help the boy Kim, his disciple:

> So thus the Search is ended. For the merit that I have acquired, the River of the Arrow is here. It broke forth at our feet, as I have said. I have found it. Son of my soul, I have wrenched my Soul back from the Threshold of Freedom to free thee from all sin – as I am free, and sinless. Just is the Wheel! Certain is our deliverance. Come! He crossed his hands on his lap and smiled, as a man may who has won Salvation for himself and his beloved.

Kipling's death in 1936 coincided with King George V's. There was another less noticed death at the time – that of Saklatvala, an Indian Parsee who had become the Communist MP for Battersea. It so happened that Kipling's cremation followed Saklatvala's, and at the crematorium there was no time to clear away the Red Flags and other communist insignia set up for Saklatvala. Truly God is not mocked.

[1965]

The Trial

Never can there have been such an age as this for political trials, investigations and interrogations; not even in the high tide of the Inquisition. As so often happens, an imaginative writer, Kafka, foresaw what was going to happen, and in his novel *The Trial* produced a sort of prototype, in which the accused has no notion what he is charged with, or who his judges are. He only knows that he is guilty. I once thought of a series of plays performed in the same symbolic set of a court, using the transcripts of all the famous trials of our time – the Moscow Trials of the Old Bolsheviks, the Reichstag Fire Trial, the Riom Trials of Blum and the other leaders of the French Third Republic, and then,

under de Gaulle, the corresponding trials of Pétain and Laval;
the Nuremberg Trials and of course, the Joseph McCarthy-
inspired charges, counter-charges and investigations under the
auspices of the Senate Permanent Sub-Committee on Investigations. If my theories were done correctly, it would surely emerge
that all these trials were concerned with one thing – loyalty; and
that all of them ended indecisively because it is impossible to
discover who or what, in the twentieth century, we are supposed
to be loyal to.

What I Believe

In trying to formulate what I believe I have to begin with
what I disbelieve. I disbelieve in progress, the pursuit of happiness,
and all the concomitant notions and projects for creating a
society in which human beings find ever greater contentment by
being given in ever greater abundance the means to satisfy their
material and bodily hopes and desires. In other words, I consider
that the way of life in urbanized, rich countries as it exists today,
and as it is likely to go on developing, is probably the most
degraded and unillumined ever to come to pass on earth. The half
century in which I have been consciously alive seems to me to
have been quite exceptionally destructive, murderous and brutal.
More people have been killed and terrorized, more driven from
their homes and native places; more of the past's heritage has
been destroyed, more lies propagated and base persuasion engaged
in, with less compensatory achievement in art, literature and
imaginative understanding, than in any comparable period of
history.

Ever since I can remember, the image of earthly power, whether
in the guise of schoolmaster, mayor, judge, prime minister,
monarch, or any other, has seemed to me derisory. I was enchanted
when I first read in the *Pensées* (Pascal being one of the small,
sublime band of fellow-humans to whom one may turn and say
in the deepest humility: 'I agree') about how magistrates and
rulers had to be garbed in their ridiculous ceremonial robes,
crowns and diadems. Otherwise, who would not see through their
threadbare pretensions? I am conscious of having been ruled by
buffoons, taught by idiots, preached at by hypocrites, and preyed
upon by charlatans in the guise of advertisers and other pro-

fessional persuaders, as well as verbose demagogues and ideologues of many opinions, all false.

Nor, as far as I am concerned, is there any recompense in the so-called achievements of science. It is true that in my lifetime more progress has been made in unravelling the composition and mechanism of the material universe than previously in the whole of recorded time. This does not at all excite my mind, or even my curiosity. The atom has been split; the universe has been discovered, and will soon be explored. Neither achievement has any bearing on what alone interests me – which is why life exists, and what is the significance, if any, of my minute and so transitory part in it. All the world in a grain of sand; all the universe, too. If I could understand a grain of sand I should understand everything. Why, then, should going to the moon and Mars, or spending a holiday along the Milky Way, be expected to advance me further in my quest than going to Manchester and Liverpool, or spending a holiday in Brighton?

Education, the great mumbo-jumbo and fraud of the age, purports to equip us to live, and is prescribed as a universal remedy for everything from juvenile delinquency to premature senility. For the most part, it only serves to enlarge stupidity, inflate conceit, enhance credulity, and put those subjected to it at the mercy of brainwashers with printing presses, radio and television at their disposal. I have seen pictures of huge, ungainly prehistoric monsters who developed such a weight of protective shell that they sank under its burden and became extinct. Our civilization likewise is sinking under the burden of nuclear defence, and may well soon be extinct. As this fact sinks into the collective consciousness, the resort to drugs, dreams, fantasies, and other escapist devices, particularly sex, becomes ever more marked.

Living thus in the twilight of a spent civilization, amidst its ludicrous and frightening shadows, what is there to believe? Curiously enough, these twilit circumstances provide a setting in which, as it seems to me, the purpose which lies behind them stands out with particular clarity. As human love only shines in all its splendour when the last tiny glimmer of desire has been extinguished, so we have to make the world a wilderness to find God. The meaning of the universe lies beyond history as love lies beyond desire. That meaning shines forth in moments of illumination (which come and go so unaccountably; though, I am thankful to say, never quite ceasing – a sound as of music, far, far away, and drowned by other more tumultuous noises, but still to be faintly and fitfully heard) with an inconceivable clarity and luminosity. It breaks like a crystalline dawn out of darkness, and the deeper the darkness the more crystalline the dawn.

Let me express it, as I have often thought of it, in terms of a stage. In the middle is the workaday world where we live our daily lives, earning a living, reading newspapers, exchanging money, recording votes, chattering and eating and desiring. I call this the Café Limbo. On the left of the stage is an area of darkness within which shapes and movements can be faintly discerned, and inconclusive noises heard; sounds and sweet airs which, as on Caliban's Island, give delight and hurt not. I call this Life. The right of the stage is bright with arc-lamps like a television studio. This is where history is unfolded and news is made; this is where we live our public, collective lives, seat and unseat rulers, declare wars and negotiate peace, glow with patriotism and get carried away with revolutionary zeal, enact laws, declaim rhetoric, swear eternal passion and sink into abysses of desolation. I call this the Legend.

Across this triple stage, between Life, the Café Limbo and the Legend, a drama is endlessly presented. Two forces shape the play – the Imagination which belongs to Life, and the Will which belongs to the Legend. Out of the Imagination comes love, understanding, goodness, self-abnegation; every true synthesis ever grasped or to be grasped. Out of the Will comes lust, hatred, cupidity, adulation, power, oratory; every false antithesis ever propounded or to be propounded. Those who belong exclusively or predominantly to Life are saints, mystics and artists. In extreme cases – Christ, for instance – they have to be killed. (This is superbly explained in the famous Grand Inquisitor passage in *The Brothers Karamazov*, Dostoevsky being, like Pascal, of the small band.) Those who belong exclusively or predominantly to the Legend are power-maniacs, rulers, heroes, demagogues and liberators. In extreme cases – Hitler, for instance – they bring about their own destruction. In Life there is suffering, deprivation and sanity; in the Legend, happiness, abundance and madness.

Most of us spend the greater part of our time in the Café Limbo, casting an occasional glance in the direction of Life, and more than an occasional one in the direction of the Legend. Laughter is our best recourse, with the bar to provide a fillip as and when required. The Café Limbo is licensed. When a character passes from the Legend into Life he brings some of the light with him; shining like a glow-worm, until gradually the light subsides and goes out, swallowed up in the darkness of Life.

This same pattern may be traced more particularly and tragically in a single countenance, as anyone will be aware who has had occasion to watch over a loved face hovering between sanity and madness. (And many have. For as we abolish the ills and pains of the flesh we multiply those of the mind, so that by the time mankind are finally delivered from disease and decay – all pasteurized, their genes counted and rearranged, fitted with new replaceable plastic organs, able to eat, fornicate, and perform other physical functions innocuously and hygienically as and when desired – they will all be mad, and the world one huge psychiatric ward.) You study the loved, distracted face as a scholar might study some ancient manuscript, looking for a key to its incomprehensibility. What you see is a fight to the death between the Will and the Imagination. If the former wins, then the flickering light will be put out for ever; if the latter, it will shine again, to burn with a steady radiance. Oh, beloved, you have come back to me.

I am well aware that, psychiatrically speaking, this is nonsensical. Yet I believe it. I see the two forces struggling for mastery in each individual soul; in mine, in all men's; in each collectivity, throughout our earth and throughout the vast universe. One is of darkness and one of light; one wants to drag us down into the dark trough to rut and gorge there, and the other to raise us up into the azure sky, beyond appetite, where love is all-embracing, all-encompassing, and the dark confusion of life sorts itself out, like an orderly, smiling countryside suddenly glimpsed from a high hill. One is the Devil and the other God. I have known both, and I believe in both.

For we Western Europeans the Christian religion has expressed this ancient, and, as I consider, obvious dichotomy in terms of breathtaking simplicity and sublimity. It was not the first word on the subject, nor will it be the last; but it is still our Word. I accept it. I believe, as is written in the New Testament, that if we would save our lives we must lose them; that we cannot live by bread alone; that we must die in the flesh to be reborn in the spirit, and that the flesh lusts contrary to the spirit and the spirit contrary to the flesh; that God cannot see a sparrow fall to the ground without concern, and has counted the hairs of each head, so that all that lives deserves our respect and reverence, and no one man can conceivably be more important, of greater significance, or in any way more deserving of consideration than any other.

It is true that these basic propositions of Christianity have got cluttered up with dogma of various kinds which I find often incomprehensible, irrelevant and even repugnant. All the same I should be proud and happy to be able to call myself a Christian; to dare to measure myself against that immeasurably high standard of human values and human behaviour. In this I take comfort from another saying of Pascal, thrown out like a lifeline to all sceptical minds throughout the ages – that whosoever looks for God has found Him.

At its most obscurantist and debased, the Christian position still seems to me preferable to any scientific-materialist one, however cogent and enlightened. The evangelist with his lurid tract calling upon me to repent for the Day of Judgement is at hand, is a burning and shining light compared with the eugenist who claims the right to decide in his broiler-house mind which lives should be protracted and which must be put out; or with the colporteurs of sterility who so complacently and self-righteously display their assortment of contraceptives to the so-called backward peoples of the world as our civilization's noblest achievement and most precious gift.

The absurdities of the Kingdom of Heaven, as conceived in the minds of simple believers, are obvious enough – pearly gates, angelic choirs, golden crowns and shining raiment. But what are we to think of the (in Johnson's excellent phrase) sheer unresisting imbecility of the Kingdom of Heaven on Earth, as envisaged and recommended by the most authoritative and powerful voices of our time? The Gross National Product rising for evermore, and its beneficiaries, rich in hire-purchase, stupefied with the telly and with sex, comprehensively educated, told by Professor Hoyle how the world began and by Canon Collins how it will end; on the broad highways venturing forth, three lanes a side, with lay-bys to rest in and birth pills to keep them *intacta*, if not *virgo*, as an extra thrill blood spattering the tarmac; heaven lying about them in the supermarket, the rainbow ending in the nearest bingo hall, leisure burgeoning out in multitudinous shining aerials rising like dreaming spires into the sky; happiness in as many colours as there are pills – green and yellow and blue and red and shining white; many mansions, mansions of light and chromium, climbing ever upwards. This Kingdom, surely, can only be for posterity an unending source of wry derision – always assuming there is to be any posterity. The backdrop, after all, is the mushroom cloud; as the Gadarene herd frisk and frolic they draw ever nearer to the cliff's edge.

I recognize, of course, that this statement of belief is partly governed by the circumstance that I am old, and in at most a decade or so will be dead. In earlier years I should doubtless have expressed things differently. Now, the prospect of death over-shadows all others. I am like a man on a sea voyage nearing his destination. When I embarked I worried about having a cabin with a porthole, whether I should be asked to sit at the captain's table, who were the more attractive and important passengers. All such considerations become pointless when I shall soon be disembarking.

As I do not believe that earthly life can bring any lasting satisfaction, the prospect of death holds no terrors. Those saints who pronounced themselves in love with death displayed, I consider, the best of sense; not a Freudian death-wish. Likewise Pastor Bonhoeffer when he told his Nazi guards, as they took him away to be executed, that for them it was an end but for him a beginning; in that place of darkest evil he, the victim, shining and radiant. The world that I shall soon be leaving seems more than ever beautiful; especially its remoter parts, grass and trees and sea and rivers and little streams and sloping hills, where the image of eternity is more clearly stamped than among streets and houses. Those I love I can love even more, since I have nothing to ask of them but their love; the passion to accumulate possessions, or to be noticed and important, is too evidently absurd to be any longer entertained.

A sense of how extraordinarily happy I have been, and of enor-mous gratitude to my creator, overwhelms me often. I believe with a passionate, unshakeable conviction that in all circumstances and at all times life is a blessed gift; that the spirit which ani-mates it is one of love, not hate or indifference, of light, not dark-ness, of creativity, not destruction, of order, not chaos; that, since all life, men, creatures, plants, as well as insensate matter, and all that is known about it, now and henceforth, has been benevolently, not malevolently, conceived, when the eyes see no more and the mind thinks no more, and this hand now writing is inert, whatever lies beyond will similarly be benevolently, not malevolently conceived. If it is nothing, then for nothingness I offer thanks; if another mode of existence, with this old worn-out husk of a body left behind, like a butterfly extricating itself from its chrysalis, and this floundering, muddled mind, now at best seeing through a glass darkly, given a longer range and a new precision, then for that likewise I offer thanks.

[1966]

The Great Charles

I first set eyes on de Gaulle in 1941, in the lift of the Connaught Hotel where he was then staying. His presence was frosty and gauche, but still decidedly impressive. I always thought of him as a man apart. His great height, his Cyrano nose, his awkward movements, all added to this impression. He seemed to have no connection even with the omnipresent war and its macabre ribaldries; with Monty slang, Churchillian rhetoric, Forces humour, and other grisly devices for keeping up morale. His gaze was fixed elsewhere.

With some of his entourage, like Soustelle and Passy, I had dealings, and so got to know them. They treated him with awe, devotion and even affection, but there was no familiarity. It has been suggested by his detractors (for instance, by Robert Mengin in his *No Laurels for de Gaulle*) that he favoured extreme Rightists. Actually, if there were some former *cagoulards* among his inner circle, there were also fellow-travellers and, I dare say, even an occasional Party member. Neither then nor subsequently did de Gaulle fall in with the fashion for seeing our times as a Western in which a good guy and a bad guy contend together, the ultimate victory of the former being of course assured. This enabled him to avoid both the ridiculous raptures over Stalin and the USSR to which Roosevelt, Churchill, *The Times* and most of those set in authority over us succumbed at the time of Yalta, and equally the frenzied and unedifying anti-communist obsessions which have so distorted American thinking and statesmanship in the post-war years. Passy told me that on one occasion, in June 1941, when the *Wehrmacht* had just invaded Russia, de Gaulle sat listening to radio reports of German successes on the new Eastern Front in the company of a number of Allied officers. They were talking, as most of them did at that time, with ill-disguised satisfaction of how the Germans would go through the USSR like a knife through butter. De Gaulle remained silent. They asked him for his views. 'I was thinking,' he replied, *qu'il faudra désormais songer aux moyens d'arrêter la progression communiste en Europe.*' It was a cool and perceptive judgement. The same attitude has enabled him, representative, as he is, of whatever remains valid in European conservatism today, to be received as an honoured guest in the Kremlin with a warmth and cordiality accorded to no other statesman from the West.

It is often forgotten how incredibly weak his position was in London in the war years. He lacked everything – money, friends, resources, an appealing personality and a facility for the sort of rhetorical claptrap which war necessitates. I saw some of his troops arriving at Sheerness, and visited them when they were quartered in Olympia. Not even Falstaff had so bedraggled a company. De Gaulle knew perfectly well that Churchill would have liked some other eminent Frenchman to provide a focus for opposition to the Pétain regime, and had even toyed with the lunatic notion of getting Weygand over. Later, he had to reckon with the unremitting hostility of Roosevelt, who, with the terrible flippancy of an abysmally shallow mind, used him as a tease in his relations with Churchill, and tried to make as much mischief as possible with his c..n puppet – Giraud. There were fiascos like the ill-fated Dakar expedition, and troubles with subordinates – for instance, Admiral Muselier. No one could possibly have had a weaker hand to play from.

Yet what a player! When he went to Broadcasting House to deliver one of his radio exhortations, it was as a bestower, not a receiver, of favours. His relations with MI6 and OSS – to whom he had to look for all operational facilities in his dealings with the *maquis* – were haughty and suspicious, if not contemptuous. Among the motley collection of heads of Allied Governments in exile (he was never accorded recognition as such) whose national anthems were played so lugubriously after the BBC News, he alone has counted for anything. Who now even remembers the names of the others? History has obliterated them.

Every attempt to exclude de Gaulle or restrict his authority proved a failure. In Algiers he soon dominated the situation. The Allied Military Government, planned for France after the Normandy Landings, and the covey of brigadiers who were to operate it, just never got off the ground. De Gaulle was everywhere received as he saw himself – as the very embodiment and voice of liberated France. When shots rang out in Notre Dame at the thanksgiving service for the liberation of Paris, everyone very properly fell flat on their faces – except de Gaulle. There was just that one ridiculously tall man who remained standing. It was a symbolic posture that he has maintained ever since.

Two years later, in 1946, he relinquished his position of unquestioned authority as abruptly and emphatically as he had assumed it. As Soustelle described the scene to me, the members of his government, Soustelle among them, were waiting for him to come and preside over a cabinet meeting when suddenly he stalked into the room, banged the table, exclaiming: '*J'en ai marre!*', and stormed out again. The others had no recourse but to follow his example and resign. There were many who were convinced that his political career must thenceforth be considered over. I myself was so accustomed to his weird infallible triumphs that I assumed he must in due course return to power on his own terms. I saw him as one of those circus trick-cyclists who ride into the arena seemingly on the point of falling off, until one comes to realize that they are in fact consummate riders.

Acting on this hunch, I sought and was accorded an interview with him at about the lowest point in his fortunes, when he had only a handful of followers in the *Assemblée*, among them the faithful Soustelle. He received me in the Rue Solférino, seated at a desk which seemed grotesquely too small to accommodate his massive bulk; his head tiny by comparison. One does not, of course, interview de Gaulle; one listens, managing at best to interpolate an occasional word. Almost without taking breath he explained to me how, with an unworkable political system, a faltering economy and the sort of scum that had come to the top in the Fourth Republic, there would infallibly be a breakdown in due course and a call for him to take over. I managed with great difficulty to put a question – one I had often puzzled over. Why, when he headed a government at the end of the war, did he not use the unlimited power he then had to institute a better and more workable system? He looked at me with the sly ferocity he reserves for awkward questioners, and roared out that it was not the right moment. Then the monologue was resumed. At the end I meekly asked him what he proposed to do now. This time he looked benignly at me, and said with great complacency: '*J'attends.*' As we now know, his waiting was not to be in vain. With a characteristic stroke, having used the slogan *Algérie Française* to get into power, he proceeded at an appropriate moment to hand Algeria over to the Algerians, thereby ensuring staying in power. In politics it is necessary, he said in extenuation, to betray either the electorate or the country. He preferred the former course.

His prowess as a general is dubious, and in any case untested; he has never, in point of fact, conducted military operations on any scale. As a mid-twentieth century politician, however, he is incomparable. His television appearances (carefully rehearsed before a mirror with the aid of a man from the *Comédie Française*) are superb; his electioneering methods more reminiscent of a Kennedy than of St Cyr. After one of his tours his hands are bleeding and swollen (stigmata of universal-suffrage democracy) like Lyndon Johnson's. This is how M. Viansson-Ponté describes what happens:

> To say that he mixes with the crowd is an understatement: he plunges into it, wallows in it. One can keep an eye on him not so much because of his height, but because he is the virtual centre of a whirlpool. Disappearing in one place, he pops up in another for a moment, then is lost to sight again for a long underwater stretch, only to surface like a diver at the other side of the street . . . He has been seen to emerge with three buttons missing, uniform torn, hands scratched, military cap askew, but eyes sparkling with pleasure.

His humour is as out-of-the-way as everything else about him. When Soustelle told him that all his (Soustelle's) friends in Algeria were horrified by de Gaulle's policy of negotiating with the Nationalists, he blandly remarked: '*Alors, mon vieux, changez vos amis.*' On another occasion, when Frey, the Minister of the Interior, remarked that if they held elections the OAS might manage to assassinate at least 50 Gaullist Deputies, de Gaulle fell into a reverie, then murmured with a sigh: '*Qu'importe, Frey! Pourvu qu'ils sont bien choisis!*' I like the item in the standing orders at the Elysée Palace: '*Ne déranger le Président de la République qu'en cas de guerre mondiale*', and his brief exchange with a parish priest in the course of one of his tours: '*Oui, mon général, je prie tous les jours pour vous.*' '*Vous faites bien.*' The egotism implied in such anecdotes is so stupendous as to be almost sublime.

How will history regard him? It all depends on how things turn out. In retrospect it may well seem that he seemed so tall only because he was matched with pygmies, that he spoke so true only because it was against such a torrent of lies and fantasies; that his dawn proved to be a sunset; spectacular, certainly, but to be succeeded by a night particularly dark. Even so, it surely cannot be doubted that he is unique among his contemporaries. Let Simone Weil, a devoted follower, have the last word. There was, she wrote shortly before she died, 'in his words an accent of sincerity and honour' – two qualities, she might have added, by no means plentiful in our world.

[1966]

Krokodil

I was much interested in some exchanges I have had recently with the editor of *Krokodil*. Round about Christmas he sent me a very affable telegram asking me to let him have an account of 'the funniest event this year that I witnessed'. After some consideration, I decided that far and away the funniest event I had witnessed was Mr Macmillan's visit to the USSR. So I wrote a brief account of it, drawing a comparison between our Prime Minister and Don Quixote, with his Sancho Panza, in the person of Mr Selwyn Lloyd, pounding along behind him. The answer I received to this offering deserves quotation:

> Excuse me for taking so much time to answer. But the matter is that after weeks of hesitation we felt that we could not publish your article. Our position is that we feel in a way responsible for the materials we publish and although it is your point of view we here do not want to laugh at Mr Macmillan. For our readers such an article would be in a way the expression of *Krokodil*'s point of view and since it is not we are forced to reject it. As you undoubtedly know, we hold Mr Macmillan in high esteem and we also think that his visit to the USSR played an important role in the relaxation of world tension. At the same time we repeat that we would be very happy to have from time to time your contributions.

In a way, I quite see his point, and shall probably have a go at another contribution one of these days. A proffered contribution to the *New Yorker* on similar lines would probably produce an almost identical reaction. The world's present insecurity is liable to create an exaggerated respect for authority. In the shadow of the mushroom cloud, we draw together, hush our voices, and keep in step. Such order as exists seems too frail to be subjected to the blasts of ridicule. Like an invalid, it has to be wrapped up, kept from the draughts, and fed on pre-digested food.

The area of life in which humour is permissible is subtly shrinking. Even sex, which gave mankind its first big laugh, has become a serious matter. An unholy alliance of advertisers, pornographers and head-shrinkers have moved in on it, driving the poor clowns away. Class, another valuable piece of humorists' real estate, has been made the object of a takeover bid by resentful beneficiaries under the Welfare State. As for the Church – the Archbishop of Canterbury has stolen the show by being funnier than any professional comedian could hope to be, and no one else can get in on the act.

Gossip

Gossip writers, I see, have been under attack again. I always feel a certain unease about this particular controversy in which they come out as so indubitably the baddies. For one thing, honesty compels me to admit that, personally, I find gossip more interesting than news, and must, therefore, acknowledge an obligation to the purveyors. After all, even if bitchily, gossip is about people, whereas news is concerned primarily with power, and has to concern itself for the most part with abstractions like votes and money and the Gross National Product, with NATO and SEATO and OPEC and UNESCO and NATSOPA, all the phantasmagoric kingdom of initials. Who sleeps with whom is intrinsically more interesting, and even more significant, than who votes for whom; I'd sooner read about John F. Kennedy's amours than what his speech-writers wrote for him to say or how his public image comported itself. In any case, pretty well all we know about him for certain is gossip, and even some of that was planted by his PR men and has to be treated with reserve. I have read that in his time in the White House a mechanical pen was set up there which reproduced the President's signature so perfectly that even handwriting experts could not tell it was a facsimile. This enabled 'personalized' letters signed by the President to be turned out by the thousand. When he was assassinated, it seems, they forgot to turn off the machine, so that the letters went on being signed and dispatched posthumously. How wonderfully symbolic! What Fearful Symmetry! In the same sort of way, his public image has gone marching on. Gossip provides, as it were, the *samizdat* version.

I Love You, England

I feel in myself nowadays an almost overpowering love for England as a place, for the English as people and for the English language. Even with the motor cars and the television aerials and the ice-cream vans, the English countryside remains greener and more delectable than any other. Already I am looking forward to the spring, so uniquely gentle and fresh and fragrant that elsewhere there never seems to be a spring at all. Where else is there such pasture, flowers so varied, birds singing so sweetly? It is true that nowadays one doesn't often hear a cock crow, with the hens all in battery-confinement; but where I live the factory farmers have still not swept the cattle indoors. The lambs will still frisk in the spring and the cows munch away in the lush meadows by the Rother.

As for the English people – bamboozled and vulgarized by advertisers, cheated by politicians, lied to by vicious with-it clergymen and teachers, sung to in abysmal bastard-Americanese, and induced to turn themselves into an inferior version (if such be imaginable) of a transatlantic moron – I still find them gentler in disposition; more humorous, original, wry, easy-going, genial and kindly, above all *more detached*, than any other.

They survey the heroes allotted to them – the Churchills and the Dimblebys – with a tolerant but quizzical eye, and endure with equanimity bordering on indifference rhetorical assaults about the Dunkirk spirit, belt-tightening, all being in this together, and other attempts to break down their propensity in all circumstances to live for the moment and take it easy. Even the Monarchy which they are supposed to revere is more a subject for ribaldry than awe. Sir William Haley's exhortations do not reach them, of Lord Reith they have never heard; they prefer *Coronation Street* to *Look Back In Anger*, hymns to sermons, dirty jokes to *Lady Chatterley's Lover*, the *Sunday Mirror* to the *Sunday Times*, *Housewives' Choice* to the Third Programme. The gap between them and the score or so of men (and what men!) who control the party machines and the mass-communication media, is vast, as one soon discovers if one happens to come under attack. The rotten eggs are thrown over the crowd's head by the cheerleaders in the rear.

Then the English language. Anyone whose trade is to use words must be aware of the fabulous riches it offers in the way of vocabulary and imagery, of its versatility and subtlety and strength, of the unique possibilities it provides for packing into the compass of a tiny unadorned phrase feeling and wisdom which whole libraries scarcely contain. By way of example, once when I was in Darwin, Australia, I got a message that a man in hospital there had asked to see me. I went along, and found that he was a retired policeman who had gone totally blind and was soon to die: a grizzled, dried-up old fellow, with, it seemed, a taste for literature. It turned out that he had heard with pleasure something I had said on the radio, and that was why he had asked that I should come and see him. In such a situation I scarcely knew what to say except to blurt out how proud I was that, in the general idiocy of public utterances, words of mine should have pleased him. I wanted to say something else, something better, and suddenly remembered a remark of Gloucester's in *King Lear* about his blindness – 'I stumbled when I saw'. He was tremendously taken with it, and kept repeating it over and over. It is difficult to see how five words could say more.

Again, soon after the end of the 1939-45 War, I got tickets to take my family to see *As You Like It* at the Old Vic. The theatre had only lately been re-opened. There was still a great hole in the roof through which you could see the stars, and only a part of the auditorium was in use, the rest being roped off. I arrived late, when the performance had already begun. I could see my family in their places, the children grouped round their mother, and all rapt and absorbed. I have no idea who the actors and actresses were, possibly students, anyway very young and fresh in their presentation of Shakespeare's enchanting comedy; probably now all famous, moaning and groaning over kitchen sinks, bathing in blood with Sade, following the Tynan trail. On that night, bringing the Forest of Arden to that battered old theatre, they seemed delectable, an image of everything most wonderful about England and being English; the more so as the dreadful buffooneries of victory – more repellent, if anything, than those of war – were still ringing in one's ears and boding ill for the years to come. After all, to have as one's mother tongue the language Shakespeare wrote in gives one a tremendous advantage; puts at one's disposal a majestic instrument which, though it may be corrupted and distorted with oven-ready, daisy-fresh, through-putting additions, still enables a writer entrusted with it, if he tries hard enough, to scratch out a phrase or two not wholly unworthy.

Thus it is not really surprising that quite a lot of highly

cultivated foreigners, washed up on our shores by the ferocious currents of the age, displaced persons whom some crazed man of destiny has liberated or emancipated to the point that they have had to make off as best they might, actually choose of their own free will to remain among us. Often they might very well move on to America where they would surely prosper, but prefer our rundown little island, even though it is governed by Wilson and Heath, resounding with nonsensical rhetoric about a non-existent Commonwealth, and drenched in the moral fatuities of permissive and teach-in dons.

These estimable DP additions to our citizenry can be set off against the so-called brain-drain. I think of them with particular satisfaction every time I read of some loud-mouthed scientist removing himself across the Atlantic. The fact is that England today is a much pleasanter place for a civilized European to live in than ever it used to be. This is partly a consequence of our having come down in the world and lost our Empire; an encumbrance which was accepted with reluctance and endured with an ill grace until it was almost over. There was a short and horrible period when imperialism was put across as a popular mystique. One recalls it now with a shudder of disgust. Empire Day! That carries you back. Yet it was going strong when I was young, with flags out in all the government schools, renderings of Kipling and Elgar, and an appropriate address by the headmaster or some local big-wig. The whole thing, mercifully, is over and done with, only lingering on in a kind of twittering, twilit way in the concept of the Commonwealth. This, too, one hopes, is reaching the last phase.

People have already forgotten the intolerable conceit this sense of imperial destiny generated, collectively, and in individuals like Indian civil servants and colonial administrators – all those Excellencies, actual and potential, in toppers and grey frock-coats. It gave the upper and middle classes and their hangers-on a taste of what Blake calls that deadly poison from Caesar's laurel crown, inducing them to see their importance, not just in terms of money or social position, but – much more sinisterly – in terms of power. It put them on the threshold of fascism, and sometimes, in their stations overseas, well over it.

Fortunately, they were brief Caesars. Nowadays, if they farm the Kenya Highlands, they must come to terms as best they may with Kenyatta; if they trade in Bengal, with Indian politicians once scornfully dismissed as 'native agitators'. Like the rest of us, too, they have to endure exhortations on the merits of majority rule from that fine old Gladstonian Liberal, the Emperor of Abyssinia and Lion of Judah, and panegyrics of one-man-one-vote from Redeemer Nkrumah and Dr Banda, the latter having recently perfected the principle's application in Malawi by instituting public executions.

All this goes to make the social atmosphere in England much sweeter and more congenial. Aspiring proconsuls, retired to Sevenoaks, take their fury out on the lawnmower. Though snobbishness is always with us, it assumes ever more bizarre forms which amuse rather than annoy. Better, after all, dukes dressed as showmen, harlequinade aristocracy, than a ruling class with pretensions to rule, if not us, then over pine and palm on our behalf. Indeed, a ruling class on the run like ours provides one of the most diverting spectacles life holds. Nothing is more conducive to the gaiety of the nation. They make every possible miscalculation; grow beards when they should shave, deck themselves out in discarded Carnaby Street models, compensate for past misdemeanours by excessive zeal for the abolition of capital punishment and making the world safe for sodomy, discover Marxism at Stalin's funeral and the poor at Beveridge's, wait with a stiff upper-lip for Godot and take the Wayland Way to bigger and better sex, infallibly mistaking bandwagons for hearses and vice versa.

It is permissible to hope that these favourable circumstances will become more marked as the English grow more accustomed to their new situation in the world, realizing, for instance, that it is as foolish for them to march through the street shouting 'Hands off Vietnam!' as for Eskimoes or Laplanders so to do. After burdensome years we are now in the happy position of not having our hands on Vietnam, or soon, with a bit of luck, on anywhere else. Nor need we any more bother with those leaden propositions about how 'as long as our two great English-speaking democracies continue to work together . . . etc., etc, . . .', annually propounded in an atmosphere of cigar smoke and brandy fumes to Your Royal Highness, Your Grace, Your Excellencies, My Lords, Ladies and Gentlemen. Sterling may be shaky, Mrs Gandhi in trouble, income and prices not all they might be, Tanzania looking askance and Sierra Leone in a denunciatory mood; but, oh! brothers, a great weight of boredom has been taken off our shoulders, and for that at least we should be thankful.

[1966]

Am I A Christian?

This is a question I mull over from time to time without finding a satisfactory or convincing answer. If I put it to myself after, say, reading one of the Archbishop of Canterbury's pronouncements on contemporary *mores* in the House of Lords, or listening to some *Ten-to-Seven* radio evangelist of Beveridgeanity, I feel greatly relieved that I can still disengage myself from any seeming commitment to attitudes such as theirs. If they are Christian, I reflect, then I emphatically am not. On the other hand, hearing *War and Peace* read aloud (which I have of late been so tremendously enjoying), or any of Tolstoy's writings, gives me an almost overpowering sense of how uniquely marvellous a Christian way of looking at life is, and a passionate desire to share it. Likewise listening to Bach, reading Pascal, looking at Chartres Cathedral or any of the other masterpieces of Christian art and thought. As for the Gospels and Epistles, I find them (especially St John) irresistibly wonderful as they reduce the jostling egos of now – my own among them – to the feeble crackling flicker of burning sticks against a majestic sunset. Is it not extraordinary, to the point of being a miracle, that so loose and ill-constructed a narrative in an antique translation of a dubious text should after so many centuries still have power to quell and dominate a restless, opinionated, over-exercised and under-nourished twentieth century mind?

I am well aware, of course, that just to be thus quelled and dominated is far from amounting to being a Christian. In any case, what is a Christian today? One may well ask. From the days when the Very Rev. Hewlett Johnson used to expatiate in Canterbury Cathedral upon the Christian excellence of the late Stalin, to the Right Rev. Bishop of Woolwich's gay endorsement of *Lady Chatterley's Lover* as an aid to Christian marriage, and on to even loftier heights of psychedelic piety, there is scarcely a contemporary absurdity which has not received some degree of clerical, if not episcopal, endorsement. Rebellious or randy Fathers come to the microphone to tell us of the doubts which have assailed them and of the hazards of priestly celibacy; learned theologians bend their powerful minds to demonstrating that God is dead and His Church, therefore, become a useless excrescence. Holy discothèques, sanctified playmates furnished by Mr Hefner, Bishop Pike of California – Dear God! how well I remember him – Bishop ('call me Jim') Pike, and his memorable observation as we made our way arm in arm to the hospitality room from the television studio where we had been doing our little stint of Soper-opera. St Paul, he said, was wrong about sex. So he was, Bishop; so he was.

One may marvel that, when pretty well every item of Christian belief and of Christian ethics has been thus subjected to some degree of denigration and attack by those ostensibly responsible for upholding and propagating it, congregations of sorts nonetheless continue to assemble in parish churches on Sunday mornings, and ordinands and novices, though in dwindling numbers, continue to come forward with seemingly authentic vocations. Vegetarians do not normally enlist themselves in the Worshipful Company of Butchers, yet the Church of Christ has to stagger on under the guidance of those who increasingly sympathize with, when they do not actually countenance, every attack on its doctrines, integrity and traditional practices. By one of our time's larger ironies, ecumenicalism is triumphant just when there is nothing to be ecumenical about; the various religious bodies are likely to find it easy to join together only because, believing little, they correspondingly differ about little. I look forward to the day when an Anglican bishop in full canonicals will attend a humanist rally on the South Downs, or a Salvation Army Band lead a procession of Young Atheists to lay a wreath on Karl Marx's grave in Highgate Cemetery. It cannot be long delayed, if it has not happened already.

It would take a subtle ear indeed to catch out of all this confusion any consistent or coherent theme. Institutional Christianity, it seems to me, is now in total disarray, and visibly decomposing, to the point that, short of a miracle, it can never be put together again with any semblance of order or credibility. In its present state of decomposition, institutional Christianity is not even an impediment to Christian belief, but just a joke. One notes the grimaces of Vatican faces as, holding their noses, they try to swallow the birth pill, the bizarre convolutions of Quakers when they venture out on the nursery slopes of sex, with the same sort of wry satisfaction as one does the tergiversations of the bishop who recently baptized a nuclear submarine.

Yet curiously enough the very intensity of all this confusion, the very preposterousness of the effort to market dust and ashes as body building, and a kingdom not of this world as profitable real estate, somehow for me clears the air for a consideration of what Christianity really is about. The surrender of Institutional

Christianity to the promoters of a kingdom of heaven on earth has been so abject, the assumptions of scientific materialism are so widely accepted and arrogantly stated, that an aspiring Christian today is left in a kind of catacomb of his own making, utterly remote from the debates and discussions going on around him, whether about 'permissive' morality (divorce, contraception and abortion – those three panaceas for all matrimonial ills), or about the basic dogma of the Christian faith.

In my copy of the New Testament (Everyman edition, chronological arrangement by Principal Thomas M. Lindsay, first published in 1906, and not, I see, reprinted since 1948) I underline passages which take my fancy. Nearly all of them are about the deceitfulness of the cares of this world and of riches, about how concupiscence and vanity separate us from God, about glorying in tribulation which brings patience, experience and hope, about the flesh lusting against the spirit and the spirit against the flesh, these being contrary to one another so that we cannot do the things that we would do, and so on. They are, I should say, about the most unpopular sentences it is possible to utter today. At religious gatherings they cause malaise and irritation; on radio and television panels derision and incredulity. When I use them I am often accused of insincerity or affectation, so rooted are the opposite assumptions – that by caring about this world we shall make it better, that we must aim collectively to get richer and richer in order to get happier and happier, that the unrestrained satisfaction of our bodily desires is the way to physical, mental and spiritual contentment.

However, I love these sentences, and often say them over to myself. I should like them to govern my every thought and activity for the rest of my life. They seem to me to be true, and the notion of making the world better by caring about it, and achieving happiness through material prosperity and sensual pleasure, quite nonsensical. In face of the otherworldliness which I still unfashionably find in the Gospels, as far as I am concerned the whole edifice of twentieth century materialism – and the utopian hopes that go therewith – falls flat on its face. The pursuit of happiness becomes a grotesque fantasy, and the Gross National Product an equally grotesque mirage. One is delivered from the myth of progress and can joyously snatch despair from the idiot jaws of hope. The terrible vision of a Scandinavian-American paradise, with longer lives, more and better aphrodisiacs and more leisure and amenities for all, dissolves into nightmare, awaking from which one advances gingerly upon the sublime truth that to live it is necessary to die, that a life can only be kept by being lost – propositions which strike contemporary minds as pessimistic, but which seem to me optimistic to the point of insanity, implying, as they do, that it is possible for a mere man, with his brief life and stunted vision, imprisoned in his tiny ego and enslaved by his squalid appetites, to aspire after a universal understanding and a universal love. Is this being a Christian? Ask me another.

[1967]

Novels

As one gets older one reads novels, I find, with increasing reluctance. Almost any work of non-fiction, whatever its character – biographies, autobiographies, histories, even sociological and anthropological studies – is bearable, and even sometimes pleasurable. But fiction! To follow the intricacies and sexual minutiae of yet one more emotional tangle! One more journey into and out of bed! Oh, no! Novelists, especially female ones, leave nothing out. Remorselessly, they take one the whole way. And nowadays they need have no prudish inhibitions, worse luck. Each matrimonial breakdown and love affair is explored to its innermost recesses and uttermost limits. It is intolerable. 'I don't care what you do, or with whom, or where, or how,' one mutters, grinding one's teeth and clenching one's fists, 'only don't tell me about it.'

Jane Austen And Iris Murdoch

I should much rather be even a minor character in a Jane Austen novel than a major figure in an Iris Murdoch one.

Refractions In The Character Of Kim Philby

Now that Philby's own story of his career as a Soviet spy in the British Secret Service has been published (*My Silent War*, MacGibbon and Kee, London and Grove Press, New York), the documentation of this weird episode may be considered complete. There are still, it is true, some gaps, but as they can be filled only from official sources it would seem to be unlikely that we shall be told any more in the immediate future at any rate – unless, of course, some cataclysm causes the archives of the Secret Service or the CIA or the KGB to be opened, as the archives of the Czarist political police were as a result of the Russian Revolution.

At the time of the defection of Burgess and Maclean – two British Foreign Office men who created a sensation in May 1951, by disappearing behind the Iron Curtain – which touched the whole affair off, a good deal was written about them, mostly of a speculative, not to say fanciful, nature. Philby's defection gave the story a new impetus, and brought him into the centre of the stage, rather dwarfing the other two figures. We have had his American wife's account of their courtship, marriage and life together in Beirut and Moscow (*Kim Philby . . . The Spy I Married*, Pan Books, London and Ballantine Books, New York), a rather touching and, I'm sure, truthful reminiscence of what was for Mrs Eleanor Philby for the most part a singularly warm and happy experience. I congratulate her on her candour in admitting this; most women who have been dismissed by their husbands, as she was by Philby, suggest the contrary. We have also had *The Philby Conspiracy* (André Deutsch, London and Doubleday, New York) by three journalists – Bruce Page, Phillip Knightley and David Leitch – on the staff of the London *Sunday Times*. Theirs is an exercise in journalism in depth – the riposte of written journalism to the visual television variety, or, in McLuhan terms, the Message struggling to exist outside the Medium. I wouldn't personally award them more than a beta minus for the result of their efforts, even though I have to admire their assiduity, which extended to sending a man after me, to ask questions about Philby, as far as the Sea of Galilee, where I was engaged in making some films for BBC Television on the New Testament. Graham Greene happened to be there at the same time; like myself, he had worked under Philby in the Secret Service in the 1939-45 War years. There was, we agreed, something hilariously funny in this quest for Philby being so assiduously conducted, and reaching so far afield. As I switched my mind from the recruitment of the fishermen and the feeding of the five thousand – sober and matter-of-fact topics compared with my questioner's – I reflected that everything to do with Intelligence infallibly ends in farce.

I first met Philby in about 1935 in the office of the *Review of Reviews*, then being edited by a friend of mine, Wilfrid Hindle. The *Review* had been started by an eccentric English journalist, W. T. Stead, who saw the advantage of piecing together and republishing material which had already appeared. He made a great success of the venture, but after his demise the publication languished, and by the time Hindle took it over, with Philby as his assistant, it was at its last gasp, soon thereafter expiring. Its soul, however, went marching on – across the Atlantic where it underwent a fabulous reincarnation as the *Reader's Digest*. To anyone like myself, ever on the lookout for what Blake calls 'fearful symmetry', it is pleasing to reflect that in some remote degree Philby may be said to have been treading on the heels of Mr DeWitt Wallace.

Philby made no particular impression on me at this first meeting. I just remembered him as a dark, quiet young man; the son, as Hindle told me, of St John Philby, one of those, to me repugnant, English Arabists, of whom there is a long unappetizing line, from Richard Burton to T. E. Lawrence. It is a fact that the Arabs have always made a great appeal to a certain type of middle- and upper-class Englishman, partly, perhaps, because they are given to sodomy – a favourite pursuit at English boarding schools – and in any case have a seeming simplicity of character and directness of manner which contrasted agreeably, in the days of the British Raj and the Palestine Mandate, with the deviousness of Indian Hindus and Israeli Jews. Certainly, Philby had a great regard for his father, though in *My Silent War* he scouts the suggestion that this influenced him much. He does say, though, that Philby senior, had he lived to know about it, would not have taken amiss his son's transfer of allegiance to the Communist side – a rather surprising attitude, one would have thought, for someone who identified himself with an extreme Rightist, if not Fascist, position, to the point that he was actually interned in the war as a subversive under Regulation 18b. Mr Ben-Gurion, it seemed to me, put the matter succinctly and well in a letter I had from him after a long and fascinating television session at the desert kibbutz where he lives in retirement. 'I knew the father of

Kim Philby,' he wrote. 'He was not a pleasant person. If father became a Moslem why should not his son become a Communist?' Exactly!

I have often wondered if Philby senior at some point worked for the Secret Service; he is just the sort of person who might have. The Secret Service anyway was bristling with old cronies from his days in the Indian Political Department, and they, no doubt, helped the son to get in. Philby himself insists that his sole sponsor was Guy Burgess, but it is difficult to believe that even the Secret Service would have accepted without additional support the recommendation of so disreputable and distasteful an individual. However, you never know; a ruling class on the run is capable of every folly; and displays a remarkable perversity in markedly preferring its enemies to its friends. In an almost hysterical passion to avoid the charge of promoting stuffed shirts it quite often prepares its own ruin. It is difficult to think of any other explanation to account for the popularity enjoyed by Burgess in upper-class circles. On the only occasion that I met him, he immediately struck me as unsavoury, untruthful, vain, dirty and rather stupid, though I suppose the credulous might have been dazzled by his fund of anecdotes about his alleged conquests of both sexes and his relations with the great, including Winston Churchill.

The next occasion that I met Philby he was definitely in the Secret Service, and so was I. My own recruitment had come as a result of my friendship with Graham Greene, whose sister worked in the organization. It seemed almost too good to be true when I was suddenly extricated from the infinite tedium of being a corps intelligence officer with little or nothing to do, and told to report to an address in London. Incidentally, this address – Broadway House, almost opposite St James's Park Underground Station – as well as the names of the chief officers in the Secret Service (or MI6, as it is called in wartime), were long considered top secret information even though they had all been given out on the German radio in the early months of the war. Security, in my experience, specializes in putting double padlocks on stable doors after the horses have gone. From a security point of view, information known to be in the hands of the enemy is, like mercy, twice-blessed – it blesseth both those that have it and those that lose it. Nowadays, of course, as a result of Philby's and other disclosures, MI6 personnel have become household words, next in fame only to the denizens of the world of James Bond – their images as reflected in Ian Fleming's sick novels.

My own assignment was to Lourenço Marques in Mozambique or Portuguese East Africa, a place I had not heard of before, and hurriedly looked up in an atlas to find out where it was, and in the *Encyclopaedia Britannica* to gather some information about it. The only fact which remains with me from these scanty researches is that at one point the Portuguese offered to sell the port of Lourenço Marques to the British Government for a million pounds sterling, but Gladstone, I daresay prudently, declined the offer. From my memories of the place it would seem that the proposed price was high. In the nineteenth century the Portuguese Empire seemed on its last legs by comparison with the British and French, and liberal politicians were always considering offering its components to the Germans to keep them quiet. How interesting, and in a way appropriate, that in the twentieth century it should be the only imperial survivor! I was instructed, before leaving for Mozambique via Lisbon (where I was to pick up a diplomatic visa as a bogus vice-consul), to acquaint myself with the various departments of MI6 that I should be serving, and especially Section V which dealt with Counter-espionage overseas. This was how I came into contact with Philby.

Section V at that time (1942) was located near St Albans, an ancient cathedral town, in what once had been a substantial country house. Later Section V was transferred to Ryder Street, in the West End. Philby was in charge of the Iberian Section, which included the Portuguese colonies, and it was to him, therefore, that I first addressed myself. Again, as on the previous occasion, he made no particular impression on me, though his subordinates, as I observed, spoke in strongly adulatory terms of him. I recall two of them especially – Trevor Wilson, a curious, eccentric, lovable individual with whom, subsequently, I had a lot to do, and Tim Milne, a nephew of A. A. Milne, only begetter of Winnie the Pooh, whom I never got to know well, but who advanced steadily in the Service with Philby. For some inscrutable reason, Milne is almost the only MI6 figure whose anonymity is scrupulously observed both in *My Silent War* and in *The Philby Conspiracy*.

The first thing one noticed about Philby in conversation was his truly appalling stutter; it was really shattering. As he struggled to get the words out, his hand would convulsively clench and unclench. Some people say – for instance, his wife Eleanor in her book about their marriage – that sometimes he scarcely stuttered at all. I never had this experience; with me he always stuttered dreadfully – which, for all I know, may indicate that there was always an undercurrent of hostility between us. If so, it was unconscious on my part. On his part – assuming, as he claims, he was already an old-established Soviet agent – it may well have been conscious; my detestation of the Soviet regime as a result of having worked as a newspaper correspondent in Moscow in the early thirties was fairly well-known from my writings on the subject, especially my book, *Winter in Moscow*. Philby's stutter was the worst I have ever known, far worse than Maugham's, which was liable to abate and even disappear in sympathetic company. Once in great trepidation I did a television interview with him – I think the only one that ever was done – and to my great delight and relief we got by almost without his stuttering at all.

To his intimates, and indeed throughout the office, Philby was known as Kim, after Kipling's hero in the book of that name. He had been born in India, and acquired the nickname as a small boy. It is interesting to reflect now that Kipling's Kim also became a professional spy, and we leave him having made the grade and well on the way to a successful career as an Intelligence agent. Such a career was liable to end in Section V of the Secret Service; Philby's immediate superior, Major Felix Cowgill, had served in India, as had Cowgill's immediate superior, Colonel Vivian. So in a sense the fictitious Kim and the real one may be said to have arrived at the same point. Moreover, when Kipling's Kim was engaged in espionage on behalf of the British Raj, the enemy was assumed to be Imperial Russia, whose troops might march any day through the Khyber Pass; his namesake turned the tables and spied on behalf of Soviet Russia to the discomfiture of the British. I have always contended that fiction is a much surer guide to human character and affairs than fact, and urged aspiring politicians to study Shakespeare's *Julius Caesar* in preference to Dr Gallup, and aspiring seducers to turn to *Anna Karenina* rather than Dr Kinsey. Philby is a case in point. If whoever was responsible for MI6's internal security (it is difficult to think of this official without a smile) had read Kipling's *Kim* with care and insight, he might have avoided much subsequent grief and woe.

A good deal has been made of Philby's charm and ability. As far as his charm was concerned, he certainly was a pleasant person, with a winning smile and, as it seemed, an essentially kindly disposition. I think his stutter drew one to him in a protective sort of way – an attitude which probably applied more to women than fellow males. Beneath the show of being a great boozer and fornicator and adventurer, one sensed a terrific vulnerability.

When, as I was given to understand, he was fired from the Secret Service for having had Burgess as a houseguest in Washington, I tried to help him get a job and generally, as P. G. Wodehouse would put it, rallied round. I believe I might do the same thing again if an occasion arose. I cannot in honesty pretend that I feel any great moral indignation about what he has done – more pity than anything. It's such a tawdry, tenth-rate story, especially as he tells it in that terrible dry style which comes of reading and writing government papers. When I read about how pleased he was to get a Soviet decoration to wear beside his Franco one (won when he was a newspaper correspondent in the Spanish Civil War) and his OBE, I felt like bursting into tears. There is, it is true, something very despicable in the callous way he describes unseating and then supplanting Cowgill, who had been particularly kind to him and was a dedicated and conscientious officer to whom we were all beholden. Yet I felt sure that the callousness was to offset acute pangs of contrition. Likewise in the case of the agents he betrayed to the Russians in Albania and elsewhere – it was dirty work for which he was ill-suited. I do not consider Philby a bad man, only a very foolish and weak one. This, as I deduce from her book, is the final judgement of his third wife, Eleanor.

Probably I should feel differently about Philby if I felt differently about Intelligence as a pursuit, but since it seems to me that it is largely fantasy, I cannot take seriously either its alleged successes or the corresponding misdemeanours and betrayals. Supposing there had been no Philby spying for the Russians, would the present Cold War alignment of forces be appreciably different? I doubt it. What did he tell them that was worth knowing? Precious little, I should say: details of the British and American Intelligence and Counter-intelligence setups, as we have had details of the equivalent Russian setup from various defectors – and where has that got us? Even the Albanian operation (which aimed at stimulating a revolt against the country's then Russian satellite regime) was, like that of the Bay of Pigs, ill-conceived and doomed from the start. I, as a matter of fact, had heard about it, so the security can't have been all that hot. In both the United States and Britain expenditure on Intelligence has gone up by leaps and bounds; we spend millions, America spends billions. Are we really the better, or even the more secure for it? Before the 1914-18 War the United States had no Intelligence setup at all, and we had at most a score of ex-Indian Army colonels in London and a few eccentric figures dotted about the world who concentrated their attention on bribing charladies to go through War Office wastepaper baskets, or on seducing the wife of an undersecretary or chef de cabinet in the hope that she might babble state secrets in bed. Now we have great hordes of agents and double agents, phony attachés and passport-control officers, vast archives and complex screening procedures, spy ships and spy aircraft, radio interception and cipher-cracking enterprises. Not even Education, the great mumbo-jumbo of the twentieth century, has produced quite such an edifice of parasitism and pretence.

I cannot say that I got to know Philby well – I wonder if any-one did – but we were on Christian name terms, had meals together occasionally, and I visited his home once or twice. His then wife, Aileen, made a most pleasant impression; she was pretty, sensible, a good but not a doting mother, intelligent rather than intellectual – just the kind of girl I like. She and Philby seemed very happy together; he was quite at his best with his children and in the sunshine of domesticity – the most agreeable form of happiness, discounting the occasional ecstasy of passion or illumination, available to us here on earth. There was, I fancy (one has to be terribly careful in matters of this kind not to mix up hindsight with genuine recollection), a certain disparity between his juvenile notions of 'bohemian' behaviour and her congenital 'respectability'. His ostentatious drinking may well have troubled her – I have no memory of her taking more than moderate amounts of liquor herself – and some of his boon companions were probably little to her taste. It is difficult to think of any wife who would find Burgess as a houseguest other than a pain in the neck. At the same time, she and Philby gave me no sense of strife or strain; all that was nicest and simplest and gayest in Philby came out, it seemed to me, when they were together with their children. What happened subsequently I know only from hearsay. One heard of Aileen becoming chronically ill, and even of mental trouble; she died when Philby's love affair with her successor, Eleanor, was in full swing in Beirut. Eleanor Philby mentions Aileen's death in her book, but does not record that Philby displayed grief or remorse when he heard about it. Aileen at some point may well have got wind of what Philby was up to with the Russians. (Who, living with him, could fail to?) Maybe she died of a broken heart – one more innocent victim in this squalid episode.

Philby's drinking has been much remarked on; it was certainly heavy and habitual. He was fond of dispensing drinker's lore, which I find as tedious as lecher's lore. I recall his elaborate explanation that a chaser of brandy after a pint of beer provided an excellent hangover specific. I never, as it happens, saw him drunk in the sense of passing out or babbling; his stutter, in any case, provided a sort of cutout as far as a tendency for drink to loosen his tongue was concerned. What a joke, incidentally, if his stutter had been adopted as a security device – a notion that assuredly would have appealed enormously to Fleming. Philby's drinking struck me as one more aspect of his essential romanticism and immaturity; he had a Hemingwayesque tendency to adulate crooks and frauds as long as they spoke the language of defiance and violence. I remember one man – a Jewish art dealer named Tommy Harris, now dead – for whom he had an inordinate veneration (and still has to judge by his references to him in *My Silent War*, where he is described as living in his house in Chesterfield Gardens 'surrounded by his art treasures in an atmosphere of *haute cuisine* and *grand vin*'). Harris struck me as a decidedly shady and second-rate individual. War, one must always remember, brings out the juvenile romanticism in everyone. It is the sport of boys, young and old, and is largely conducted by people like Montgomery and Patton who are obvious cases of arrested development. I have always contended that the old *Boys' Own Paper* is a much better guide to war than Clausewitz, let alone Tolstoy's *War and Peace*. As an ageing junior officer I was very conscious of a certain detachment from the boy-scout atmosphere which prevailed in officers' messes, as it did in MI6. Philby just seemed one more example of how the ungrown-up come into their own in wartime, and I accepted him as such. In his war trilogy, Evelyn Waugh has explored with incomparable skill and wry comedy the plight of the middle-aged in mind and body like myself thrown by the accident of war into close companionship with juvenile warriors of all ages.

Looking back and searching my mind for anything in Philby's behaviour which might have alerted me to his duplicity, I can only think of his financial circumstances, which were certainly better than his pay warranted. Though what we were paid was supposed to be secret, we naturally had a pretty good idea of our colleagues' earnings; Philby's grade in Section V of MI6 entitled him, roughly speaking, to the pay and allowances of an army major, with the additional advantage that Secret Service emoluments were not assessed for income tax – a terrific bonanza which spies and their operators used to enjoy in the good old days. Thus Philby's pay was about what I got myself, with some extra allowances when I was abroad, and provided for no more than a decidedly modest middle-class standard of life. His domestic circumstances, as I recall them, were markedly superior to this, and I assumed that either his wife had some private means or his father helped with an allowance. I now know that Aileen had no money of her own, and that Philby senior was himself chronically impecunious. It is generally assumed, and Philby himself implies, that he received no financial reward for his work as a Soviet agent. I doubt this; spy masters always seek to give their men money because accepting it leads to subservience, and Philby, who had expensive tastes and a great need for money, would not have required too much persuasion, I should have thought. We know, in any case, from Eleanor Philby's book, that the KGB provided £4000 a year free of tax for his family in England when he decamped to Moscow. If, as seems to me virtually certain, he was on the Soviet payroll, it would account for his higher standard of life.

Nothing in Philby's conversation ever gave me the notion that he was a Communist zealot, or even particularly interested in politics. I think I can say with confidence that I know what to look for in matters of this kind, and Philby manifested none of the usual symptoms. He was, in fact, rather a boring companion; not particularly well-read or interested in ideas as such, adhering in a general way to the left-wing opinions which were the conventional wisdom of his generation and class, addicted to cricket and the sort of, to me, unfunny humour that I had to grapple with when I became editor of *Punch*. This essential banality of disposition is very apparent in *My Silent War*, which is precisely the sort of book he might have been expected to write on retirement, loaded with honours, after a blameless career as a public servant. All the right complimentary remarks are made about his superiors like the head of the Secret Service in his time, Sir Stewart Menzies, or 'C' as he is always rather absurdly called inside the organization; the original, of course, of Fleming's 'M'. Philby gives a positively sanctimonious impression of dedication to his work, and one has to keep on reminding oneself that however hard he may have exerted himself on behalf of MI6, he was exerting himself even harder on behalf of the KGB. In Intelligence, as in so many other ways, the 1939-45 War was a cockeyed affair, with Philby working for the Russians, and Admiral Canaris, the head of the Abwehr, working for us. I found the Admiral's role, when I learned of it, decidedly disconcerting; it was like hearing that, in what one fondly supposed to be a hard-won victory in a game of football, the goalkeeper on the opposing side had deliberately let the balls through.

Philby's undoubted attractiveness then was not due to any particular gifts or graces of mind or body (though he was quite pleasant looking). There was just something appealing in him; some warmth of disposition to which one responded, something affectionate and aspiring that, one felt, life had stunted. I can see him now seated at his desk, wearing his father's old army tunic, endlessly smoking; shaken from time to time by that devastating stutter which, in its intensity, was almost like a fit; his black eyes bright, but not glowing; I used to think they were the eyes of an animal, a wounded animal. My own strong impression was that he would have chosen, had it been possible, to be a combatant soldier, and I assumed that his stutter had incapacitated him. Of all things he wanted glory, and I suppose he may be said to have found it – of a kind. It happened by chance that shortly after the end of the war I was asked quite casually what I thought of Philby's suitability to remain on in the Secret Service as one of its career officers. It was when they were weeding out the wartime personnel, and, I may add, nearly always making the wrong choices. I said that he had every sort of qualification, in my opinion, except that I detected some strain of violence, something farouche in him which would make me hesitate, if it rested with me, to take him on. It was not a bad judgement.

Without any question Philby's abilities were greatly over-estimated among MI6 personnel. He was, for instance, spoken of with awe as a man who might easily, had he wished, have become editor of *The Times*. Actually, his performance as a *Times* correspondent on the Franco side in the Spanish Civil War was no more than average, and his dispatches from the Middle East after his downfall in the Secret Service were commonplace, though conscientious. Again that terrible banality manifested itself in his style and diction. One of the weaknesses of the Secret Service higher echelons in my day was that they really had very little notion of what the outside world was like, and so tended to have an excessive respect for quite ordinary achievements, like holding down a job as a *Times* correspondent. I found them – especially the ones from the Forces – quite remarkably unworldly and gullible; the most obvious charlatans and frauds easily impressed them. In a way it was very charming, but expensive – in mistakes as well as money.

Philby's most notable talent, as is apparent in *My Silent War*, was for office infighting, something to which all Intelligence services are particularly prone. I often used to reflect that if only we could have directed against the enemy the venom and cunning exercised in interdepartmental warfare, victory would have been ours in no time. In *My Silent War* Philby explains in great detail how he first disposed of poor Cowgill, and then proceeded to get himself appointed to head the new anti-Soviet department (Section IX) set up at the end of the war. It was a shrewdly calculated and wholly successful operation. At one point Graham Greene was involved, in that Philby's plans required that Greene should be promoted. Greene refused, and, indeed, resigned rather than acquiesce; his chief, if not his only, criticism of Philby was that he was unduly given to intrigue in the furtherance of his power mania.

In theory at any rate, this office revolution engineered by Philby was at the behest of his Soviet contacts. So at least he would have us believe. I personally remain skeptical about the whole notion, assiduously put out by Philby and now generally accepted, that he entered the Soviet Intelligence Service in his early thirties, impelled thereto by the spectacle of the great Depression and the treachery of Ramsay MacDonald in forming in 1931 a National Government, predominantly Conservative in composition, thereby reducing the Parliamentary Labour Party, whose leader he had been, to minute proportions, and keeping it out of office for years to come. It is easy to see why this notion appeals now to Philby and his Soviet bosses; in its light the whole episode seems much more creditable than it would if Philby had been seduced to work for Soviet Intelligence while a serving officer in the British Secret Service. Yet I find it very difficult, in the light of his character and temperament, to imagine him dedicating himself to this long-drawn-out deception. It would seem to me that the vaguely Fascist leanings he displayed in his early years were much more likely to have been genuine, derived from paternal influences, than assumed in order to build up cover as a Soviet agent. Authoritarian government appeals to a certain sort of person and is repellent to others; and, as has been shown again and again, those with a taste for it like it in any version, and vice versa. Philby, I should have said, is the classic type to find authoritarianism appealing: ambitious, romantic, weak and violent. As in so many cases, the appeal of the Soviet regime to him is unlikely to have been its Marxist theory, or its utopian aims (the withering away of the State, with the proletariat of the world living happily ever after), but rather its inexorably brutal practice. I never detected in him the faintest indication that he had studied or cared about dialectical materialism, but he constantly betrayed his admiration for ruthless action, whatever its aim and auspices. For instance, he once said to me of Goebbels, when we were discussing the Nazi leaders: 'That's a man I could have worked with.' It was, I'm sure, no idle boast.

Probably Philby himself does not know precisely when his feelings about the USSR under Stalin turned from sympathy to actual allegiance; when his partisanship, from being purely emotional, became 'n the legal sense treasonable – the more so because at some point he must have been functioning as a double agent with the approval of his Secret Service and KGB superiors alike. No one who has not engaged in such practices can form any conception of the blurring of identity and mental confusion involved. One creates a fantasy, and then becomes a part of it; the false ego and the real one become interchangeable, and finally indistinguishable. When I was in Lourenço Marques this happened in a mild degree to me. In the way of espionage I became involved in certain more or less intimate relationships with the local enemy. It was exactly like writing a novel, sent in coded instalments to MI6 and Philby in London. Soon the plot and the characters took charge; fantasy was piled on fantasy for fantasy's own sake, and I should have been hard put indeed to say what precisely was my own role, whether in my own capacity or as an MI6 agent. On my way home through Lisbon in 1943 – after the victory at Alamein, Mozambique ceased to have any strategic importance – I felt an almost irresistible impulse to make my number with the German Embassy there; not from any desire to be a traitor, or to risk my neck in some crazy double-agent venture, but just to embark upon one more level of fantasy. Incidentally, had I committed this imprudence, as I now know, I might well have been received more respectfully than at the time would have seemed possible. Thanks to the researches of Dr David Irving, I have been able to read the reports on me and my activities sent to Berlin from the German Consulate-General in Lourenço Marques. In them I appear enormously more important and formidable than was, in fact, the case. All espionage agents may be relied on thus to enhance the importance of their opposite numbers in order to enhance their own. They are always eager to upgrade one another.

In the last year of the war, I was given the task in Paris of looking over the dossiers of a number of double agents who had worked for us and the Germans, with a view to deciding whether they could be said to have been on our side or the enemy's. It was, I soon realized, an impossible decision to make; since the individuals themselves obviously did not know where their own ultimate loyalties lay (apart from an evident desire, in most cases, to come out finally on the winning side), how could I or any other outsider hope to assess where they stood? Philby must have been in a like situation. No doubt his flight at last to the USSR represented a final decision in favour of the KGB as against the Secret Service, but everything suggests it was actuated more by fear of the consequences of staying than a positive desire to go. Had there not been this occasion for fear I suspect that Philby would still be playing out his fantasy in Beirut in the manner of *Our Man in Havana*, Greene's brilliant study of Intelligence fantasies. It is not for nothing that James Bond became a hero of our time; Fleming's dream figure, with his ferocious appetites, his snob accomplishments, his sadistic propensities, achieves what modern man most craves – the dissolution of his identity. In the climate of ideological conflict the spy is king; from Bulldog Drummond to James Bond, from Kipling's Kim to Kim Philby, is the course our world has run.

Philby, in other words, may be regarded as a real-life James Bond. His boozy amours, his tough postures, his Intelligence expertise are directly related to the same characteristics in Fleming's hero. Take, for instance, the following account by Mrs Eleanor Philby of Philby as lover:

'Whenever we met, in the market café or some other favourite haunt, he slipped under my coffee cup a tiny note written on a flimsy piece of paper, half the size of a playing card – sheets of paper taken from boxes of local cigarettes. These notes marked the tender stages of our relationship. On one day in June 1957, Kim slipped me three *billets doux*, at 11.10 in the morning at Biblos, after lunch at 2.30 in a restaurant overlooking the old Phoenician port, and in a nearby village at 6.30 that evening. The first note read simply: "Deeper in love than ever, my darling. XXX from your Kim"; and later that day it was: "Still deeper. XXX from your Kim"; and later still, as the sun was setting over the sea, it was: "Deeper and deeper, my darling. XXX from your Kim." '

The tone of the messages, Mrs Philby justly observes, 'was often that of a romantic novelette, with only occasionally a note of banter creeping in'. Though Bond would have conducted the operation more expensively and flamboyantly, the epistolary style is very similar; Philby is to Bond, one might say, what Uncle Tom is to Black Power. What Mrs Philby failed to note was that Philby used the same devices as a lover as he did as a spy; the flimsy notes were standard MI6 practice, as were his instructions to her for destroying the notes: 'Please, sweetheart, when the impulse seizes you to destroy this, burn it, put the ashes in a little bottle (preferably Manhattan) and toss the bottle into the sea.'

There must, of course, have been a Rubicon that Philby crossed when he started passing material to the Russians unbeknownst to MI6, receiving, as I believe, relatively substantial money payments in return. When was this? One can only hazard a guess; mine would be: in the war soon after the Nazis invaded the USSR. As is now well-known, quite early on in the war first the Japanese and then the German military and diplomatic codes were cracked, with the result that a great deal of operational and other Intelligence, some of it relating to the Eastern Front, flowed from Bletchley where the job was done. I shall never forget this curious establishment, where I spent a few days. It was almost entirely manned by eggheads of various kinds, many of them markedly eccentric; the atmosphere was strikingly like any university faculty, in the vein of *Who's Afraid of Virginia Woolf?*, with a good deal of bickering, shrill talk and adultery. No one could possibly have guessed, unless in the know, that these weird individuals were making a more substantial contribution to the war effort than whole armoured divisions. Even generals find it difficult to lose battles when they have the enemy's operational orders for the day on their breakfast table, and it was just precisely this that Bletchley provided.

After their midday meal the code breakers commonly threw themselves with great ardour into a game of rounders on the lawn in front of the house where they lived and worked. What a target, I reflected, watching them, for Hitler's bombers! How much more rewarding, had he but known it, than some ostensibly important military installation like GHQ Home Forces, whose loss might have been a positive gain to the Allied side! The Bletchley output relating to Russia was not initially passed on to the Soviet Government on the ground that the security of the source would thereby be jeopardized, although particular items – for instance, the date and place of Hitler's attack on the USSR – were transmitted to Stalin through the British Embassy in Moscow without disclosing how they were obtained. Stalin, needless to say, treated them with contemptuous incredulity. Some Section V officers, I know, considered it disgraceful that valuable Intelligence should thus be withheld from the Russians, or passed to them on terms which invited disbelief. Was it, I ask myself, to rectify this state of affairs that Philby first got into the way of passing MI6 documents to the Russians? It is possible. In the end, I may add, the Russians did get all relevant Bletchley material, routed to them via the 'Lucy' setup in Switzerland, whence it was transmitted to Moscow as having come from dissident German staff officers. I like very much the notion that Stalin, in his old-fashioned way, could never bring himself to trust the Intelligence provided by his British and American allies, but was persuaded to accept the bona fides of an obscure undercover agent in a neutral country.

My course of training before leaving for Lisbon and Lourenço Marques was not arduous; after my visits to Section V and Bletchley I received instruction in the use of secret inks from a large sad-faced man in a house in Chelsea. He taught me to write with a ball-point pen without pressing on the paper, and explained how, if all else failed, a satisfactory secret ink could be made from bird droppings – known in the trade as BS. In Amsterdam, he told me, where he had once been stationed, he had found the birds curiously recalcitrant when it came to providing droppings; he would lure them on to his window ledge with bread crumbs, and they would eat the crumbs and depart, leaving nothing behind. In the end he had found a solution – to take a stroll in the parks which abounded in Amsterdam, and then, when he saw a good cache of bird droppings, drop his handkerchief on it as though by chance and, in recovering his handkerchief, scoop up the bird droppings as well. It was experiences like this which made me wonder whether what was presented to me as MI6 was in reality no more than a façade deliberately set up for deception purposes, and I half expected in due course, when my reliability had been established, to be introduced to the genuine article. Nothing of the sort happened, and by the time I came to leave for Lisbon I had been forced to conclude that the bizarre individuals I had met and the bizarre procedures I had been shown did veritably constitute the far-famed British Secret Service.

In Lourenço Marques I had no direct communications from Philby, though presumably he was responsible for the service messages I received. If so, I cannot say that they betokened any particular efficiency or dynamism on his part. Graham Greene was on the other coast, in Freetown, and we occasionally communicated in cipher, scrupulously using one-time pads – an arrangement that sounds like a personal-hygiene device, but is actually designed to safeguard the security of codes by adding arbitrary numbers to each encoded group. The nature of our exchanges scarcely rated such precautions. I lived in the Polana Hotel, as did my Italian and German opposite numbers – Signor Campini and Dr Leopold Wirtz. Occasionally we would stumble into one another on our way to the dining-room or the lavatory, but otherwise held rigidly aloof. It was a curious existence, seemingly so infinitely remote from the war – which however, we, too, in our own fantastic way, were supposed to be waging. Campini, an ebullient Italian and ardent Fascist, has, I have heard, now fallen on lean times; Wirtz on the other hand, who also in my Lourenço Marques days gave every indication of being a strong Axis man, would appear to have resumed his promising diplomatic career in the service of the German Federal Republic. There was one small link, as it turned out, with Philby; a diplomatic exchange with Japan, which took place in Lourenço Marques while I was there, washed up on our Mozambique shores, among other English diplomats, one Steptoe, who announced in tones of breathless secrecy that he had been working for MI6 in the Far East. I gladly attached him to my minute setup and grew very fond of him – a small and essentially ridiculous little man with a portentous manner and a tremendous sense of self-importance (he was convinced that if he returned to England by sea the Germans would hear of it and send a submarine to take him off), but a kind heart and a certain vein of shrewdness which only added to the Gogol-like comedy of his character. After his return to London he was posted to Section IX, the new anti-Communist department of the Secret Service whose head Philby became. Poor Steptoe! I can just imagine how he irritated Philby who, like all power maniacs, was disdainful of the weak and the absurd. In *My Silent War* he describes with obvious relish how Steptoe was got rid of. By way of compensation Steptoe was made His Britannic Majesty's Minister in the Republic of San Salvador, in whose capital the good man died.

Shortly before leaving Lourenço Marques I decided on an impulse late at night to conclude my Mozambique fantasy with an attempted suicide. Was it an act of despair? Or one more elaboration of the web of deception I had spun? Perhaps neither, or both; to this day I do not know for sure. I took my car to a remote part of the shore where there was a Greek café I sometimes visited, took off my clothes and stepped naked into the sea. First I waded, then swam on and on until I began to feel drowsy. It was the end, I decided, and turned for one more look at the shore. I could see the lights of the Greek café, and suddenly they were welcoming me; I felt as I never had before how marvellous the world was, how marvellous to be alive. It was like Bunyan in reverse; all the trumpets were sounding for me on my own side. With great difficulty I managed to swim back to shallow water, to lurch ashore, find my clothes, dress and make off. Never thereafter have I forgotten, nor could I ever forget, that the world is a home for us where we must live until our true release comes. To cover myself, as in duty bound, I took out my one-time pads and sent off a report of what had happened to London; Dr Wirtz likewise, as I learned from Dr Irving's material, sent off a report to Berlin. Only Graham Greene (by this time working at headquarters under Philby) with his novelist's perception understood that there was more in the episode than met the enciphered eye.

Back in London I saw Philby once or twice, but since I was moved to a liaison job with the French I had little to do with him professionally. He seemed to be flourishing, but Cowgill had begun to show signs of strain, I thought. My liaison duties took me to Algiers and then to Paris, where I lived in the Rothschild mansion in the Avenue de Marigny, requisitioned for the purpose by Lord Rothschild, also serving in Paris as a British Intelligence officer. The house had been occupied during the German occupation by a Luftwaffe officer who, rather to my surprise, had left everything intact. When I mentioned this to M. Felix, in charge in the Avenue de Marigny establishment under all regimes, he smiled and remarked that no doubt the general had reflected that Hitlers come and go but Rothschilds go on for ever.

Though my liaison duties were negligible, I had a spacious office overlooking the Bois de Boulogne, in the Boulevard Suchet where the French *Services Spèciaux* had established themselves. Much elegant Boulevard Suchet furniture, I fear, went into the boilers to keep us from freezing to death that first bitter winter of Paris's liberation. My chief French contact was Jacques Soustelle, who later on was to have so turbulent a political career. I found him a cultivated and agreeable man, and continue to regard him with affection and respect. For the most part I contented myself with trying, sometimes with success, to save suspected collaborationists from the guilty wrath of their compatriots. Looking back now, it seems to me that this was the only useful thing I did in the whole war.

Some time after I had been settled in Paris, Philby paid a visit there, staying with us at the Avenue de Marigny. He and I dined together; as far as I can remember, it was the only social occasion on which there were just the two of us. We had a good dinner and a lot to drink, and then strolled out by the river, feeling, as one does in such circumstances, lighthearted and full of beneficence. I even had a sense of intimacy with Philby – no doubt alcoholically generated – such as I had never experienced before. At one point he indicated a shadowy building where, he said, he had lived with his first wife long ago. It was the first time I had heard that he had been married to someone before Aileen; I learned afterwards she was an Austrian Jewess and Communist militant whom he had met in Austria and married more for her protection than anything else. Then there was a most curious development; he suggested we have a look at the Soviet Embassy in the Rue de Grenelle, and there we duly went. We stood in the road outside the Embassy, and Philby started muttering, to himself rather than to me: 'How shall we ever be able to penetrate this place? How get inside?' – words to that effect. Perhaps I was too tipsy to react properly; I just contented myself with saying that I personally had no intention of even trying, that as far as I was concerned journalism with all its deficiencies seemed a less reprehensible way of earning a living than spying. With that we returned to the Avenue de Marigny, and Philby went off the next morning early.

What did the incident signify? I really have no idea. Was Philby clowning for some obscure purpose of his own? Or working out something in his own mind, the conflict of two loyalties still not wholly and finally resolved? Was I being subjected to some kind of test? Or was there behind the Soviet Embassy's drawn blinds someone else peering out at us, deriving, if not enlightenment, then amusement from the spectacle we presented? Was it for him that the show was put on? I should certainly have reflected, had I been completely sober and in my right mind, that it was, to say the least, highly unprofessional for an important counter-espionage officer like Philby thus to expose himself to his putative enemies. No such thought, I have to admit, occurred to me at the time; I accepted the incident as perfectly normal, and never gave it another thought until I learned of Philby's defection.

It was, presumably, Section IX business which brought Philby to Paris, but I cannot remember discussing it with him. In any case, had he brought it up, my interest would have been but languid; I was heartily sick of espionage, including particularly its jargon ('letter box', 'cutout', etc.), and longed to be shut of it. Thenceforth I occasionally received queries from London relating to Communist matters for transmission to the French. They were mostly, as I recall, of a very elementary nature; one that particularly amused Soustelle asked for the address of French Communist headquarters – which, as Soustelle pointed out, could have been obtained more readily from the Paris telephone directory. There was also an eccentric French colonel who provided me with a lot of information purporting to reveal Communist infiltration at a very high level in the then government. This I duly sent on to London, receiving in reply a note from Philby in his own hand to the effect that it was clearly nonsensical, and recommending me to consign any further communications of the kind to the waste-paper basket. Philby's estimate may well have been correct; on the other hand, it may not, and I daresay I should have looked further into the matter, though I may plead in my own defence that the French *Services Spèciaux* were at least as infiltrated by Communist agents as MI6, and that anything coming into or going out of the Boulevard Suchet, I am sure, was sped on its way to the Rue de Grenelle.

After the war I occasionally heard of Philby, mostly from Dick Brooman-White, a charming and sensitive MI6 figure who subsequently became a Conservative Member of Parliament for a Scottish constituency. He was one of Philby's most devoted admirers, recounting his doings with a distinct note of awe in his voice. Incidentally, the three authors of *The Philby Conspiracy* are hopelessly wrong about Brooman-White, whom they present as a tough, moneygrabbing, right-wing politician. Nothing could be further from the truth; he was diffident to a fault, comfortably off himself and almost childishly disinterested where money was concerned, and – as I often had occasion to point out to him – disastrously prone to a sentimental liberal outlook. His hero worship of Philby, like that of so many others, arose out of a romantic temperament; he saw Philby as a kind of Elizabethan in a world full of little prudent men, and he quite failed to realize that Philby's swashbuckling qualities were born, like his apprecia-tion of them, of highly twentieth century longings and frustra-tions.

It was Brooman-White who first told me that Philby had come to grief in Washington through having harboured Burgess, and who enlisted my help in finding him work as a journalist when, as must inevitably happen, he was sacked from the Secret Service. Before going ahead I asked Brooman-White for an assurance that there was nothing against Philby other than imprudence, and received it, I am sure in the utmost good faith. The notion, I was told, that Philby had tipped off Maclean that his exposure as a Soviet spy was imminent, thereby facilitating his escape with Burgess, was nonsensical. On that understanding I tried to get him taken on by *The Daily Telegraph*, whose deputy-editor I then was, the idea being to send him to India; when that failed, I wrote to David Astor, proprietor and editor of *The Observer*, explaining how Philby came to be needing employment, and suggesting that he would be well worth taking on. While this was afoot I saw Philby once or twice; he struck me as being decidedly subdued, which was scarcely surprising in the circumstances, and I was touched to find that he had already started reading up about India on the assumption that *The Daily Telegraph* job might come off. When Harold Macmillan, as Foreign Secretary, gave him a clean bill in the House of Commons, and he brilliantly vindicated himself at a press conference of his own, I was delighted and rejoiced with Brooman-White, who told me there was no pressing financial problem, as the Secret Service had provided an ample golden handshake. This strengthened my conviction that Philby's innocence was assured; I could not believe that even the Secret Service would provide generous severance pay to someone still open to a charge of treason. When I heard from Brooman-White that Philby was again working for the old firm in the Middle East I assumed it had now been finally settled, after exhaustive inquiry, that without any possibility of doubt his association with Burgess was purely personal, and that he had no hand in helping Burgess and Maclean to flee to the USSR. Philby's own flight from Beirut proved how false these assumptions were. When I heard of it I tried without success to get in touch with Brooman-White, and learned soon afterwards that he, too, had died.

In *My Silent War* Philby gleefully described how he took us all in. It does not make pleasant reading. After all, it is the easiest thing in the world to deceive well-wishers; one believes one's friends, and if they lie to one the chances are their lies will be believed. In Washington, for instance, Philby was well-liked, and naturally his American associates took his loyalty and reliability for granted; that terrible system whereby, in Communist and other totalitarian countries, everyone is suspect and required continuously to demonstrate their innocence has not yet, thank God, been adopted in America or Western Europe. Occasional Philbys are the price we pay for working still on the assumption that our friends and colleagues are honest, truthful and loyal. This by no means excuses the lamentable inadequacy of MI6's screening procedures, or the imbecilic credulity displayed in dealing with Philby by senior personnel who were in a position to know better. Yet I must say, speaking for myself, if I have to choose between freedom and security I will always choose freedom – the more so because history shows that security purchased with freedom is in the long run not even secure.

In London in the war we saw the beginnings of what was to

become the awesome CIA; Harvard dons, military and naval misfits, linguists of various categories, from professors of Sanskrit to tourist couriers and travelling salesmen, nested under the eaves of MI6, studying that crazy structure in order in due course to be able to construct an even crazier one of their own. Philby, I remember, took the greatest possible interest in this development, as though he foresaw the benefits that would accrue to him personally, and to the cause of espionage throughout the world. I myself was correspondingly saddened – like watching some sweet young ardent virgin disappear through the portals of an old-established house of ill fame. Things have gone Philby's way; espionage has undergone a fantastic development everywhere; not even the electronics industry has expanded at such a rate. What is more, as always happens in such cases, espionage has developed its own trade unionism and its own brand of loyalty. There is more in common, one feels, between the CIA, the KGB and MI6 than there is between any one of these organizations and the society it is supposed to be servicing. In that sense, when Philby said that, for him, going to Moscow was going home, it may be taken as signifying a move from a branch office to headquarters – a move which, for him, involved dismissing his American wife and setting up briefly with Melinda Maclean, who had followed her English diplomat husband to Moscow.

There is nothing in the millions of words which have by now been written about the Philby affair (including Philby's own, and these) which sheds any appreciable light on what went on inside his mind. The reason may well be that nothing went on there at all; that he proceeded mindlessly, like a somnambulist. I do not see him thinking things out; he belongs to the category of man of action, and is no intellectual. This is the conclusion of Professor Hugh Trevor-Roper (another MI6 old boy) in a sparkling piece which appeared in the sometime CIA publication, *Encounter*. The period of Philby's greatest activity as a Soviet spy, Trevor-Roper points out, was during the worst excesses of Stalinist terrorism and the Nazi-Soviet Pact. It seems inconceivable, he argues, that anyone actuated by serious and thought-out ideological considerations should have been able to absorb these monstrous episodes without one squeal. Another gloss is provided by John Le Carré in his introduction to *The Philby Conspiracy*. He sees the whole thing as an Establishment misdemeanour, an old school-tie operation, with everyone covering up for Philby because he had been to the right school and spoke with the right accent. I should say myself that almost the precise reverse was the case.

Philby, as I see it, represents not the Establishment's strength but its decrepitude; he was its sanctified Judas, its chosen betrayer. Far from being the Establishment's favourite son because he seemed to conform to its code, it was the other way round – because he was so contemptuous of Establishment ways of thought and behaviour, so open in his preference for a Burgess over a Colonel Vivian, for 'X', 'Y', and 'Z' over 'C'. Civilizations, like individuals, in their decrepitude develop a death wish, which makes them seek to encompass their own destruction, by damning their friends and lauding their enemies, by advancing the causes which seek their ruin and impeding those which might safeguard their interests; by promoting moral squalor with a view to inducing inertia and indifference. I see Philby quite simply as an instrument – possibly a largely unconscious instrument – of this process.

[1968]

James Bond

Ian Fleming had very clear notions about what Bond had to be and do to endear himself to eighteen million readers. He knew the requisite ingredients for a dish to set before them – money, sex and snobbishness, beaten into a fine rich batter, with plenty of violence to make it rise in the pan, then served hot and flambé with Sade flavouring, and washed down by a blood-red wine.

A Nightmare

There is a nightmare which often assails me. I imagine myself waking up one morning and finding that England has become overnight a monolithic, totalitarian state, without anyone noticing; without revolution of the Left or of the Right, or any large constitutional controversy or last stand by defenders of individual liberty.

Wax To Wax

What glory remains for a man who is exhibited as a wax-work at Madame Tussaud's? Groping about in the dark there I stumbled against someone about my own height and found he was me. The moment of recognition was fateful for both of us. You! ... You! The only difference between us was that he kept his ground, remaining *in situ*, whereas I hurried shame-facedly away. Now I often think of him standing there and woodenly surveying a sort of turning cylinder which momentarily illuminates things in his (my?) past – a fat baby, a plump boy, an earnest youth in Indian *kadi*, a soldier of sorts, a wizened telly sage, etc., etc.; surely a one-man waxwork show rather than anyone's life, least of all mine. So, good luck to you, *mon semblable* (as T. S. Eliot might have put it), and continue to enjoy the company of all those interesting people you've been thrown amongst. Like an air-hostess, or even – no kidding – the face behind the guichet in the ticket office of an underground station, or one of those hand-of-officer-only secretaries in MI6, no doubt you are accustomed to saying that you like your job because you 'meet such interesting people'.

Dear Doppelgänger, it's not just that you meet interesting people; you live among them. Looking fixedly at your back is a massive plaster De Gaulle who occasionally bursts into speech – that rumbling, unforgettable voice ever delectably in your ears. Then, on one side are the Burtons, 'For ever warm and still to be enjoyed/For ever panting, and for ever young'; their transplant loves undying in their breasts, an umbrella protecting them from the rain which falls on the just and unjust alike – but not on them. On the other side, Twiggy – who else? – in delicate china clay at her ablutions. (Ah! not in wax, my heart, for fear our fiery appetites, inflamed by your limpid eyes and scrawny limbs, should daily melt you down.)

Across the way, Frank Sinatra, in a wineglass and wearing such a grin! – a mere slip of a boy of some fifty summers, magnificently unprepared for the long littleness of death. And Cassius Clay, pirouetting like Nureyev (also present). And Robert Kennedy – was there ever such a broth of a boy as Bobby, even younger than Frank (in his middle forties), even more magnificently unprepared, just a kid, with a kid's adventurousness, tousled head, impulsive ways; a kid-Senator, maybe a kid-President? Goody goody, goody!

Sombre old Hitchcock taking a shower, Nobby Stiles on the run, glittering Cordobes tossed in the air by a non-existent bull, and, of course, the Beatles, done in colour by Scarfe – dear bulbous boys, full of noises, sounds and sweet airs that give delight and hurt not. All 'Heroes – Live' (as the company are called), and you, old alter ego, one of them. What an honour! If only I could borrow you from time to time, to go on the telly for me, sit through a literary lunch, deliver a lecture, write a review of Miss Iris Murdoch or Svetlana Hallelujah, be Rector of Edinburgh University, and advise the students on family planning. I am a birth pill. Anyway, I'll tell you one thing – your wax heart is all your own, not to be donated to anyone, not even to Mme du Barry down below breathing so convincingly through the ages; nor received from anyone, not even from Jomo Kenyatta, also down below, standing among the captains and the kings. 'My true love hath my heart, and I have hers'; 'Maid of Athens, e'er we part,/ Give, oh! give me back my heart;/ But since that has left my breast,/ Take, oh take, oh take the rest' – this to include kidneys, liver, testicles and any other odd organs.

How were you made? How did you come to be? Well, the eyeballs were matched from a large selection on a tray; likewise the white thatch, little tufts mingled with my thin thatch to get the exact equivalent. As we're both in loose-fitting macintoshes, the anatomy between neck and calf scarcely matters, but the head does – battered old cranium minutely measured with calipers, and all the little pits and abrasions carefully reproduced; tints and bags and scars and discolourations likewise. Stringy neck, lean shanks, hands, ankles and feet, all done in wax more or less accurately. Then the clothes. A slight embarrassment here; somehow picking out a shirt, socks, shoes and tie for my wax sibling irresistibly reminded me of those people I noticed once when I was hanging about outside Forest Lawn in Los Angeles, discreetly bringing along bundles of clothes, lingerie etc., especially made backless for convenience and economy, to adorn the cadavers of Loved Ones.

Leaving the Other One (as Mrs Webb used to call Sidney) upstairs to wait his (our?) turn to be lit up and say his piece, then relapsing into darkness and silence while Twiggy, Sinatra, Cordobes and the others had their turns, till his (ours?) came round again – leaving him, I ventured among the other waxworks, all silent and immobile in the old Tussaud style. In the Grand Hall the government, some seated and some standing; Mr

Wilson, it seems, having needed to be redone quite a number of times owing to changes brought about in his phiz as a result of being Prime Minister – some additional wax around the jowls, a tightening up of the corners of the mouth, something about the eyes that required adjustment.

The interesting thing is that great ones, actual or potential, are wax anyway; nature seems to have made them so in preparation for their subsequent greatness. Thus Jenkins is unmistakable wax, whereas Gordon Walker, you feel, would never melt down even in a fiery furnace. Our party bosses looking for their lamas should look for wax and they'd never go astray. Macmillan – pure wax; Maudling likewise; whereas in, for instance, Hogg's case the iron – or maybe just flesh – has entered into his wax, while Powell might almost be a man.

As for the Royals – pure wax every one of them. They really shine in Madame Tussaud's; only the Duke of Edinburgh, I thought, looked a bit wilted, as though he was melting inside his admiral's uniform. He is, I gather, due for a refit anyway. Snowdon, Ogilvy, the young Duchess of Kent, wax to their fingernails, and, of course, the Queen herself – radiant wax. I suspect that the Royals like being on show more than the rest of us. They're to the wax born; in their case, as I should suppose, life in Madame Tussaud's is to a great extent indistinguishable from life elsewhere; the whole tableau could be moved to Windsor, and they substituted in Baker Street, with no one any the wiser.

Apart from the Royals, one may note among the waxworks a terrific levelling process – the wax is the wax for a' that. Attlee, Ramsay MacDonald, Gaitskell, scarcely to be distinguished from Asquith, Monty and Nkrumah (incidentally still among those present; a tiny crumb of comfort, I daresay, in his long, lonely exile). The writers are rather a disappointing lot – nothing beyond Maugham, and artists and musicians pretty well non-existent. Surely Picasso would make a Hero – Live, and Marshall McLuhan; especially him, flashing out his wisdom in coloured psychedelic rays.

The clerics stand up well; waxmen all, though Newman, I thought (it may be just a personal partiality), with faint traces of humanity breaking through the wax. The soldiers also excellent, and the coloured folk – a fine Emperor of Abyssinia and Obote; Gandhi less impressive; but, oh! my goodness, what a splendid Ayub Khan! Nelson on his deathbed, and Napoleon – the original Mme Tussaud's own masterpiece, piously preserved – greatly to be admired. By the time I had been through the Battle of Trafalgar my spirits were restored, and I could think with relative equanimity of that sinister double upstairs, even though I knew I was absolutely certain sooner or later to humiliate him in the eyes of the other Heroes – Live by getting myself praised by John Gordon or written up in the *Church Times*.

Down below in the cellars there's a sort of wax abattoir, with spare Wilson and Heath heads about the place, and Sophia Loren's torso, and Gandhi's leg – a sight to rejoice a transplant surgeon's heart. There's even Isadora Duncan's thigh and Dr Ramsey's shoulders, with many another treasure. How long, I wonder, before I get relegated to this slag-heap of notoriety? They're all the time taking in and throwing out; scarcely a day passes but someone's melted down to make room for someone just made. I doubt if I'll last long; before long I'll be a Hero – Dead, and then just dead. From wax to wax, oh! oblivion, where is thy sting? Meanwhile the public continue to pour in and stare. It might be supposed that what with telly and the colour supplements wax would lose its appeal. Not so. Only the Chamber of Horrors, as I learn, is less of a draw since the death penalty was abolished – an interesting commentary on the larger world of wax in which we live.

[1968]

Marilyn Monroe

I once asked Arthur Miller what it was like being married to a sex symbol. He said that, in his eyes, Marilyn Monroe was no such thing, but very much an individual woman who happened to be his wife. Then I ran into him in a Harlem restaurant on the night of the last presidential election. His marriage to Marilyn had just bust up and he looked pretty miserable. It occurred to me then one might write a contemporary version of the Sleeping Princess in reverse – the Waking Princess, in which the arc lights under which she lies keep her awake, until a fairy prince comes along, turns them off and she falls asleep in his arms. Miller tried to do just that, but succeeded only momentarily in dimming the ever-watchful lamps. She had to find more effective means of extinguishing them. Alistair Cooke, as usual, had the best comment:

This orphan of the ruthless City of the Angels at last could feel no other identity than the one she saw in the mirror: a baffled, honest girl forever haunted by the nightmare of herself, 60 ft tall and naked before a howling mob.

Newzak

It is often said nowadays that thanks to our mass-communication media – especially television – people are better informed than ever before and so harder to deceive. They see for themselves what is going on in the world, it is argued – for instance, in Vietnam; they even see Senator Robert Kennedy just after he has been assassinated, with his grief-stricken family and associates gathered tragically round him. Whereas formerly only a small privileged minority were in the know, now everyone is, with the result that it isn't possible any longer to throw dust in their eyes.

Isn't it just? Television, I should say, *is* dust and viewers' eyes are full of it. What is seen on the screen, what purports to be reality, is not reality at all but a fantasy or legend, served up, as it were, oven-ready and daisy-fresh; confectioned with ever greater skill and celerity. It is Instant Legend, brought to you in living colour – the blood redder than red, the grass greener than green. Within a stone's throw of where Senator Kennedy was struck down in Los Angeles there must have been at least six studios where shots were likewise ringing out and bodies slumping to the ground as his did. Only in their case, unlike his, when the mystic word 'Cut!' was pronounced the dead rose up, and a little water cured them of their wounds. In Senator Kennedy's case, there was no rising up; the blood was real, though in living colour it looked just like the other. For him 'Cut!' was only pronounced at Arlington Cemetery.

It used to take centuries for a legend to establish itself; from the Crucifixion to the Holy Blood miraculously liquefying once a year in Bruges might be a thousand years: now it happens overnight. Senator Kennedy's halo sprouted in a matter of hours; before one's very gaze he was transformed from a presidential candidate avid for votes, and in his quest for them pouring out money and speech-writers' rhetoric without stint, into a martyred saint who had laid down his life for the poor and the oppressed.

Our Prime Minister, as usual, struck the right note; the Senator, he said, had died for democracy. So, I suppose, in a manner of speaking he had; it was his advocacy of arms for Israel, with an eye to the important Jewish vote in New York, which inflamed his Jordanian Arab assassin. If that is democracy, he may be said to have died for it.

It is to the fabricating of Instant Legend in all its different aspects that the media are dedicated. Day by day they churn it out, in still and moving pictures, in spoken, and, to a decreasing extent, written words. The part of the written word in this process, already becoming minimal, is likely in due course to disappear altogether, as one sees very clearly in America, where newspapers, like prehistoric monsters, get weightier (in every sense) and fewer all the time. Soon, following the railways, they will become extinct, though doubtless the Smithsonian in Washington, DC will display a few choice specimens – among others, the great, jumbo *New York Times* Sunday edition, for sure. In this connection, I may mention that the Smithsonian already displays as a precious antiquity the teleprompter version of Eisenhower's speech at the first inauguration. It was an exhibit which I observed, attracted a good deal of attention, the enormous platitudinous words on the fat roll of yellow paper exercising some weird fascination.

This fabrication and presentation of Instant Legend amounts to a sort of Newzak, comparable with the Muzak which endlessly plays in American hotels, lifts, airports and other public places, including jet planes high up in the stratosphere. Muzak consists of tunes and musical compositions all mixed up together to form a flabby, shapeless, sickly, interminable wash of sounds and sweet airs; a musical drooling, unidentifiable except for occasional recognizable snatches and echoes. Newzak likewise is an interminable wash of news, with occasional recognizable fragments of happenings. It takes up more and more time on American radio and television. Indeed, there are flourishing radio stations which transmit Newzak round the clock, and nothing else, largely for the benefit of motorists, who switch it on as an alternative to pop music when they are driving along the freeways. They take it in drowsily, as it might be some crooner twanging away; Paris, West Berlin, Biafra, Vietnam, floating into their minds and then out again, interspersed, of course, with the ads – it's richer, it's warmer, it's better – delivered in that ingratiatingly persuasive voice to be heard in every language everywhere.

On the television, naturally, things are done on a grander scale.

Cronkite in living colour; likewise Huntley and Brinkley, so that you can see the very veins on their noses, and even the soft colourful insides of their mouths when they happen to open them rather wider than usual. (I found myself looking into the inside of Martin Luther King's mouth when a very close close-up of him holding forth was shown within minutes of his assassination.) These pundits intone Newzak like priests each evening, every now and again breaking off for a 'message', this being the consumer aspect of Newzak; an integral part of it nonetheless, which we might call Conzak. Thus the Abbé Cronkite will be telling us about student rioting at the Sorbonne, and then, just at the most exciting moment, switch us over to an attractive young couple by a waterfall both puffing away with evident satisfaction at a particular brand of cigarette. The sunshine, the sound of the water, Muzak gently playing, the girl lightly clad, the man bronzed and fit – whatever will they be up to when they stub out their cigarettes? Before we can find out, we're back at the Sorbonne, with the Abbé in his most incantatory voice filling us in about the latest developments there.

This alternation of Newzak with Muzak and Conzak goes on for an hour or so, and may well in time come to fill all the evening viewing hours; perhaps in the end, like the Radio-Newzak shows, go on round the clock, so that at any moment, day or night, Tele-Newzak will be available, with a whole succession of Abbé Cronkites, indistinguishable from one another, working in shifts. It might be thought that this would set a strain on the reporters and camera crews out in the field collecting material for Newzak, but I don't believe so. Already a close viewer (if there are any such) may notice that, for instance, the same Vietnam shots make frequent appearances, and as time goes on stock material for any given situation will be increasingly drawn on, I am sure. In fact, I anticipate a Newzak bank which will suffice for all but the most unforeseeable contingencies. As it is, footage gets used again and again in compilation TV programmes. (There are shots of Jarrow hunger marches and of trade unionists marching under a banner in the General Strike, which have become as familiar inside the trade as pictures of Highland cattle used to be in seaside boarding houses when I was young.)

Come to that, why have the happenings at all when filmed versions of them will do perfectly well instead? When I was in Israel last autumn the authorities there were busy filming a lively reconstruction of the recent fighting in Jerusalem. Then what's the necessity for the original fighting? I asked. Why not, instead of going to war, arrange for their own Newzak in which they are the victor? Then they'd never need to fight. It seemed like a good idea.

The result of all this, of course, is that the ordinary citizen gets ever further separated from reality. The world he lives in is increasingly one of fantasy whose living colours make the actual earth's seem drab; whose drama is for his living-room, not for living; whose loves, like the ones of Keats's Grecian Urn, are 'For ever warm and still to be enjoyed./ For ever panting and for ever young'. In the end fantasy takes over. He can no longer distinguish between life and the screen (I see in the latest top 10 ratings that *The Saint* and the Kennedy Assassination tie for ninth place). His rulers belong to a Western – sometimes actually, like Governor Reagan. Instant Legend possesses him wholly; he shall have Newzak wherever he goes. Well was the camera originally named obscura. It is the ego's very focus, with all the narcissism of the human race concentrated into its tiny aperture. It advances upon one in a television studio like some ferocious monster, ravening and bloodshot eyed. Of all the inventions of our time it is likely to prove the most destructive. Whereas nuclear power can only reduce us and our world to a cinder, the camera grinds us down to spiritual dust so fine that a puff of wind scatters it, leaving nothing behind.

[1968]

Obituaries

I have always enjoyed writing obituaries almost more than any other kind of journalism. What is more pleasurable than to begin: 'We deeply regret to announce the death of . . .' and then go on to expatiate upon the civic virtue, kindly generous disposition and discerning mind of some portentous public figure still out and about, seemingly with many more years of active life before him. One always had a vague hope that perhaps it might serve to abbreviate his days. Alas, in my experience, it nearly always works the other way; just preparing someone's obituary seemed to make him immortal.

My True Love Hath My Heart

There is a story going around (it might even be true) of a donor who was lined up for a heart-transplant operation. The recipient, however, at the last moment decided against having a transplant, and died; the putative donor was recently discharged from hospital. This certainly could happen. As everyone now knows, only a living heart can be transplanted, so the donor cannot be dead in the hitherto accepted sense. Thus the fact must be faced that heart transplanting amounts essentially to experimenting with human beings, as has hitherto been done with animals – especially dogs. It is highly significant that the ice should have been broken for such experimentation in South Africa.

I raised this question on a television programme with Dr Christiaan Barnard himself. Why, I asked him, had the first heart-transplant operation been conducted in his hospital in Cape Town? Was it because the surgeons and equipment there were better than anywhere else? Or, as I believed, because the vile doctrine of apartheid devalued life itself, turning all our bodies into carcasses fit for experiment. The question was ill received. Dr Barnard evaded it; the twenty or so distinguished doctors on the set with me barracked, and one of them got up to dissociate them all from my ill-chosen observations. Afterwards I was accused of bringing politics into a discussion about medicine and ethics. A number of letters I received in connection with the programme were more understanding – one particularly, which related to a doctor who had worked in South Africa and then decamped because, as he put it, the prevailing attitude to the black African patients was veterinary rather than medical.

It is, indeed, the moral rather than the political implications of apartheid which make it so hateful. Politically speaking, it amounts to rule by a white oligarchy, who no doubt will in due course be succeeded by a black oligarchy, as has happened in all the former African dependencies. The world today is largely governed by entrenched oligarchies, whether party machine-men, money-men, communist *apparatchiks* etc., etc. The replacement of one oligarchy by another can be exciting, and raise extravagant hopes, especially in the young, but when the dust has settled and the rhetoric spent itself, there are the same old police, the same old prisons and the same old cant. When the anarchists marched with their black flags in a procession in Paris led by party-line communists like Aragon, I remembered how Kropotkin was given a state funeral in Leningrad when he died there in 1921. The procession passed the prison where his followers had already been incarcerated. Some of them were able to get their arms through the bars and salute his coffin, loaded with flowers, as it passed. It was the last anarchist demonstration ever to be permitted in the USSR.

How sinister that the South African achievement which has won esteem everywhere should be the very one that most exemplifies the true moral horror of apartheid! How disturbing that drawing attention to this should so enrage, not so much the upholders of apartheid, as those who ostensibly oppose it on the highest ethical grounds! The really terrible thing about apartheid is that it reduces the status of human souls, in Christian terms all equally dear to their Creator and made in His Image, to two categories – the driver and the driven. Seen so, their mortal shape deserves no particular respect. It can veritably be regarded as a collection of spare parts, to be sliced off and grafted on as required. In South Africa Dr Barnard could chance his arm without fear of serious opposition; in California and Texas – where the moral climate comes nearest to South Africa's – they could follow suit. London came next, and soon, we may be sure, the knives will be out, and the quest for donors be on, all over the place. Then factory farming and the broiler house will loom up as our human lot and way of life, as the dark visions of the future of an Orwell and an Aldous Huxley have envisaged.

The most ardent advocates of heart transplants are prepared to admit that there will never be enough donors in the foreseeable future for the operation to be available for more than a minute proportion of those who might benefit from it. This is even taking into account all that the roads offer on a bright weekend – a fruitful source of spare organs, as could be gathered from an aside when Dr Barnard was on the prowl for a donor. For the moment, it was said, no one suitable had shown up, but over the weekend they might have better luck. Properly organized, the roads should yield quite a harvest of serviceable spare parts, in flesh as well as metal. Nothing wasted on our motorways this weekend! Moreover, the possibility is bound to come under consideration of using the organs of incurables to service productive citizens. After all, imbeciles have hearts and kidneys – often quite good ones. Since they cannot be fitted with new brains, why not put their organs to good use?

One wonders on what basis the fortunate recipients are to be chosen. Presumably, in America millionaires would have first call, followed by the luminaries of show business; in Russia, the party hierarchy, followed by spacemen and nuclear physicists. Fitting ex-president Eisenhower with a new heart was, it appears, seriously considered. It was a pity in a way that this need for one did not coincide with Senator Robert Kennedy's assassination. Eisenhower with a Kennedy heart would have been a very powerful ticket. In this country one scarcely knows. Leaving aside the royal family, probably some weird protocol would prevail, with the Archbishop of Canterbury, the Lord Chancellor and the Earl Marshal heading the queue, and Lord Thomson and Mr Clore able to jump it.

Another question I tried, without success, to raise with Dr Barnard was that of the priorities involved. Can it be seriously maintained that the dedication of such rare skills and resources to protracting the life of a middle-aged Cape Town dentist for a few extra months or years can be justified in a continent where doctors and medical supplies are so woefully lacking? Doctors themselves have spoken out about this. Even in England, as we all know, patients sometimes have to wait an inordinate time for life-and-death operations, and hospital staff and accommodation are desperately short. Surely the resources tied up for heart transplants are out of all proportion to what has been, or may be, achieved in the way of advancing medicine's true aims – to heal the sick and alleviate suffering. So far the chief result of the transplants has been to advertise the transplanters in a highly distasteful and unprofessional manner, and to raise hopes in sufferers from heart complaints which can never be realized.

I have in honesty to admit that I feel in myself – as I know others do – a deep, instinctive repugnance for this spare-part surgery which is not capable of a wholly rational explanation. Such feelings, I am well aware, can be, and have been, dismissed as mere obscurantism and atavism. Yet the feeling of revulsion persists. It is to do with a sense that all creation pre-eminently deserves respect – the animals, the plants and trees and grass, the folds of the hills and the sweep of the plains, the very stones and soil, and especially Man. That our present way of life is carrying us in the opposite direction – towards using creatures and crops and one another without respect; greedily, arrogantly, bulldozing out whatever stands in our way, breeding weird animal grotesques for our meat, subordinating crops, fruits, the forests and the water springs, everything, to our purposes without reference to nature and its exigencies.

Somehow, to me, the heart transplants are part of this process. Man trying to grasp at some kind of crazy renewal of himself – of heart, of kidney, of liver. Toying with the notion, perhaps, deep in his unconscious of reanimating his waning fertility. Envisaging, even, a self-induced immortality. Living for ever, like an old vintage car – each part replaceable, even the battery or headpiece – as it wears out. Man achieving everlasting life, not because his soul is immortal and belongs to eternity, but because his body can continue to exist in time till the end of time. What an immortality that would be! It recalls Swift's terrible account of the Struldbrugs, those melancholy creatures of the Kingdom of Laputa, who, unable to die, spend their days envying the dead.

[1968]

Apologia Pro Vita Sua

I am 65 this year, which means that I qualify for the old age pension and enter the NTBR (Not To Be Resuscitated) belt. On the one hand, a grateful state will, if I stop working, provide me with a modest competence, and, on the other, should I fall seriously ill, some doctor, or even nurse, will decide whether I rate the attentions requisite to keep me alive. As prices go on rising and the value of money declines (as, it seems to me, must inevitably happen), it will become increasingly difficult to support life on an old age pension however abstemious one's ways, and, to judge from a telly-encounter I had the other day with Dr Christiaan Barnard and the flower of our medical profession, the chances that any of them would strive officiously to protract my few remaining years would seem to me to be slight indeed.

This prospect, I can say in honesty, does not appal me. I expect for a while yet to keep such wits about me as will prevent dependence on the state's munificence, and to go on evading a considered medical execution. I have never found death particularly frightening and, following Pascal's famous wager, incline to bet on its having some sequel. In any case, as Pascal points out, should this prove not to be the case, one will never be called upon to pay up.

What gives me more apprehension than considering the future is looking back on the past. As a communicator, or vendor of words (St Augustine's term), have I, I ask myself, shed more darkness than light? Have I, in the dear words of the *Book of Common Prayer*, followed too much the devices and desires of my own heart? They are difficult and rather dreadful questions. These contemporary, mass-communication media whose servant I have been are liable to take over the communicator, to re-vend the vendor; Marshall McLuhan had a great moment of insight with his 'the medium is the message'. When one takes a pen in one's hand one has only one's own vanity, deceitfulness and vainglory to contend with; speaking into a microphone, or standing before a camera, one has all mankind's. The clapperboard claps, the voice cries 'Action!' and, like a flower unfolding in the sun, the ego expands.

The first thing I remember about the world – and I pray it may be the last – is that I was a stranger in it. This feeling, which everyone has in some degree, and which is, at once, the glory and the desolation of *homo sapiens*, provides the only thread of consistency that I can detect in my life. Christian brass today, from Lambeth to Woolwich, and on into the canonries and archdeaconates of the remoter dioceses, tend to condemn the feeling as unduly pessimistic, though to me it seems the most optimistic of all attitudes – almost to the point of insanity – and the one that most clearly emerges from the New Testament. I cannot myself imagine a more fearful fate for our species than that they should so habituate themselves to their earthly circumstances as to be finally contented with them, or a more sublime one than they should continue till the end of time to peer into the Cloud of Unknowing.

In my early days this sense of being a stranger was closely related to political zealotry; the Left is for strangers, who persuade themselves that the causes they espouse are on behalf of the weak against the strong, of the poor against the rich. They sing their Magnificat lustily, only to discover that the humble and meek, exalted, become mighty in their turn, and so fit to be put down. In my case, the discovery was dramatically made in the course of a journalistic stint in Moscow; the spectacle of all my heroes abasing themselves before a great tyrant, and purporting to justify all his doings and all his works, cured me of hero worship for ever. I understood then how it came about that the kingdoms of the earth are in the devil's gift, and why the founder of the Christian religion declined them.

It was not just that a particular regime had been discredited in my eyes, and a particular set of hopes and desires shown to have been fraudulent. The whole notion of progress died on me, and I saw our way of life based on it as crazy and hollow – a death-wish inspired slide, into total fantasy; getting richer and stronger and wiser, moving faster and further, pursuing happiness ever more avidly, and leading all mankind into the same pursuit. Where the riches? – in the Pools. And the strength? – in the sky. Where the wisdom? – on a screen. Whither the movement? – into space. And the happiness? – in a pill, or soaked up in blotting paper. As for mankind – here, we watch our coloured dreams come true, and over there they count their ribs in cold perplexity; in the one case listening to the rattle of dice, in the other of their bones.

So it came to be for me the spirit of progress brooding over a world in dissolution; the most frightened men with the mightiest weapons in their hands; the streets of Calcutta littered with the dying and the dead, and ours glowing and shining with ex-hortations to eat, drink and fornicate. How randy and how sterile (*Playboy* and the Pill)! How humane and how cold-hearted (spare human parts salvaged from the murderous tarmac)! How enlightened and how base! How free and how confined! Four Freedoms leading to forty times four servitudes; racial equality washed away in oceans of racial bloodshed; comprehensive streams of illiteracy, planned non-families – all examples of Fearful Symmetry, as Blake called it; the fearful matching up of ostensible intent with actual outcome.

It is, of course, perfectly possible to see it quite differently, as the great majority of people do, or imagine they do – with every-one getting richer and richer and therefore happier and happier. Are not the young today, as the *Guardian* puts it, 'better educated and more aware of the problems that confront them and society than any previous generation'? I should say! Dear old *Guardian*! With abortions and divorce (later, I daresay, euthanasia) available on request, and birth pills handed out with the free orange juice, surely the spaced kiddies will be born into happy uninhibited broiler homes with happy uninhibited broiler lives before them. As for war – once the Americans are dislodged from Vietnam, leaving the peace-loving Vietnamese to settle their own affairs, the rest of mankind will be able to live peaceably together; except in the Middle East, where some confusion exists as to which is the peace-loving side.

Such is the liberal dream on which Western Man has largely subsisted (when he was not waging ferocious war – which was most of the time) during the half century or so that I, as a journalistic power-voyeur, have been keeping watch, if not over him, then over the six or seven newspapers, the two or three periodicals, the radio and television channels which record his doings, attitudes and intentions. To me, I confess, the dream is a nightmare; I can't believe in it, and stare with a wild surmise at those who do. If I project the dream into the future, there seems no outcome; only an infinitely extended projection which at last disappears into grey nothingness – Gross National Product rising year by year, to double, treble, quadruple, and hire-purchase indebtedness rising correspondingly; colour television, three-dimensional, on a large screen, on a still larger screen; more and more motor cars, wider and wider roads, faster and faster aeroplanes, supersonic, supersupersonic, with louder and louder bangs; anti-missiles, anti-anti-missiles, anti-anti-anti-missiles, and so on *ad infinitum.*

How you see it depends on whether you are inside or outside the dream. From within out, it all makes sense; from without in, no sense at all – just lunacy. We who ride on the periphery, looking both ways, tend to be buffoons; for us this is the most acceptable role, certainly the most profitable. In times like these people rather like it; hence the popularity of 'satire'. Gargoyles are put on cathedrals to modify the portentousness of the steeple; in the same sort of way, by being absurd it is possible to be serious, as by being serious, it is all too easy to be absurd. At the very core of our twentieth century liberal dream – in the Pentagon, say, or inside Mr Jenkins's ear – there is total seriousness; as there is at the dream's remote extremities – in the Kremlin, say, or under General de Gaulle's *képi*. Somewhere between the two it is permissible to laugh, there the clowns of one sort and another disport themselves.

I admit to having appeared, with advantage to myself, in this arena. Yet in the end clowning does not suffice; and anyway it becomes increasingly difficult to make a Harold Wilson, a Lyndon Johnson or a Ted Heath seem more ludicrous than they naturally are, or even to distinguish between them. So nowadays I find myself brooding on the show itself rather than elbowing a way on to the stage in a piebald coat and cap and bells. Who put it on? I keep on asking myself. Who wrote the lines, devised the characters? Surely the run must be nearly over now. Or has it always been so – playing to full houses despite the same old gags, and working up to the same climax; the curtain coming down only to rise again on the same scenery and the same players?

Yes, I decide, it has always been so, and always will be so; the significance, if any, must be looked for elsewhere. I feel enormously grateful to have lived at a time when the actors and acting are so shoddy that this conclusion is inescapable. Inconsistent on my part? I daresay – easy, in any case, to catch me out; you said this, that, or the other thing. In my own mind, however, there is no sense of inconsistency; only of being engaged in a search for what, once looked for, is found.

[1968]

Germaine Greer

The Women's Lib movement finds in Miss Germaine Greer, author of *The Female Eunuch*, one of its most audacious and vociferous champions. Indeed, her book reads like nothing so much as the wild cries of a woman at bay. One sees her (if she will pardon the liberty) naked and beating her breasts in fury over the monstrous regiments of men who exploit, degrade and corrupt her sex, making of women their servants and their playthings. A photograph on the dustjacket shows her as a dark, rather tragic looking female with large, lustrous eyes and long, curling lashes. I note that she writes regularly for a magazine with the unappetizing name of *Suck*, and that she is a lecturer in English at Warwick University – something that no lady of her mettle should be required to be.

Miss Greer's strictures on the romanticization of sex in the interests of salesmanship and sugar-daddy pleasures are apposite and apt. Why, she asks, should female smells have to be pomaded and perfumed out of existence when male ones – sweat and grime and beery breath – are considered not only permissible, but positively alluring? When will justice be done, and the female genital organ become a thing of joy and beauty in its own right? Why should a hairy chest on a Hemingway hero add to his charms, whereas women are expected to go to great expense, trouble and sometimes suffer excruciating pain in order to have hair removed from all but a few specialized areas? (Here, as a matter of fact, she might have recalled the famous lady of Lisbon whose luxuriant beard was said to have attracted suitors from all over the world.) Why, in short, must women suffer the indignity of living in a society whose male-oriented standards require them to be conformed to an image bearing no relation to their true nature, appetites and rights? An image, as she justly points out, as abhorrent in the works of a D. H. Lawrence or an Ian Fleming as in those of the sob sisters of present day fiction.

If, however, one may sympathize with Miss Greer's contemptuous exposure of the squalid role allotted to women in contemporary erotica in its manifold forms, the solution she offers strikes me as lacking in both practicality and charm. Take, for instance, SCUM, the Society for Cutting Up Men, which, Miss Greer tells us, received a great impetus when a Miss Valerie Solanas shot – alas, not fatally – Andy Warhol. Miss Solanas, Miss Greer considers, in advancing the proposition that the best way for women to move back to humanity is simply to exterminate men, worthily serves the cause of Women's Lib. It was probably, she writes, 'the fierce energy and lyricism of her uncompromising statement of men's fixation of the feminine, and their desperate battle to live up to their own penile fixation, which radicalized Ti-Grace Atkinson and eventually gave birth to WITCH Women's International Terrorists Conspiracy from Hell'.

Yet would even the final triumph of SCUM reinforced by WITCH serve to realize all Miss Greer's hopes and desires? One may presume to doubt it. A pyrrhic or cockless victory, I should have thought. Miss Greer's other proposal – to take a large farmhouse in Italy where she and other professional ladies could give birth to babies and bring them up collectively – has been often enough entertained and put into practice, always with unsatisfactory results. With her powerful, vigorous and well-stocked mind, Miss Greer is worthy of better things. Will she perhaps in time discover that the duties and joys of motherhood provide the true alternative to the indignities of female involvement in the gilded pigsty of the prevailing erotomania; that love and fulfilment begin where the animal exigencies of the body end? Beneath the libidinous Lib shrew and scold I seem to detect the lineaments of a Florence Nightingale or Mary Wollstonecraft (whom she quotes much), or even – dare I say it? – a St Theresa.

Women's Lib

I have never been able to understand precisely what Women's Lib is aimed at achieving. That all women should become men, and vice versa? That reproductive arrangements should be transferred to the laboratory, thereby eliminating the necessity for women at all? That men should develop mammary glands so as to be able to take a turn at suckling? I just don't know.

The Great Liberal Death Wish

Searching in my mind for an appropriate name for the seventies, I settle for The Decade of The Great Liberal Death Wish. It seems to me that this process of death-wishing, in the guise of liberalism, has been eroding the civilization of the West for a century and more, and is now about to reach its apogee. The liberal mind, effective everywhere, whether in power or in opposition, particularly so during the present period of American world domination, has provided the perfect instrument. Systematically, stage by stage, dismantling our Western way of life, depreciating and deprecating all its values so that the whole social structure is now tumbling down, dethroning its God, undermining all its certainties, and finally mobilizing a Praetorian Guard of ribald students, maintained at the public expense, and ready at the drop of a hat to go into action, not only against their own weak-kneed, bemused academic authorities, but also against any institution or organ for the maintenance of law and order still capable of functioning, especially the police. And all this, wonderfully enough, in the name of the health, wealth and happiness of all mankind.

Previous civilizations have been overthrown from without by the incursion of barbarian hordes; ours has dreamed up its own dissolution in the minds of its own intellectual élite. It has carefully nurtured its own barbarians – all reared on the best Dr Spock lines, sent to progressive schools and colleges, fitted with contraceptives or fed birth pills at puberty, mixing D. H. Lawrence with their Coca-Cola, and imbibing the headier stuff (Marcuse, Chairman Mao, Malcolm X) in evening libations of hot chocolate. Not

Bolshevism, which Stalin liquidated along with all the old Bolsheviks; not Nazism, which perished with Hitler in his Berlin bunker; not Fascism, which was left hanging upside down, along with Mussolini and his mistress, from a lamp-post – none of these, history will record, was responsible for bringing down the darkness on our civilization, but liberalism. A solvent rather than a precipitate, a sedative rather than a stimulant, a slough rather than a precipice; blurring the edges of truth, the definition of virtue, the shape of beauty; a cracked bell, a mist, a death wish.

I was fortunate enough myself, while still in my late twenties, to be presented with a demonstration of the great liberal death wish at work, so manifest, so incontestable in its implications, and, at the same time, so hilariously funny, that I have never subsequently felt the smallest doubt that here lay the key to the tragicomedy of our time. It happened in Moscow, in the autumn of 1932 and spring of 1933, when I was working there as correspondent for the, then, *Manchester Guardian*. In those days, Moscow was the Mecca for every liberal mind, whatever its particular complexion. They flocked there in an unending procession, from the great ones like Shaw and Gide and Barbusse and Julian Huxley and Harold Laski and the Webbs, down to poor little teachers, crazed clergymen and millionaires, and drivelling dons; all utterly convinced that, under the aegis of the great Stalin, a new dawn was breaking in which the human race would at last be united in liberty, equality and fraternity for evermore.

Stalin himself, to do him justice, never troubled to hide his contempt for them and everything they stood for, and mercilessly suppressed any like tendencies among his own people. This, however, in no way deterred them. They were prepared to believe anything, however preposterous; to overlook anything, however villainous; to approve anything, however obscurantist and brutally authoritarian, in order to be able to preserve intact the confident expectation that one of the most thoroughgoing, ruthless and bloody tyrannies ever to exist on earth could be relied on to champion human freedom, the brotherhood of man, and all the other good liberal causes to which they had dedicated their lives. It is true that many of them subsequently retracted; that incidents like the Stalinist purges, the Nazi-Soviet Pact, the debunking of Stalin at the Twentieth Party Congress, the Hungarian and Czech risings, each caused a certain leakage among liberal well-wishers. Yet when the dust settles, the same old bias is clearly discernible. It is an addiction, like alcoholism, to which the liberal mind is intrinsically susceptible – to grovel before any Beelzebub who claims, however implausibly, to be a prince of liberals.

Why? After all, the individuals concerned are ostensibly the shining lights of the Western world; scholars, philosophers, artists, scientists and the like; the favoured children of a troubled time. Held in respect as being sages who know all the answers; sought after by governments and international agencies; holding forth in the press and on the air. The glory of faculties and campuses; beating a path between Harvard and Princeton, and Washington, DC; swarming like migrant birds from the London School of Economics, Oxford and Cambridge into Whitehall. Yet I have seen their prototypes – and I can never forget it – in the role of credulous buffoons capable of being taken in by grotesquely obvious deceptions. Swallowing unquestioningly statistics and other purported data whose falsity was immediately evident to the meanest intelligence. Full of idiot delight when Stalin or one of his henchmen yet again denounced the corrupt, cowardly intelligentsia of the capitalist West – viz., themselves. I detect in their like today the same impulse. They pass on from one to another, like a torch held upside down, the same death wish. Editors come and go, newspapers decline and fold, Labour Governments form and unform; after Roosevelt, Truman and then Eisenhower; after Kennedy, Johnson and then Nixon; but the great liberal death wish goes marching on.

In those far-off days in Moscow it was possible to discuss matters like distinguished visiting intellectuals with officials of the Press Department of the Soviet Foreign Office, with whom, of course, we foreign journalists were in constant contact. Most of them were Russian Jews who had lived abroad before the Revolution. Unlike the usual sort of wooden-faced Soviet functionary, they had a sense of humour and a taste for irony. One and all, as it happened, were fated to be shot when, later on, Stalin swung the regime back to traditional Russian anti-Semitism. Yes, of course, they said, people like Shaw and the Webbs were natural stool pigeons, historically destined to play a Judas part and betray – admittedly, rather out of vanity than cupidity – their own phony liberal principles to a triumphant Marxist revolutionary movement in whose eyes they were, and must always be, anathema. Meanwhile, they had their usefulness, if only in reassuring the Soviet authorities that, whatever they might feel bound to do in the way of terrorism and dictatorial practices, they never need worry their heads about hostile reactions in enlightened circles and newspapers in the West. The Foreign Office men told me that they even on occasion amused themselves by seeing how far they could go in gulling distinguished visitors, fabricating production statistics and Stakhanovite feats at the factory bench which could not possibly be true. However tall their stories, they were invariably believed, and often quoted in learned publications abroad; the credulity of their visitors was, it seemed, fathomless.

To the fevered mind of a Senator Joseph McCarthy, or the more sedate, but still irascible one of a Vice-President Spiro Agnew; even to so erudite and responsible a citizen as Enoch Powell, it all smells unmistakably of conspiracy. How otherwise to account for the fact that the liberal mind, like deathwatch beetles, seems to be active in all the rafters and foundations of the State? So, they imagine suborned men, and hurl wild accusations and denunciations. Ah, if only it were a conspiracy! How easy, then, to apprehend the principals and subdue their dupes! But a death wish subconsciously entertained in newspaper offices and college faculties, in television and radio studios, in churches of all denominations, wherever two or more illuminati are gathered together – that is something else. To suppress a death wish it is necessary to proclaim a corresponding life wish – which is just what a Senator McCarthy, a Vice-President Agnew, an Enoch Powell cannot do; with the result that their wild accusations only serve to advance the very thing they believe they are attacking. They remind me of an old evangelical missionary I came across years ago in South India when I was living there. This good man had got in the way of appearing each year at a local Hindu festival and denouncing the God Shiva, before whom devotees were prostrating themselves. At first he was stoned, then just cursed and insulted, and finally taken for granted. When the time came for him to retire, the organizers of the festival petitioned his missionary society to send a replacement. He had become part of the show.

Recalling, in the light of these experiences, my time as an editorial writer on the *Guardian* before going to Moscow, I realized that there, in that citadel of liberalism, we were engaged in spelling out the essential terms of the great liberal death wish. All our protestations and prognostications were governed by its exigencies. Thus, in our editorials, it was a basic principle that our enemies were always in the right and our friends in the wrong. If, for instance, a British soldier was killed anywhere, it was an unfortunate consequence of the brutal and crooked policies the poor fellow was required to implement; if, on the other hand, a British soldier killed someone, the victim was automatically a blessed martyr, to be mourned, and possibly made the subject of a demonstration, by all decent liberal people. Like-wise, any Indians who were misguided enough to be our friends became thereby worthless and despicable figures in our eyes – with the exception, curiously enough, of the Aga Khan, who really was worthless. The repute in which he was held, however, was not due to any appreciation of his political views, but rather to his eminence on the racetrack; something so esteemed by the English that it covers even being on our side. Other Indians, like Nehru, who specialized in holding us up to hatred and contempt, were treated with the utmost consideration. I note that a similar role has come to be adopted by *The New York Times*, *The Washington Post*, and other high-toned American newspapers, as well as by the more eminent radio and television commentators, who pour out their wrath and derision on any poor sucker who is fool enough to support the American side anywhere, but are quick to offer sympathetic treatment to a Castro, a Ho Chi Minh, a Che Guevara, none of whom can be regarded as exactly Americanophil. As far as the death wish or Gadarene stakes are concerned, I calculate that America is running a shade behind us, but is going hard in the direction of the same cliff.

In the view we propounded of Europe in the *Guardian*'s columns in those just pre-Hitler years, the villain was France, armed to the teeth, and, we insisted, ruthlessly pursuing selfish national ends: the hero, a much-wronged Germany, disarmed, bankrupted, victimized by the greedy, revengeful victors of the 1914-18 War. No view could have better pleased the then emerging Dr Goebbels, or have been more conducive to the disaster of September 1939; more especially as it was combined with an unwavering, sancti-monious refusal to countenance anything in the nature of re-arming, and a naïve, obstinately held faith in the ramshackle League of Nations as a peace-keeping instrument. In this way our national interests were damaged far more drastically than by any-thing a specifically conspiratorial body like the Comintern could hope to achieve. We were led into a war we had little chance of winning, and whose outcome, whether we were on the winning or the losing side, was bound to be, as far as we were concerned, ruinous. A bull's eye for the great liberal death wish.

In the same sort of way, today's version of the liberal mind makes America the universal villain. Sinister American pressures and stratagems are detected behind every financial and economic crisis anywhere in the world; as are the machinations of the CIA behind every reactionary regime or take-over. America is seen as the watchdog of a capitalist-imperialist *status quo*, just as France was in the post 1914-18 War years. No doubt, in due course there will be a similar awakening. Such an attitude, contradictorily enough, is combined with an eager acceptance of current American styles and practices. Veterans of American campus fighting are to the fore in student disorders in London, Paris and Berlin; American pot, pornography, Andy Warhol films, and other intimations of decadence and decay find a ready market across the Atlantic. The demonstrators who advance on London policemen guarding the United States Embassy in Grosvenor Square are mostly jeans-clad, infantile slogan-chanting, obscenities-mouthing, tousled, tangled bearded baboons, who yell 'Pigs!' and 'Fuzz!' in the true Berkeley manner. In other words, what is objected to is the, now waning, American endeavour to underpin crumbling West European economies, and reinforce such defences as can be mustered there against an attack from the East. The incursions of American decadence are as eagerly welcomed as these efforts are abhorred – a characteristic death-wishing stance.

Again, when the final decomposition of the British Empire took place, the death wish, operating through the liberal mind, ensured that, having shed a real empire, we should have a phantom one on our hands in the shape of the so-called British Commonwealth – the most ephemeral setup of the kind since the Holy Roman Empire – involving us in the cares and expense of an empire with none of the compensations. Thus, we have been forced to finance, and sometimes defend, demagogue-dictators of the most unedifying kind, who have ridden to power on the one-man-one-vote principle so dear to liberal hearts. It is a case of responsibility without power – the opposite of the prerogative of the harlot. A similar process may be detected at work in America, whereby the liberal mind's proneness to excessive guilt feelings has induced so fawning and sycophantic an attitude towards Negro discontent and subversion that lifelong white agitators for civil rights, inveterate freedom-marchers and admirers of Martin Luther King, integrationists who have squatted and howled and been carried screaming away by the police for years past, nowadays find themselves being kicked in the teeth by Black Panthers and other Negro militants with a ferocity which might seem excessive directed against the reddest of red-necks.

I ask myself how this predilection for enemies and distaste for friends came to pass in what many of us have been brought up to regard as the most cultivated and enlightened minds of our time. Why it has seemed so obvious to them that whatever commends itself to our well-wishers must be despicable, and whatever serves the interests of our ill-wishers must be beneficial. Why, for instance, there should be so unanimous a feeling in such circles in the United States that the discrediting of American policies and the defeat of American arms in Vietnam represents a progressive aspiration, and the converse a reactionary one. Why, in a world full of oppressive regimes and terrorist practices, in England the venom and fury of the liberal mind should pick on the white South Africans with particular spleen when their oligarchic rule only differs from that of a dozen others – Tito's, Franco's, Ulbricht's, Castro's, etc., etc. – in that they happen to be anxious to be on good terms with the English.

What but a death wish could bring about so complete a reversal of all the normal worldly considerations of good sense, self-interest and a desire to survive? I remember reading in Taine's *Origines de la France Contemporaine* of how, shortly before the Revolution, a party of affluent liberal intellectuals were discussing over their after-dinner cognac all the wonderful things that were going to happen when the Bourbon regime was abolished, and freedom à la Voltaire and Jean-Jacques Rousseau reigned supreme. One of the guests, hitherto silent, suddenly spoke up. Yes, he said, the Bourbon regime would indeed be overthrown, and in the process – pointing round – you and you and you will be carried screaming to the guillotine; you and you and you go into penurious exile, and – now pointing in the direction of some of the elegant ladies present – you and you and you will hawk your bodies round from sansculotte to sansculotte. There was a moment of silence while this, as it turned out, all too exact prophecy sank in, and then the previous conversation was resumed. I know several fashionable and affluent households in London and Washington and Paris where similar conversations take place, and where similarly exact prophecies might be made, without, as on the occasion Taine so appositely described, having the slightest impact.

It would seem to be clear, then, that the great liberal death wish arises out of a historical, or maybe biological, necessity, rather than out of any rational, or even irrational, considerations. Civilizations, like classes and families and regimes, degenerate, and so must be wound up. Just as the great-grandson of some famous ducal figure or billionaire may have thrust upon him the disagreeable fate of ending his line, and, drooling and dissolute, duly ends it, so the liberal mind, likewise drooling, has been entrusted with the historic task of bringing to an end what we are supposed to be defending with might and main – I mean what we still like to call our free way of life and the free institutions which have sustained it. On such a basis, all the views, attitudes, values and recommendations of the liberal mind today make complete sense. Going back to my Moscow experience, those eminent intellectuals abasing themselves before Stalin, and so fatuously accepting his bona fides as a lover of human freedom and enlightenment, were simply fulfilling a manifest destiny to abolish themselves, their culture and their world.

Suppose that somehow or other a lot of contemporary pabulum – video tape of television programmes with accompanying advertisements, news footage, copies of newspapers and magazines, stereo tapes of pop groups and other cacophonies, best-selling novels, films, and other such material – gets preserved, like the Dead Sea Scrolls, in some remote salt cave. Then, some centuries, or maybe millennia, later, when our civilization will long since have joined all the others that once were, and now can only be patiently reconstructed out of dusty ruins, incomprehensible hieroglyphics and other residuary relics, archaeologists discover the cave, and set about sorting out its contents and trying to deduce from them what we were like and how we lived. (This is assuming, of course, that we do not, in the process of working out the great liberal death wish, blow ourselves and our earth to smithereens – a large assumption.) What will they make of us? I wonder. Materially, so rich and so powerful; spiritually, so impoverished and fear-ridden. Having made such remarkable inroads into the secrets of nature; beginning to explore, and perhaps to colonize, the universe itself; developing the means to produce in more or less unlimited quantities everything we could possibly need or desire, and to transmit swifter than light every thought, smile or word that could possibly delight, entertain or instruct us. Disposing of treasure beyond calculation, opening up possibilities beyond conception. Yet haunted and obsessed by the fear that we are too numerous; that soon, as our numbers go on increasing, there will be no room or food for us. On the one hand a neurotic passion to increase consumption, sustained by every sort of imbecile persuasion; on the other, ever-increasing hunger and penury among the so-called backward or underdeveloped peoples. Never, our archaeologists will surely conclude, was any generation of men intent upon the pursuit of happiness more advantageously placed to attain it, who yet, with seeming deliberation, took the opposite course – towards chaos, not order; towards breakdown, not stability; towards death, destruction and darkness, not life, creativity and light. An ascent that ran downhill; plenty that turned into a wasteland; a cornucopia whose abundance made hungry; a death wish inexorably unfolding.

Searching about in their minds for some explanation of this pursuit of happiness that became a death wish, the archaeologists, it seems to me, would be bound to hit upon the doctrine of progress; probably the most ludicrous, certainly the most deleterious, fancy ever to take possession of the human heart; the liberal mind's basic dogma. The notion that human beings, as individuals, must necessarily get better and better is even now considered by most people to be untenable in the light of their indubitably outrageous behaviour towards one another; but the equivalent collective concept – that their social circumstances and conduct must necessarily improve – has come to seem almost axiomatic. On this basis, all change represents progress, and is therefore good; to change anything is, *per se*, to improve or reform it.

For instance, to dilute the marriage tie to the point that it no longer impedes virtually unrestrained promiscuity, or provides the possibility of a stable home to bring up children in, is a reform; to oppose this, reactionary. Likewise, to abolish all restrictions on what may be published, or publicly shown as entertainment, is a reform, even though it opens the way for an avalanche of pornography, and gives full freedom to operate to the sinister individuals and interests engaging in this unsavoury trade. Again, the legalization of abortion is a reform, as, we may be sure, will be claimed in due course for the legalization of euthanasia. In Germany, under the Nazi regime – a decidedly liberal one in this field – sterilization of the allegedly unfit was practised with a zeal and expedition that must be the envy of our eugenists, forced, as they are, to adopt such paltry devices as offering transistor radio sets to putative Indian sterilees. The Nazis were able, too, to dispose painlessly and expeditiously of unproductive citizens – what the French, with their usual brutal realism, call 'useless mouths' – without any questions being asked, and to conduct experiments in transplant surgery that would have uplifted Dr Christiaan Barnard himself. All this Nazi-sponsored progress was summarily interrupted by Germany's military defeat in 1945, but after a decent interval has been resumed in the victor countries. It will surely lead to a decision – which I have an uneasy feeling has already been taken, at any rate subconsciously – not to go on much longer bearing the burden of caring for the senile and incurable mentally sick. Hence the starving of these services for funds and personnel, the noticeable reluctance to build new accommodation, when expenditure on public health generally has been soaring. I anticipate quite soon a campaign, conducted at the most elevated moral level, to dispose painlessly of incurables in gerontological and psychiatric wards, no doubt acquiring a useful reserve of transplantable organs in the process. It will represent an important advance for the liberal mind – and for the great liberal death wish.

It was, of course, Darwin's theory of natural selection which first popularized the notion that Man and his environment are involved in an endless and automatic process of improvement. Who can measure the consequences of this naïve assumption? What secret subversive organization, endowed with unlimited funds and resources, could hope to achieve a thousandth part of what it achieved in the way of discrediting the then prevailing moral values and assumptions, putting in their place nothing more than vague, sentimental hopes of collective human better-ment, and the liberal mind to entertain them? It is interesting to reflect that now, in the light of all that has happened, the early obscurantist opponents of Darwinian evolution seem vastly more sagacious and farseeing than its early excited champions. There must be quite a number today who, like myself, would rather go down to history even as a puffing, portentous Bishop Wilberforce than, say, a Herbert Spencer, or a poor, squeaky H. G. Wells, ardent evolutionist and disciple of Huxley, with his vision of an earthly paradise achieved through science and technology; those twin monsters which have laid waste a whole world, polluting its seas and rivers and lakes with poisons, infecting its very earth and all its creatures, reaching into Man's mind and inner conscious-ness to control and condition him, at the same time entrusting to irresponsible, irresolute human hands the instruments of universal destruction. It must be added that, confronted with this prospect when, at the very end of his life, the first nuclear explosion was announced, Wells turned his face to the wall, letting off in *Mind at the End of its Tether* one last, despairing, whimpering cry which unsaid everything he had ever thought or hoped. Belatedly, he understood that what he had followed as a life-force was, in point of fact, a death wish, into which he was glad to sink the little that remained of his own life in the confident expectation of total and final obliteration.

The enthronement of the gospel of progress necessarily re-quired the final discrediting of the gospel of Christ, and the destruction of the whole edifice of ethics, law, culture, human relationships and human behaviour constructed upon it. Our civilization, after all, began with the Christian revelation, not the theory of evolution, and, we may be sure, will perish with it, too – if it has not already. Jesus of Nazareth was its founding father, not Charles Darwin; it was Paul of Tarsus who first carried its message to Europe, not Karl Marx, or even Lenin. Jesus, by dying on the Cross, abolished death-wishing; dying became thenceforth life's glory and fulfilment. So, when Jesus called on his followers to die in order to live, he created a tidal wave of joy and hope on which they have ridden for two thousand years. The gospel of progress represents the exact antithesis. It plays the Crucifixion backwards, as it were; in the beginning was the flesh, and the flesh became Word. In the light of this Logos in reverse, the quest for hope is the ultimate hopelessness; the pursuit of happiness, the certitude of despair; the lust for life, the embrace of death.

The liberal assault on Christianity has been undertaken with a fury and fervour which today, when the battle seems to have been conclusively won, is difficult to comprehend. I well remember my surprise, in a television encounter with Bertrand Russell, at discovering in him an almost demented hatred of Christ and Christianity, to which he attributed all the horrors and misfortunes mankind has had to endure since the fall of the Roman Empire. As I attempted to confute this view, I found myself watching with fascination a red flush which rose steadily up his thin stringy neck and spread to his face. The receding chin, the pasty flesh, the simian features struck me then as suggestive of a physical degeneracy (doubtless to be expected in view of his family history) matching the moral degeneracy he had done so much to promote. It was a cruel, and doubtless unfair, light in which to see him; a product, I daresay, of the passionate and physically agonizing conflict in which I found myself involved. At the time, however, the impression was particularly vivid and convincing, and abides with me still.

The script of this strange encounter is still extant, and reveals the philosopher in a most unphilosophic mood; roaring and bellowing like any atheist orator at Hyde Park Corner. In the light of it, I derived a lot of quiet amusement from the tributes paid to Russell by eminent churchmen when he died. To the best of my knowledge, there was not one single ecclesiastical or clerical voice raised to point out that the great influence Russell undoubtedly exerted was inimical to the Christian faith and the moral standards derived therefrom. It is rather as though one were to find in the literature of the Royal Society for Prevention of Cruelty to Animals a panegyric of bullfighting or fox hunting, or to fall in with a party of total abstainers on their way to a wine festival in Provence. Yet even these comparisons pale into insignificance when we have clergymen who find an echo of the Gospels in the brutal materialism of Marx and Engels; who lay wreaths on shrines to Lady Chatterley, or even to *Playboy* magazine. Or – what must surely be the final *reductio ad absurdum* – a sometime lecturer in biblical studies at Manchester University who detects in the New Testament the encoded version of a phallic-narcotic cult based on the consumption of particular mushrooms.

It is, indeed, among Christians themselves that the final decisive assault on Christianity has been mounted; led by the Protestant churches, but with Roman Catholics eagerly, if belatedly, joining in the fray. All they had to show was that when Jesus said that His kingdom was not of this world, He meant that it was. Then, moving on from there, to stand the other basic Christian propositions similarly on their heads. As, that to be carnally minded is life; that it is essential to lay up treasure on earth in the shape of a constantly expanding Gross National Product; that the flesh lusts with the spirit and the spirit with the flesh, so that we can do whatever we have a mind to; that he that loveth his life in this world shall keep it unto life eternal. And so on. One recalls a like adjustment of the rules in Orwell's *Animal Farm*. A whole series of new interpretative 'translations' of the Bible have appeared supporting the new view, and in case there should be any anxiety about the reception of these adjustments in Heaven, God, we are told on the best theological authority, has died.

To counteract any anxiety on earth, there is the concept of situational ethics, whereby our moral obligations are governed, not by a moral law or moral order underlying all earthly ones, but by the circumstances in which we happen to find ourselves. Thus, the Ten Commandments have only a conditional validity; it may, in particular circumstances, be positively virtuous to covet a neighbour's goods or seduce his wife. Reacting accordingly, Roman Catholic priests and religious are walking out in shoals to resume the material and sensual preoccupations they once thought it proper to renounce, or from within demand the right to follow Demas and love this present world. As for the congregations – not surprisingly, they are dwindling fast. Situational ethics prepares the way for situational worship – a state of affairs not remedied by introducing pop groups, folk singers, and I daresay in time LSD and striptease to enliven divine service. The new enlightened clergy positively revel in the decline in church attendance, gleefully recommending selling off redundant churches and their contents, and looking forward to the time when institutional Christianity, like the State in Marxist mythology, will have withered away. In this aspiration, at any rate, they are unlikely to be disappointed.

In the moral vacuum left by thus emptying Christianity of its spiritual or transcendental content, the great liberal death wish has been able to flourish and luxuriate; the more so because it can plausibly masquerade as aiming at its opposite – life enhancement. Thus, our wars, each more ferocious and destructive than the last, are to establish once and for all the everlasting reign of peace. As the media spout better and bigger lies, their dedication to truth is the more insistently proclaimed. One thinks again of Orwell, and the Ministries of Truth and Peace in *Nineteen Eighty-Four*, the former, as he told me himself, being based on the BBC, where he worked for a while during the 1939-45 War. Again, in a frenzied quest for the physical and mental well-being which should accompany the pursuit of happiness as naturally as a tan comes from lying in the Mediterranean sun, resort to drugs steadily increases, as does the variety available; while medicine men (doctors, psychiatrists and the like) are in ever greater demand, assuming the role of priests, advising and moulding their flock, uplifting and depressing them, keeping them alive and killing them off as they think fit. Just where happiness seems most accessible – in the happy lands, the Scandinavias and Californias – many jump after it from upstairs windows, or gulp it down in coloured barbiturates, or try to tear it out of one another's bodies, or scatter it in blood and bone about the highways, along which, with six lanes a side and Muzak endlessly playing, automobiles roll on from nowhere to nowhere.

Pascal says that when men become separated from God, two courses present themselves; to imagine that they are gods themselves, and try to behave as such, or, alternatively, to seek for enduring satisfaction in the transitory pleasures of the senses. The one sends them, like Icarus, flying into the bright furnace of the sun, there to perish; the other reduces them to far below the level of the farmyard, where the cows with their soft eyes, and the hens with their shrill cries, and the strutting peacocks and the grunting pigs, down to the tiny darting flies and wasps and insects, all live out whatever span of animal existence is vouchsafed them, under God's kindly gaze. Men are denied this satisfaction. If they set up as a farmyard, it is a place of dark fantasies and weird imaginings – Prometheus, unbound, chaining himself to the rock, and there, day by day, gorging his own entrails.

Both these recourses have played their part in the unfolding of the great liberal death wish. In their laboratories, men like gods are working on our genes, to remake them after their own image; with computers for minds, and all our procreation done in test tubes, leaving us free to frolic with our sterilized bodies as we please in unconstrained and perfect bliss. Other men like gods build Towers of Babel in glass and chromium, reaching higher and higher into the sky. Yet others prepare the broiler houses and factory farms for men, not fowl and beasts; even designing for us, as gods should, a kind of immortality; keeping us on the road indefinitely, like vintage cars, by replacing our organs as they wear out – kidney, heart, lungs, genitals, brain even – with spare parts from newer models. Young heads on old shoulders; new ballocks on old crotches.

As for the farmyard – what a gilded sty has been devised! What ambrosial fodder! What perfumed rutting, melodious orgasmic grunts, downy straw and succulent swill! If the purpose of life is, indeed, to pursue happiness here and now, on this earth, then, clearly, it can only be realized in terms of what this earth provides – that is, of goods and toys, of egotistic success or celebrity, of diversions like speed and travel and narcotic fantasies; above all, of sexual pleasure and excitement which alone offers an additional illusory sense of transcendental satisfaction notably lacking in another Cadillac, a trip to Tibet or to the moon, or a press of autograph hunters.

Sex is the only mysticism materialism offers, and so to sex the pursuers of happiness address themselves with an avidity and dedication seldom, if ever, surpassed. Who among posterity will ever be able to reconstruct the resultant scene? Who for that matter can convey it today? The vast, obsessive outpouring of erotica in every shape and form; in book and film and play and entertainment, in body and word and deed, so that there is no escape for anyone. The lame and the halt, the doddering and the infirm, equally called upon somehow to squeeze out of their frail flesh the requisite response. It is the flesh that quickeneth, the spirit profiteth nothing; *copulo ergo sum*, I screw, therefore I am – the new version of Descartes's famous axiom. All possible impediments swept away; no moral taboos, no legal ones, either. An orgasm a day, however procured, keeps the doctor away. Pornography, like Guinness, is good for us, as numerous learned doctors and professors have been at great pains to establish. For instance, a Dr O. Elthammer of the Stockholm Child Psychiatric Department, who, I read in a letter to the *New Statesman* – that faithful chronicler of the liberal mind through every twist and turn and tergiversation for half a century past – has 'proved conclusively' that pornography does not have a corrupting effect, by showing to some children between the ages of eleven and eighteen a film of a woman being raped by a group of intoxicated louts and then forced to have intercourse with a dog. 'None of the children,' the doctor triumphantly concluded 'was frightened during or after the film, but a proportion of the older girls did admit to being shocked,' while two adults also present 'needed psychological treatment for a month afterward'. One idly wonders what, if anything, happened to the dog.

Each seeming impediment provides an occasion for another spurt. If one Cadillac fails to produce the requisite yield of happiness, then two assuredly will; if not two, then three, or four, or five. If going to bed with one particular woman proves wearisome, then try another. Or two at a time. Or an orgy. Or jumping from a candelabrum. Or any other device or combination. For fuel to keep this fire going, the pornography of the ages is dredged and dredged again, as are the sick memories and imaginings of popular novelists. The fire's extinction would spell, not just impotence, but exclusion from life itself; like those poor souls in Dante's *Inferno* without a place in either Heaven or Hell. Whatever else may be the case, the magic formula itself cannot be wrong. It must, it must work. So try again! The psychiatric wards fill to overflowing with deluded pursuers of happiness whose quest has proved abortive; guiltily conscious that happiness has eluded them in a society in which it is the only good. There, the children of affluence wail and fret over their broken toys and broken hopes and unresponding flesh. No matter; press on, grasping after new toys, new hopes and new flesh.

In the birth pill, quasi-divine invention, a little death wish in itself, may be seen the crowning glory of the pursuit of happiness through sex. Adapting Voltaire's famous saying, if the pill had not been invented it would have been necessary for it to exist. What laborious days and nights to bring it into existence! What ingenuity and concentration of purpose on the single objective – the achievement of unprocreative procreation, of *coitus non interruptus* that is guaranteed also to be *non fecundus*! What armies of mice and rats and rabbits and other such small deer to be experimented upon, until – oh! glory hallelujah! – their tiny wombs, minutely dissected out, are seen to be blessedly vacant despite prior coupling, holding out to all mankind the sublime prospect – the converse of what was vouchsafed the Virgin Mary – of likewise being able to couple without conceiving. A Minificat rather than a Magnificat.

With the pill, the procreative process has at last been sanctified with sterility. Aphrodite sinking into the sea, unmenstrual, and forever sterile; unending, infertile orgasm – a death-wish formula if ever there was one. Is it not remarkable? – millions upon millions of women dedicated to the pursuit of happiness, all pummelled and perfumed and pomaded, all coiffured and clothed and contained in accordance with the best television and glossy-page recommendations; stuffed full of vitamins, fruit juice and rare steaks, with svelte, sun-tanned, agile bodies; their hands beseechingly outstretched, insistently demanding a specific against conception. Ready to run any risk, make any sacrifice, suffer any disability – loss of appetite, if not of wits, growing sick and languid, sexless even, and fat – provided only they can be guaranteed fool and accident-proof sterility.

This neat compact death wish, so easily swallowed, is for export as well as home consumption. Under the auspices of the World Health Organization and other enlightened agencies, earnest colporteurs of contraception carry the good news to darkest Africa; awesome lady missionaries of family planning take their coils and caps and pills, as traders once did coloured beads, to the teeming populations of Asia and Latin America. Only among the Western educated, however, do they find any appreciable number of clients. In the countryside their product has few takers. The result is that it is the new bourgeoisie, admirers of *Oh! Calcutta!* rather than residents of Calcutta proper, who take to the pill. The others continue to procreate regardless, leaving the apostles of the liberal mind to the self-genocide they have chosen.

If sex provides the mysticism of the great liberal death wish, it needs, as well, its own special mumbo-jumbo and brainwashing device; a moral equivalent of conversion, whereby the old Adam of ignorance and superstition and the blind acceptance of tradition is put aside, and the new liberal man is born – enlightened, erudite, cultivated. This is readily to hand in education in all its many branches and affiliations. To the liberal mind, education provides the universal panacea. Whatever the problem, education will solve it. Law and order breaking down? – then yet more statistics chasing yet more education; venereal disease spreading, to the point that girls of ten are found to be infected? – then, for heaven's sake, more sex education, with tiny tots lisping out what happens to mummy's vagina when daddy erects, as once they did the Catechism; drug addiction going up by leaps and bounds, especially in the homes where educational television is looked at, and the whole family marches to protest against the Vietnam war? – surely it's obvious that what the kids need is extra classes under trained psychiatrists to instruct them in the why and the wherefore of narcotics. And so on.

On radio and television panels, on which I have spent more time than I care to remember, to questions such as: What does the panel think should be done about the rising rate of juvenile delinquency? the answer invariably offered is: more education. I can hear the voices ringing out now, as I write these words; the male ones throaty and earnest, with a tinge of indignation, the female ones particularly resonant as they insist that, not only should there be more education, but more and better education. It gives us all a glow of righteousness and high purpose. More and better education – that's the way to get rid of juvenile delinquency, and adult delinquency, for that matter, and all other delinquencies. If we try hard enough, and are prepared to pay enough, we can surely educate ourselves out of all our miseries and troubles, and into the happiness we seek and deserve. If some panel member – as it might be me – ventures to point out that we have been having more, and what purports to be better, education for years past, and that nonetheless juvenile delinquency is still year by year rising, and shows every sign of going on so doing, he gets cold, hostile looks. If he then adds that, in his opinion, education is a stupendous fraud perpetrated by the liberal mind on a bemused public, and calculated, not just not to reduce juvenile delinquency, but positively to increase it, being itself a source of this very thing; that if it goes on following its present course, it will infallibly end by destroying the possibility of anyone having any education at all, the end product of the long, expensive course from kindergarten to postgraduate studies being neo-Stone Age men – why, then, a perceptible shudder goes through the other panelists, and even the studio audience. It is blasphemy.

The bustling campuses multiply and expand, as do their faculties and buildings. More and more professors instruct more and more students in more and more subjects, producing barely articulate graduates, who irresistibly recall to me the *bezprisorny* I remember so vividly from my time in the USSR – those wild children whose parents and guardians had died in the great Russian famines of the early twenties, but who had somehow lived on themselves to race about Moscow and Leningrad and Kiev like wolf packs. Their wild, pinched faces, their bright animal eyes, suddenly glimpsed when they rushed out from under some bridge or embankment – have I not seen them again among our own pampered children, wearing their proletarian fancy dress, on any campus between the Berlin Wall and the California coastline? Here, too, the death-wish cycle completes itself. Pursuing knowledge, we find ignorance, and join hands across the civilized centuries with our own primitive, savage origins. A Picasso, after a lifetime's practice, arrives at the style of the cave drawings in the Pyrenees, and Beethoven is drowned in the insistent beat of jungle drums and jungle cries. The struggle to extricate meaning and order from confusion and chaos is abandoned, and literature itself reverts to total incoherence, in the process disappearing. Fiat Nox!

I see the great liberal death wish driving through the years ahead in triple harness with the gospel of progress and the pursuit of happiness. These our three Horsemen of the Apocalypse – progress, happiness, death. Under their auspices, the quest for total affluence leads to total deprivation; for total peace, to total war; for total education, to total illiteracy; for total sex, to total sterility; for total freedom, to total servitude. Seeking only agreement based on a majority, we find a consensus based on a consensocracy, or oligarchy of the liberal mind, of whose operation an admitted maestro – R. H. S. Crossman, former minister in Harold Wilson's Government and *New Statesman* editor – has written in his inimitable way: 'Better the liberal élitism of the statute book than the reactionary populism of the marketplace.' Seeking only truth supported by facts, we find only fantasy supported by celluloid or video dreams, seen through a camera-eye brightly (the camera, like the pill, a minuscule death wish). All the world compressed into a television screen; seen with, not through, the eye, and so, as Blake tells us, leading us to believe a lie. What lies believed! So many and so varied; from far and near, satellite-carried, earnestly spoken, persuasively whispered, in living colour. The lie, the whole lie, and nothing but the lie.

Demonstrators waiting, bearded men and bra-less girls poised to emit their shrill cries, placards grounded, police standing by, their van discreetly parked, one or two journalists looking at their watches and thinking of editions. Everyone waiting. When, oh when, will they come? At last, patience rewarded; the cameras arrive and are set up. Sound-recordist ready, cameraman ready. Action! And lo! magically, action it is. Beards wag, breasts shake, placards lift, fists clench, slogans chant, police charge, van loads. Screaming, yelling – Pigs! Until – Cut! All is over. Slogans die away, beards and breasts subside, cops and vans drive off. All depart, leaving the street silent. From Action! to Cut! – oh, death wish, where is thy sting?

As the astronauts soar into the vast eternities of space, on earth the garbage piles higher; as the groves of academe extend their domain, their alumni's arms reach lower; as the phallic cult spreads, so does impotence. In great wealth, great poverty; in health, sickness; in numbers, deception. Gorging, left hungry; sedated, left restless; telling all, hiding all; in flesh united, forever separate. So we press on through the valley of abundance that leads to the wasteland of satiety, passing through the gardens of fantasy; seeking happiness ever more ardently, and finding despair ever more surely.

[1970]

A Kingdom Not Of This World

Jesus, for me, has been a long process of discovery – a process that is by no means over, and never can be. Like an infinitely precious and rewarding human relationship which goes on developing and constantly reveals new depths and possibilities of intimacy. Only, of course, much more so.

As a child in a socialist home in the early years of this century, I first heard of Jesus as having been an exceptionally public-spirited man of impeccable virtue who valiantly championed the downtrodden and oppressed and supported all our good causes. This, I was given to understand, naturally made him abhorrent in the eyes of the authorities. So it was perfectly appropriate that they should have brought about his public execution. If he was not actually a paid-up member of the Labour Party, it was only because there did not happen to be a Labour Party in Palestine in his time. Had there been one, Jesus would assuredly have joined it and doubtless become in due course the Honourable Member for Galilee South.

In those far-off days, I may add, such a view of Jesus was highly distasteful to all varieties of denominational Christians (apart from a few eccentric individuals, mostly Quakers and Unitarians),

and w   o held it were anathema to them. Sixty years later –
from my point of view, ironically enough – the pendulum has
swung the other way, and our then view of Jesus has become the
orthodoxy of most of today's trendy churchmen, who at the drop
of a TV studio floor-manager's hand call down anathema on anyone who does not hold it.

I remember in some vague way, even at the time, that the sheer
drama of Jesus's life, ministry, death and resurrection, as described in the Gospels, was too strong, too sublime, to be encompassed in so paltry a theme as just amending our human circumstances. It was like seeing Shakespeare's *King Lear* as, essentially, a
plea for better care of the aged. Later, I was to read and echo
words about Jesus in a similar vein by C. S. Lewis:

> You can shut him up for a fool; you can spit at him and kill
> him as a demon; or you can fall at his feet and call him Lord or
> God. But let us not come up with any patronizing nonsense
> about his being a great human teacher. He has not left that
> open to us. He did not intend to.

For myself, I could not shake off a conviction that, somehow,
the key to Jesus and the Kingdom not of this world that he proclaimed, must be sought rather on Golgotha than on the hustings
or the barricades. That giant Cross rising inexorably into the
sky was veritably his emblem – at the time, sombre and sinister
enough, yet to become the source and focus of the fiercest joys, the
most audacious hopes, the craziest expectations, ever to take
possession of the human heart.

To Jesus I owe an awareness of this so mysterious and so en-
trancing a dichotomy, built into our mortal existence, whereby
the negation of life is its fulfilment. Whereby the world dismissed
as of no account glows with new beauties and delights. Whereby
the Self discarded comes to life in fellowship with all others, as an
infinitesimal element in God's all-embracing love – like a particle
of sea-spray tossed into the sun's radiance. Whereby the universa-
lity of brotherhood takes precedence over the particularities of
equality; the perfect freedom which is service over the perfect
service which is freedom, the absolutes of love over the relativities
of justice.

So, the scene on Golgotha haunted me – more than I ever let on
even to my closest intimates, or for that matter to myself in my
introspective scribbling. Brooding on it, the dreadful certainty
possessed me that the Man on the Cross was real, whereas the

others – Pontius Pilate, the vacillating colonial governor, Herod, the puppet king, Caiaphas, the conniving High Priest – belonged to fantasy. They were history, which is, after all, only a glorified soap opera directed and produced in the victor's camp; they were news, ebbing and flowing as the editions came off the presses; they were the kingdoms of this world, which, when the Devil offered them to Jesus – rightly claiming that they were in his gift – Jesus resolutely rejected.

Precisely how a man nailed to a cross 2000 years ago, who claimed to be the Son of God, came to signify reality, in contra-distinction to the sawdust men of destiny with their fraudulent wars and revolutions and liberations, is something that can be understood, but not explained. You either see it, or you don't. Likewise, how the drama enacted on Golgotha can both belong to a remote past and still be happening, making Now Always, and Always Now. How the central character, Jesus, in his Manhood, suffers this cruel and shameful death, and, in his Godhood, rises from the dead to be for ever alive.

All I can say is that, in my experience, in surrendering to Jesus's importunities of love, life, as it were, comes into focus. Then the thorns are seen beneath the crown, the wounds beneath the purple robe. Then the cheers sound ribaldly, and the chanted slogans all resolve themselves into: Crucify him! Crucify him! Then defeat is victory, failure is success, and to die is to be born again – as a seed planted in the dark earth germinates to become a green shoot. Then, in the tiny, dark, suffocating dungeon of the Ego, a window is seen, letting in light, and with it the hope of release into what the Apostle Paul called the glorious liberty of the children of God – the only enduring liberty there is. Even this does not exhaust the potentialities of Jesus. Into the splendour of his truth there comes the warmth of his being: a helping hand accompanies the helping words. As he promised, he is with us always. It was on the road to Emmaus once, when we were filming in the Holy Land, that I sensed this most strongly. We had been trying to reconstruct what happened there – how two men walking to Emmaus from Jerusalem on the day after the Crucifixion were joined by a third man who fell into step beside them. Only later, when they had arrived at their destination and sat down to table, and the third man broke bread and offered a blessing, did they realize that he was no stranger, but their Saviour.

In the succeeding centuries, innumerable Christians were to testify that they, too, journeying through life, had been joined by another Presence, to their great comfort and joy. Were they all fools? For what it is worth, I add my testimony that wherever the walk and whoever the wayfarers, there always is this other Presence ready to emerge from the shadows and fall into step along the dusty s   way.

[1975]

Albion Agonistes

Of all the Great Issues which confront us today, none can be considered of greater moment than the manifest threats to the survival of our Western civilization. Spengler's *The Decline of the West* made a considerable stir in my young days. Has the decline Spengler observed fifty years ago now become an irreversible stampede to destruction?

Let it not be supposed that I am thinking only, or even primarily in terms of such outward and visible intimations of dominance in the world as power and wealth and influence. It is true, of course, that on this count both England and America have suffered of late a notable decline. When I first went to India in 1924 the voyage took five weeks, and pretty well every port we stopped at was flying the Union Jack. At that time we ruled over a quarter of the world and most of my countrymen firmly believed that this was an arrangement ordained by God and likely to continue indefinitely. Well, in one lifetime an Empire on which, we boasted, the sun never set, has become one on which it never rises. Again, when I first came to Washington, DC as a newspaper correspondent in 1946, America was incomparably the richest and most powerful country in the world. Now, some three decades later, largely as a result of the home thrust of the Sir Galahads of the Media, that advantageous situation has been transformed into the present shambles. Even so, in industrial and agricultural production, and even in available weapons, the people of the West are still preeminent, particularly in the American hemisphere.

No, what is at issue, as I see it, is not the means to survive, nor even the will to survive, but the *faith* to survive. It seems to me clear, beyond qualification or equivocation, that what we call Western civilization was born of the great drama enacted in Palestine two thousand years ago, the drama of the Incarnation, the Passion and the Resurrection, and all that flowed therefrom. This is what has inspired and nourished the art and literature and music and architecture and learning which are, and forever will be, the glory of our civilization, besides giving rise to innumerable lives of dedication to the love of God and of our human family. If it should prove to be the case that Western man has now rejected these origins of his civilization, persua g himself that he can be master of his own destiny, that he can shape his own life and chart his own future, then assuredly he and his way of life and all he has stood and stands for must infallibly perish.

In other words, the real crisis which confronts us is about faith rather than power, about the question 'Why?' rather than the question 'How?', about Man's relationship with his Creator rather than about his energy supplies, his currency, his balance of trade and Gross National Product, his sexual fantasies, and his other passing preoccupations, with which the media interminably concern themselves. These are essentially trivial matters, easily adjusted when the need so to do is apparent, as in time of war; whereas the God we serve, the salvation we hope for, the light we live by in this world, and, when we come to leave it, the vista reaching before us into eternity – these concern the very fundamentals of our mortal existence.

If, by way of illustration, I look at the parlous plight of my own native land, England, it is not, God knows, to glory in its present discomfiture, or to preen myself on prophecies which may seem to have come true. Never have I felt so much love as I do now in old age for the English countryside, for the English people and their history, yes, and their humour (and this from an ex-editor of *Punch*, who for some four desolating years had the thankless and hopeless task of trying to make the English laugh!); above all for the English language and literature. What blessing, I have often asked myself, could equal having for one's native tongue the language in which Shakespeare wrote, and into which the Authorized Version of the Bible was translated?

At the same time it has to be admitted that our national affairs are in great disarray, if not worse, that our institutions of government and of justice seem to be afflicted with dry rot, and that not even that Joan of Arc of suburbia, Mrs Margaret Thatcher, seems equal to the task of getting us out of our present mess. Statistics, the dismallest of all stock-taking, suggests a birth rate falling below zero, juvenile delinquency, crimes of violence, and racial antagonism rising alarmingly, divorces and bankruptcies alike multiplying, a health service and an education system slipping towards collapse, and many other unmistakable indications of wrath to come. I would say myself that some sort of civil war followed by authoritarian government of one stamp or another is a more present prospect today that it has been at any time since the time of Cromwell.

A new feature in this melancholy accounting are the media, especially television, whose immense power to influence and shape public attitudes is exercised with little regard for any consideration except profit and self-importance. With the same sublime unction it will destroy a presidency and recommend the magical qualities of a new detergent, lose a war and promote a cake-mix. Posterity will surely marvel at the tolerance accorded to this instrument of persuasion, and its operators, so immensely more powerful than anything of the kind which has ever existed before, and at the manner in which its pundit-salesmen have been able, with equal impunity, to topple institutions and undermine authority, and to sing the praises of some potion or pill capable of delivering us from pain, anxiety, body odour, acidity, and other infirmities.

How I envy the historian who, looking back across the centuries at the decline and fall of our Western civilization, as Gibbon did on that of Rome, will remark on how, as we systematically destroyed or allowed to be destroyed, all the values and restraints of the Christian way of life which we had inherited, we remained convinced that each innovation, each new assault on marital fidelity, on the sanctity of the home and the responsibilities of parenthood, was bound to be conducive to our well-being and enlightenment. There is a nightmare which from time to time afflicts me. I find myself in a BBC studio deep underground, while up above the mushroom cloud gathers and the last vestiges of civilized life disappear. In our studio the discussion proceeds, and a lady participant with a particularly shrill voice is insisting that if only the school age might be raised to twenty and the age of consent lowered to ten, if only birth control pills could be distributed to Brownies with their morning milk and extended to tiny tots in the play-schools, if only marriage counselling might begin in the cradle and *Lady Chatterley's Lover* get into the comics, all would yet be well. The barbarians who overran Rome came from without, but ours are home products, trained and suitably brainwashed and conditioned at the public expense. In the light of their antics, it is difficult to resist the conclusion that Western Man, having wearied of the struggle to be himself, has decided to abolish himself. Creating his own boredom out of his own

243

affluence, his own impotence out of his own erotomania, his own vulnerability out of his own strength; himself blowing the trumpet that brings the walls of his own city tumbling down. Convincing himself that he is too numerous, and labouring accordingly with pill and scalpel and syringe to make himself fewer in order to fall an easier prey to his enemies. Until at last, having educated himself into imbecility and drugged and polluted himself into stupefaction, he keels over, a weary battered old brontosaurus, and becomes extinct.

Before such a prospect, are we then, as Christians, to fold our arms in resignation? On the contrary, it is the breakdown of power which provides Christianity with its greatest opportunity. After all, it was to the Rome of the Emperor Nero – a ruler who makes even some of ours seem, by comparison, positively enlightened and humane – that the Apostle Paul carried the Gospel with such fantastic success, founding a universal religion which has endured through twenty centuries because, and only because, it has never finally identified itself with any earthly power.

This might seem like mere words to keep up our spirits, but actually a sign in the same sense has been accorded us so extraordinary that it amounts to one of the great miracles of history. I refer to the Christian testimony of Alexander Solzhenitsyn, who makes the point in a letter he addressed to the Soviet Government just before he was sent into compulsory exile, that what is wrong with his country is not so much its political or economic system as the Marxist materialism which is its ideology. To this, he insists, the only valid answer is provided by Christ and his teaching; the only possible response to the pretensions of absolute power is the absolute love proclaimed in the Gospels.

As a young journalist in the USSR in the early thirties, it would have seemed to me utterly inconceivable that after more than half a century of the most absolutist rule ever known on earth, under a regime dedicated to the destruction of the Christian religion and disposing of powers hitherto unimaginable over the lives, thoughts, hopes, and values of its citizens, a voice would make itself heard and be heard through the whole world stating once more in luminous words of truth the great proposition on which the Christian religion is founded – that through love, not through power, men may find their way in this world, and in humbly seeking to fulfil their Creator's purposes for them, look beyond it into the eternity which is their true habitat. And this voice – one among many and speaking for many – coming from among the regime's favoured élite, those who in worldly terms have everything to gain from adhering to its rules and principles.

The whole stupendous effort, that is to say, made at such a cost in blood and tears to condition man to a purely terrestrial existence – what is called social engineering – has been a gigantic failure, a fiasco, as such efforts must always be. Including, I may add, crazed projects in our part of the world to sort out our 'genes into some more appropriate order, dispose of lives we consider worthless, and decide ourselves who shall be born and who exterminated, even in the womb.

Should we not, then, rejoice that once more it has been demonstrated to us unmistakably that God never abandons us; that however sombre the darkness, His light still shines; and however full the air may be of the drooling of Muzak, and the cackling of Newzak, truth will make itself heard, and shall make us free. I think of Augustine in Carthage when the news came that Rome had been sacked and the great Roman Empire was nearing its end. If it be so, he told his flock, it is only what happened to Sodom; men build cities and destroy them, but there is also the City of God which they did not build and which they cannot destroy. So it is today.

I am an old man, already past the allotted three score and ten years and, as the old do, I quite often wake up in the night, half out of my body, so that I see between the sheets the old battered carcass I shall soon be leaving for good, and in the distance a glow in the sky, the lights of Augustine's City of God. Let me, in conclusion, pass on two extraordinarily sharp impressions which accompany this condition. The first is of the incredible beauty of our earth, its colours and shapes and smells and creatures; of the enchantment of human love and companionship, of the fulfilment of human work and human procreation. The second, a certainty surpassing all words and thought, that as an infinitesimal particle of God's creation I am a participant in His purposes, which are loving not malign, creative not destructive, orderly not chaotic – and in that certainty a great peace and a great joy.

[1976]

245

Epilogue

Delving into the accumulated verbiage of fifty years in the life of a professional communicator or vendor of words must be an awesome undertaking, especially for someone as discriminating as Professor Ian Hunter, henceforth to be referred to as the Compiler. A chef might contemplate the meals prepared and served over a lifetime, or a long-distance lorry-driver the mileage covered; I knew a postman in the days when postmen went on foot who calculated that in the course of a lifetime spent delivering mail he had trudged twice round the circumference of the world. The meals, however, have been eaten, the lorry-loads and the mail have been delivered. It is all over and done with; whereas the words are extant – in back numbers of magazines and newspapers, on film and video tape. I feel about them as Macbeth did about Banquo's ghost:

> The time has been,
> That, when the brains were out, the man would die,
> And there an end; but now they rise again . . .
> And push us from our stools.

In exploring this great waste of words, the Compiler has come up with some, from my point of view, startling discoveries, unearthing pieces that I had not only forgotten, but quite failed to recognize. There are others that I remember well, and thought never to set eyes on again; a few that I hoped never to set eyes on again. It was a temptation to suggest dropping one or two of these – I leave the reader to decide which – but on consideration I decided that this would be cheating. After all, it is the Compiler's selection, not mine, and I have every reason to be grateful that one so conscientious and adept should have fallen to my lot. Furthermore, I can take comfort in the thought that at least he has been spared from reading unsigned editorials such as at different times I have produced in great profusion. The authorship of these, I am glad to think, is beyond discovery even by the author himself, as proved to be the case when, in the course of recording the commentary for a television programme about India (*Twilight of Empire*), I had occasion to look through the editorial pages of the *Calcutta Statesman* during the years that I worked on it, and quite failed to identify my own contributions.

In the items the Compiler has collected together I note two recurring preoccupations which truly reflect my state of mind as I now recall it. The first derives from a stint I did in Moscow in 1932-3 as *Manchester Guardian* correspondent there, when I was confronted with the spectacle of some of the most eminent contemporary intellectuals prostrating themselves before Stalin and the regime he shaped and dominated. An honourable exception, I should mention, was Bertrand Russell, who as early as 1920 visited the USSR, and reported that the Soviet regime was bound to become one of the most thorough and odious tyrannies the world has yet known. Even he, however, as he recounts in his *Autobiography*, saw fit to yield to the pressure of his then wife, Dora, and if not retract his opinion, at any rate keep quiet about it.

This spectacle of *traison des clercs* at its basest made an imperishable impression upon me, the more so because the persons concerned had been in my eyes the elect, the samurai of our time. I revered and adulated them, and now, by way of reaction, came to despise them and hold them in abhorrence for the inexhaustible credulity and sycophancy they displayed in their attitude to the Soviet Union and its bosses. See, for instance, 'To Friends of the Soviet Union'. In the succeeding years, I went on belabouring them, recognizing in them the twentieth century cast of Dostoevsky's amazingly prophetic novel, *The Devils*. My feelings were so strong that some would say they amounted to an obsession which has infiltrated much of my writing and distorted my attitude to all sorts of different, but to me cognate, matters. Certainly, the subject has had a way of turning up, as well as the various characters concerned, notably the Webbs, whom I had a chance of observing at first hand, Beatrice being my wife's Aunt Bo. This estimable, and, when I knew them, venerable couple provided a perfect illustration of what I was getting at. So industrious in their researches, so virtuous and respectable in their ways, so sincere and tireless in their desire to plan a better, more easeful and brotherly future for their fellows, and yet led thereby into upholding with passionate and block-headed intensity Stalin's blood-thirsty practices and dictatorial rule. Solzhenitsyn's hilarious account of Mrs Eleanor Roosevelt's visit to a Soviet labour camp might just as well have applied to the Webbs.

This brings me to the second preoccupation noticeable in the Compiler's selection from my writings - my revulsion against the liberal mind as such and all its works. If these prophets of a soon-to-be-realized kingdom of heaven on earth had shown themselves to be so abysmally credulous and misleading in their accounts of the Soviet regime and biased in the judgements they passed upon it, so callous in their readiness to justify oppression and terrorism so long as they were associated with ostensibly revolutionary and progressive aims, then, it seemed to me, their utopian expectations must be seen as not just illusory but as positively disastrous; a sick fantasy, a death-wish.

In the light of this conclusion, the contemporary scene presents itself as a tragi-comic spectacle in which what pass for being humane and enlightened purposes give rise to the exact opposite of what is intended. Thus, by a strange irony, a continuing revelation of what Blake called Fearful Symmetry, illiteracy increases along with expenditure on public education, the demand for sedatives with increased leisure or affluence, and crimes of violence (particularly rape) with libertarian schemes to prevent them and rehabilitate their perpetrators. The more pacifists and internationalists in the world, the more belligerancy; the more free speech, the less truth spoken; the more maternal and child care, the more foetuses aborted and thrown away with the hospital waste. Oh, the terrible inhumanity of the humane, the fathomless gullibility of the enlightened! the relentless egoism of the well-intentioned! As *Things Past* sufficiently indicates, it is a theme to which I often return - too often for some tastes.

These ironies, I decided, must be saying something. But what? Surely, that the quest for a kingdom of heaven on earth leads infallibly to anarchy or a Gulag Archipelago, and is in any case a cul-de-sac, the trouble being that Man, a fallen creature, is incapable of achieving perfection, though he can, in certain elevated states of mind, conceive it. Like Moses, he is taken to a high point where he can see the Promised Land, but in the certainty that in this world he will never himself get there. So I came to realize that the Apostle Paul spoke truly when he said that here we have no continuing city. At the same time, there is St Augustine's City of God, which men did not build and cannot destroy, but which, for those that have eyes to see, can be glimpsed from the Earthly City. There is also, running between the two, a cable bridge, very frail and swaying in the wind, but passable. This is the Incarnation.

Thus my disillusionment with the notion of a predestined progress towards a kingdom of heaven on earth led me inexorably to the kingdom not of this world proclaimed in the Christian revelation, and a realization that for us mortals living in Time, this alone is reality, all else being fantasy. The Compiler has unearthed some early intimations of this realization, thereby confuting the widely held belief that my transcendental aspirations afflicted me suddenly in old age when I was past appreciating fleshly pleasures, and had altogether wearied of trying to make sense of the hopes and desires of this world and of the ideas pertaining to them. There is a funny book to be written about becoming a Christian in the latter part of the twentieth century. The comedy arises from the prevailing assumption that there must be some extraneous circumstance, such as senility or the fear of death, to account for so outmoded and reactionary a step. Mere acceptance of the intrinsic truth of what the founder of Christianity had to say and the drama of his life, ministry, death and resurrection as recounted in the Gospels, in no wise suffices. *Things Past*, I hasten to add, is not this book, but contains much relevant data were it ever to be undertaken. For this and for all his labours I owe the Compiler hearty thanks. No author could have hoped for a more zealous, painstaking and understanding anthologist.

Malcolm Muggeridge,
Robertsbridge,
Sussex.
21 April 1978.

Acknowledgements

'An Elderly Teacher', *New Statesman*, 1 December 1928; 'Europe, 1934', *Nineteenth Century and After*, 1934; 'Roots', *Time and Tide*, 19 May 1934; 'The Sear, The Yellow Leaf', *Fortnightly*, May 1934; 'To Friends Of The Soviet Union', *English Review*, January 1934; 'Utopias And Heaven', *Time and Tide*, 19 May 1934; 'Plus Ça Change', *Fortnightly*, August 1936; 'London Bridge Is Falling Down', *Time and Tide*, 20 April 1935; *Winter in Moscow*, Eyre and Spottiswoode, 1934; 'Moscow Farewell', *Time and Tide*, 26 May 1934; 'Why I Am Not A Pacifist', *Time and Tide*, 28 November 1936; 'Whom God Hath Joined', *Time and Tide*, 24 April 1937; 'What Is My Life?', *Time and Tide*, 12 and 19 June 1937; 'The Revolutionaries', *Time and Tide*, 1937; 'Faith', *Time and Tide*, 23 October 1937; 'Those Put In Authority Over Us', *New Statesman*, 8 November 1958; 'Power', *New Statesman*, 3 January 1959; 'Money', *Esquire*, February 1965; 'Time and Eternity', *Time and Tide*, 6 February 1937; 'Rome, Sweet Rome', *Esquire*, April 1965; 'Authority in Drag', *New Statesman*, 15 August 1975; *Ciano And Mussolini*, Heinemann, 1947; 'Humility', *New Statesman*, 2 August 1968; 'Fie On Neutralism', *Time*, 2 November 1953; 'The Art Of Non-Conforming', *Vogue*, 1 August 1953; 'Journalism', *New Statesman*, 19 June 1964; 'Farewell To Freedom?', 1954 *Queen's Quarterly*; 'Lord Beaverbrook', *New Statesman*, 24 December 1955; 'Fact And Fantasy', *New Statesman*, 27 September 1963; 'In Defence Of Bad Taste', *Maclean's Magazine*, 3 August 1957; 'Collected Speeches', *New Statesman*, 22 June 1965; 'Pursuit Of Happiness (International) Inc.', *New Statesman*, 13 September 1958; 'Eisenhower', *New Statesman*, 4 April 1959; 'America', *New Statesman*, 4 April 1959; 'Harold Ross And The *New Yorker*', *New Statesman*, 4 July 1959; 'Who Betrays Whom?', *The Twentieth Century*, Winter 1962; 'Oratory', *New Statesman*, 5 April 1962; 'Whitman', *Esquire*, December 1971; 'The *New Statesman* And I', *New Statesman*, 19 April 1963; 'G.K.C.', *New Statesman*, 23 August 1963; 'Evelyn Waugh, R.I.P.', *Esquire*, August 1966; 'Kipling Sahib', *The Listener*, 30 December 1965; 'The Trial', *Esquire*, April 1972; *What I Believe*, Allen and Unwin, 1966; 'The Great Charles', *New Statesman*, 15 July 1966; '*Krokodil*', *New Statesman*, 20 February 1960; 'Gossip', *New Statesman*, 15 August 1975; 'I Love You, England', *New Statesman*, 21 January 1966; 'Am I A Christian?', *New Statesman*, 10 March 1967; 'Novels', *Esquire*, January 1965; 'Jane Austen And

Iris Murdoch', *Esquire*, January 1965; 'Refractions In The Character Of Kim Philby', *Esquire*, September 1968; 'James Bond', *Esquire*, December 1964; 'A Nightmare', *New Statesman*, 2 November 1957; 'Wax To Wax', *New Statesman*, 26 January 1968; 'Marilyn Monroe', *New Statesman*, 10 August 1962; 'Newzak', *New Statesman*, 21 June 1968; 'Obituaries', *Esquire*, January 1972; 'My True Love Hath My Heart', *New Statesman*, 4 October 1968; 'Apologia Pro Vita Sua', *New Statesman*, 5 March 1968; 'Germaine Greer', *Esquire*, April 1971; 'Women's Lib', *Esquire*, January 1972; 'The Decade of the Great Liberal Death Wish', *Esquire*, December 1970; 'A Kingdom Not Of This World', *The Listener*, 3 April 1975; 'Albion Agonistes', *The Alternative*, February 1976.